MW01629986

Imagery and Visual Expression in Therapy

EMOTIONS, PERSONALITY, AND PSYCHOTHERAPY

Series Editors:
Carroll E. Izard, *University of Delaware, Newark, Delaware*
and
Jerome L. Singer, *Yale University, New Haven, Connecticut*

Imagery and Visual Expression in Therapy

Vija Bergs Lusebrink
University of Louisville
Louisville, Kentucky

Plenum Press • New York and London

Library of Congress Cataloging-in-Publication Data

```
Lusebrink, Vija Bergs.
    Imagery and visual expression in therapy / Vija Bergs Lusebrink.
        p.   cm. -- (Emotions, personality, and psychotherapy)
    Includes bibliographical references.
    ISBN 0-306-43453-9
    1. Imagery (Psychology)--Therapeutic use.  2. Psychotherapy.
I. Title.  II. Series.
    [DNLM: 1. Art Therapy.  2. Imagination.  3. Psychotherapy.
4. Visual Perception.   WM 420 L968i]
RC489.F35L87  1990
616.89'14--dc20
DNLM/DLC
for Library of Congress                                    90-6901
                                                              CIP
```


© 1990 Plenum Press, New York
A Division of Plenum Publishing Corporation
233 Spring Street, New York, N.Y. 10013

All rights reserved

Printed in the United States of America

To Ingrid, Karen, and Anita

Preface

Images as means of expression have fascinated and spoken to me for a long time. Yet it has been a far-reaching and circuitous journey to synthesize imagery and visual expression in the present form. Early in my life my interest in images expressed itself in art, first as a young child drawing, then responding to works of art and enjoying the life conveyed through colors, forms, and lines that created recognizable images and suggested different moods. The centering, transformative, and spiritual aspects of art emerged as I sought out art in times of personal turmoil. I returned to the expressive aspects of art through my training as a painter. Later I discovered in my own art, as well as in others' expressions, as a teacher and an art therapist, that many times we express more through visual means than we are consciously aware of doing.

The writings of art therapy pioneers Naumburg (1950, 1953, 1966) and Ulman (1961, 1965) and Rhyne's (1973) gestalt art therapy provided a framework for my own observations. Workshops and literature on guided imagery opened another door to the inner experience through images. The discovery of Jung's concept of archetypes helped me to integrate images into a mind/body frame bridging from the biological roots of the archetypal images to the spiritual aspects of our existence. The validity of my beliefs in imagery and its expression through visual means was reinforced and elaborated upon by additional exposure to the work and ideas of the early supporters of the use of visual expression of symbolism and symbolic realignment (Perry, 1953, 1962), and imagery in therapy (Horowitz, 1970; Singer, 1974), as well as by my own clients and my observations of their visual expressions. During my doctoral studies I pursued my interest in the psychophysiological components of imagery. I was fortunate to be able to do research for my dissertation under Dr. F. J. McGuigan, whose model of the neuromuscular circuits of information processing (McGuigan, 1978a, 1978b) provided another view of the components of imagery.

Imagery as a cognitive component of information processing has gained rapidly increasing recognition and application in therapy in the last 25 years. The psychophysiological components of imagery have taken longer to investigate and map, possibly because of the complexity and fluidity of imagery. The visual expression of imagery and its role in affective and creative integration have been the predominant components of art therapy. The growth of art therapy as a discipline itself has paralleled the rediscovery of imagery in psychology and psychotherapy. Holt's article on imagery, "Imagery: The Return of the Ostracized" (1964), was published within 3 years of the start of the *American Journal of Art Therapy* (originally titled the *Bulletin of Art Therapy*) in 1961 and only 5 years prior to the establishment of the first art therapy graduate programs at the University of Louisville in Louisville, Kentucky, and the Hahneman Medical School and Hospital in Philadelphia in 1969. Nevertheless, the interaction between the two aspects of expression, namely, imagery in verbal therapy and its visual expression, has been slow. The present book is the first major effort to combine these two aspects.

Images as means of expression and representation have a sequence of cognitive levels and depth of the emotional experience. The visual expression of images, in turn, is multileveled and has its own formal elements and syntax. Internal images emphasize the spatial, operational component, or they can represent a subjective internal experience. In the latter case the flow of imagery changes with the emotions associated with the imagery as it can be seen in daydreams and dreams (Klinger, 1971).

The present volume explores the different components and developmental, cognitive, and emotional aspects of imagery, visual expression, and the interaction of the two. Chapter 1 introduces different approaches to art therapy and creativity. The different components and aspects of imagery and visual expression discussed in the first four chapters of the book provide the basic building blocks for using imagery and visual expression in therapy: different types and levels of imagery, developmental aspects of imagery and symbolism, and the formal elements and syntax of visual expression. Chapters 5 and 6 introduce a systems approach using imagery and visual expression on different levels. The Expressive Therapies Continuum (Kagin & Lusebrink, 1978) provides a conceptual model of using visual expression without an emphasis on a particular therapeutic school of thought, and thus the different levels of expression and use of media can be accommodated to the therapist and client's preferences. Chapter 7 deals with the flow of thought and images, especially as it is influenced by emotions in dreams, active imagination, and daydreams. Daydreams and adolescent depression are discussed in Chapter 8. It is hoped that the psychotic and schizophrenic art and visual expressions discussed in Chapter 9 will be helpful not only in dealing with patients in these diagnostic categories but also in serving as the basis for further insights in the formations of imagery and its role in information processing. Chapter 10 concentrates on the body/mind connection with a particular emphasis played by emotions in either establishing these connections or disconnecting them.

I hope that this book as a whole will generate further development and interaction between the two aspects of the same coin: imagery and its visual expression. The volume is designed to assist the therapist, the student of imagery and art therapy, and also to some extent the investigator of imagery. I also hope that the information presented here will help the reader discover and understand the influence of and interaction between the different components and aspects of imagery and its visual expression, and their application in therapy.

Acknowledgments

The material for this book has been gathered over the last 20 years from my experience as an art therapist; from my studies of the diverse material related to the many aspects of art therapy and imagery; from my teaching, supervision, and interactions with many art therapy students; and from my interactions with many art therapists and other professionals. It is difficult to mention all the individuals and sources separately without leaving some out, but I do want to acknowledge my indebtedness to all of them. My special thanks, though, goes to all my students who shared their ideas, observations, and experiences with me.

Specifically, I would like to thank my friends and fellow art therapists Janie Rhyne, Ph.D., ATR; Janet Long, M.A., MFCC, ATR; and Linda Kotcher, M.A., for the stimulating discussions about art therapy and its theoretical implications. My special thanks go to Sandra Graves, Ph.D., ATR, whose collaboration and enthusiastic response to and cross-fertilization with my ideas helped to formulate the concept of the Expressive Therapies Continuum. Aina Nucho, Ph.D., ATR, has enriched my thinking in different aspects of art therapy, including the application of systems approach to art therapy. I cherish and appreciate our interaction and her feedback on and encouragement of the early versions of several chapters in this book. Similarly, I greatly appreciate the reactions to the different chapters by Marcia Rosal, Ph.D., ATR, and Melissa Gaskins, M.A. Melissa and other graduate students over the period of a number of years have helped me with gathering the material and compiling the bibliography. I deeply appreciate Nancy Roubieu's dedicated help and professional expertise in editing and word-processing the manuscript, and Kathleen O'Connell's editorial comments. Bill Karlen, at the Instructional Communications Center of the University of Louisville, took the photographs of the various artwork, and I am thankful for his assistance.

I would like to thank Jerome Singer, Ph.D., for his ideas and studies in imagery, which I had followed in the literature over the years. My deep appreciation goes to my clients who shared their experiences with me, and I especially thank those whose work is reproduced here. I also wish to thank my students who shared their dreams as part of their class assignments and then allowed their dream images and descriptions to be included in this book.

Contents

PART I. LEVELS AND COMPONENTS OF IMAGERY
AND EXPRESSION

Chapter 1. Imagery in Verbal Therapy and Art Therapy . .   3

Chapter 2. Images and Information Processing   27

PART II.   FUNCTION AND PROCESSES OF IMAGERY AND VISUAL EXPRESSION IN THERAPY

List of Tables

List of Figures

Imagery and Visual Expression in Therapy

Part I

Levels and Components of Imagery and Expression

CHAPTER 1

Imagery in Verbal Therapy and Art Therapy

Mary, a woman in her thirties, was in a psychiatric unit because of depression, dissociative tendencies, and violent nightmares. In an art therapy session she chose to portray her depression by using paints. She worked intensively in silence on the first picture (Fig. 1.1) without displaying any dissociation in her manner of working. After finishing the painting she described the meaning of the sequence of forms as she had painted them. The black diagonal area represented her deepening depression. Mary portrayed herself as a crouching faint figure in the lower right corner. The vertical line on the right side stood for a bloody path back to the top area representing hope and healing. A narrow black line separated her from the path to recovery. The therapist suggested that Mary explore what kept her from getting on the path.

The second painting (Fig. 1.2) showed the enlargement of the lower black line, which looked to Mary like a "mother's breast." The upright path to hope led through this area. In this picture Mary had changed her position from a crouching figure in the first picture to a faintly painted kneeling figure in the second. This visual exploration of the imagery differentiated the most pressing issue represented by the black line and expressed Mary's need for a nurturing support, which she had lacked in her infancy and childhood.

INTRODUCTION

Imagery and expression in visual media have common components. Most obvious is the image itself, experienced internally, expressed ver-

3

Figure 1.1. "Depression."

bally, or constructed and represented through the media. In any case, the images carry a meaning and also have an emotional value. The process of forming the images and the structures supporting them is similar to experiencing inner images and visual perception. Internal imagery is made accessible to consciousness through the same motoric, sensory, and visual perceptual systems as external perceptions. Internal

Figure 1.2. Elaboration of 1.1: "What Keeps Me from Going on My Path Upward: Mother's Breast."

perception can interfere with and thus is presumed to use the same channels of processing information as external perception (Sheehan, 1972).

This book explores (1) the processing of inner experiences and feelings through images, and (2) the interacting of individuals with art media to express and externalize inner images. These processes are discussed from the standpoint of imagery and art therapy, combining the two into a systems perspective. Expression through art media is referred to as "visual expression" throughout the book, and is used as a generic term in that it refers to expressions through media perceived visually and tactilely, as compared to the aural perceptions of speech.

Inner experiences of images and their external representations influence each other. At the same time they also differ, in that the media in which the images are presented and represented are different. The internal image is based on sensory, affective, and thought processes. The image is externalized either through verbal descriptions or through manipulation of media. In either case the expressive medium has its own qualities and limitations. The representations of inner images in turn are perceived internally by the viewer or listener. Thus the external images interact with and influence the internal experience.

What are the other components that contribute to and influence this interaction? What would be an effective way to conceptualize this reciprocal influence? As is discussed in the following three chapters, both inner experiences and external representations consist of several main components which interact with each other in varying combinations to create a whole. The interaction can occur on different levels in different combinations of the constituent parts.

The crossover of the two modes of expression in therapy—verbally expressed images versus visually expressed images—has been slow. This is especially true of using visual expression of images in verbal therapy. The approaches to the use of imagery in art therapy are discussed first in this chapter. The specific characteristics of the use of imagery in verbal and art therapy will be examined subsequently. Elaboration on the characteristics of the creative person, the creative climate, and the psychodynamics of the creative process gives the background of an important aspect of art therapy: creativity.

COMPONENTS OF IMAGERY AND MODES OF REPRESENTATION OF THOUGHT

The different imagery approaches are multidimensional in the modalities of imagery and the modes of representation involved. The imagery can be present in the following modalities: kinesthetic, somatosensory and visceral, visual, and verbal. The images themselves are complex and can have affective, somatic, and meaning components.

Ahsen (1973, 1982, 1984) conceptualizes images as a three-dimensional unity between vivid visual or "light" images, somatic pattern, and a meaning. The tripartite structure of these images is indicated by the term ISM. The sequence of the ISM indicates that an image is followed by the somatic response or meaning (Ahsen, 1982). The image serves as a stage for the expression of the body response and meaning. The sequence also can start either with the somatic response or with a meaning in any combination with the other two components. There is a tendency for the link between the three components to weaken; nevertheless, the visual image retains the capacity to revive the three-dimensional unit (Sheikh, 1978).

Horowitz (1970, 1978, 1983) conceptualizes images as one of three proposed modes of representation of thought: enactive, image, and lexical. Enactive representation is based on memories of motor actions and the retention of imitative behavior of others' actions. Enactive thought is conceptualized as thinking in action, with the tensing of different muscle groups constituting covert trial actions. In addition to the skeletal musculature, the enactive mode also involves the visceral neuromusculature.

Images as representational thought are based on perceptions, memories, and fantasies. Images also give a "sensory configuration to emergent ideas and feelings" (Horowitz, 1983, p. 40). Visual images are especially effective in representing information about form and spatial relationships. Images incorporate emotional responses; the latter can be delayed in turn by the inhibition of image formation.

The lexical mode of representation is seen as the most rational one, serving advanced levels of abstraction and conceptionalization. In Horowitz's (1983) model of the three modes of representation of thought, the lexical mode is regarded as an emerging development from the earlier modes of enactive and image representation. This sequence of development was based originally on Bruner's (1964) proposed course of cognitive growth and three systems of information processing and representation of thought: enactive, iconic, and lexical.

Horowitz (1983) posits that both the enactive and image modes of representation continue to develop and interact with the schemata formed by lexical representation. Each mode of representation has its own innate manner of processing information: visual images process information predominately in a simultaneous manner. The lexical representations are usually organized in a sequence.

The images are appraised for their emotional response and conceptual content. At the same time they undergo two transformations: they decrease in intensity and vividness, and they are translated in other forms of representation. The emotional aspect of images is especially important in that traumatic images retain their intensity for prolonged periods of time, and the strong emotions associated with traumatic images make the verbal labeling and categorization more difficult.

The stream of ongoing thought (Klinger, 1978; Singer, 1978, 1988) incorporates imagery related to inner experiences along with verbal and/or logical processing of external tasks. Singer (1988), in reviewing studies of ongoing thought, points out that in processing external information, individuals also process a private stream of thought either by sequential shifting or in parallel processing. The basic imagery modalities contribute to the formation of the privately generated phenomena. Sequences of information are stored in molar storage structures or *schemata*. A schema consists of image-like representations, along with a verbal label of an event, object, or person. According to Singer and Kolligian (1987), "Schemas . . . provide selection criteria for regulating attention and lend a focus to the encoding, storage, and retrieval of information in a domain" (p. 555). Schemata are conceptualized as the starting point of "top-down" information processing as compared to the previously discussed sequences from enactive to lexical processing. As knowledge structures, schemata may be tied to affective experiences and influence the cognitive processing of information, and schema perseverance may interfere with the incorporation of new data and experiences. Schemata may be combined in action sequences of scripts.

In the case vignette the images (Fig. 1.1) incorporate the sensation and meaning of being depressed. At the same time the elaboration of the immediate depressive issue (Fig. 1.2) shows the schema of perceiving lack of support and nurturance in the environment as based on childhood experiences.

The different aspects of imagery and the ensuing schemata are elaborated in art therapy through depicting the images and the feelings associated with them by using art media.

CHARACTERISTICS OF USING IMAGERY IN THERAPY

Imagery in both verbal therapy and art therapy focuses on the imaginal mode of information processing; this characteristic distinguishes these two forms of therapy from other approaches.

The uses of imagery in therapy have been discussed extensively in the literature, and summarized in reviews (Singer, 1974; Singer & Pope, 1978; Sheikh, 1986; Sheikh & Jordan, 1983). The approaches are so many and varied that Singer has already described them as forming a "Tower of Babel." These approaches to the use of imagery have been presented as based on different theoretical backgrounds. Meichenbaum (1978) states that "the number of proposed mechanisms underlying imagery therapy seems to be no fewer than the number of techniques available" (p. 382).

The theoretical bases for imagery approaches to therapy range from operant conditioning in Wolpe's systematic desensitization (1958, 1973) and Cautela's covert conditioning (Cautela, 1979; Cautela & McCullough, 1978) to psychoanalytical in Reyher's emergent uncovering psychotherapy (Reyher, 1977, 1978; Reyher & Smeltzer, 1968) and Leuner's Guided Affective Imagery (1977, 1978, 1984). The intermediary range of imagery approaches are based on social learning theory in Kazdin's (1978) symbolic modeling and Meichenbaum's (1977, 1978) cognitive behavior modification.

Sheikh and Jordan (1983) outline the following general characteristics of imagery which contribute to its effectiveness in therapy. Imagery carries intense affective charges and evokes emotional reactions with associated psychophysiological changes. Images and emotions contribute to the meaning of words, providing detailed information, especially of past occurrences and preverbal memories. Words, on the other hand, have a tendency to become abstract. Imagery, in spanning the continuum between the unconscious and consciousness, is effective in presenting clients' problematic areas and uncovering repressed material and defenses. Images also have a futuristic dimension as motivators to action, and a predictive dimension presenting ideas and actions that manifest themselves only later in verbal cognition and behavior. Strosahl and Ascough (1981) point out that imagery also serves abstraction.

In therapy, free imagery and guided imagery produce therapeutic changes without the mediating action of interpretation.

Characteristics of Using Visual Expression in Art Therapy

Art therapy emerged from the interaction of art, creativity, and psychotherapy. It also incorporates the characteristics of using imagery in therapy.

There are three major differences between art therapy and the use of verbal imagery in therapy. The most obvious difference is the use of art media to express internal images, feelings, thoughts, and sensations in a concrete form and the visual feedback of these products. The visual expressions produce a tangible, permanent record of the images that does not undergo changes and/or distractions through later recall from memory. The intrinsic qualities of the media, however, differentially influence the portrayal of the images on different levels of expression.

Second, art therapy differs from verbal imagery therapy in the emphasis on the structural aspects of the media use and visual expression. The structural aspects represent images and their relationship to each other through the organized use of the formal elements of visual expression, such as line, form, color, and location. The physical manipulation of materials and the conscious thought processes involved contribute to control.

The third dissimilarity between imagery and art therapy is that through the expression in art media, art therapy also has a creative or emergent component in creating order out of chaos and giving an image or feeling a form. Visual expression facilitates the dialogue between inner and outer reality, whereby the media can be used as symbolic agents. Different art therapy approaches vary in their emphasis on the creative aspect of expression. In some approaches (Kramer, 1971, 1979; Ulman, 1975a, 1975b) the creative aspect is either the primary goal, or at least an important aspect of it. In other approaches, the creative aspect becomes secondary to insight and expression of feelings (Wadeson, 1980; Landgarten, 1981).

Compared to the use of imagery, art therapy does not have an empirical basis for the different use of media and their influence on the expression, except for clinical observations.

Different Approaches to Art Therapy

The different approaches to art therapy are based on their proponents' experience and opinions, the latter being influenced to some extent by the therapeutic model to which the particular proponent adheres. Descriptions of several different approaches to using art in therapy follow. They are selected as representative, but are not all-inclusive of the different practitioners' variations of the techniques or theoretical references used in art therapy.

The approaches to art therapy discussed here are divided into art as therapy and art psychotherapy. The amount of verbalization by the client associated with these expressions varies depending on the different art therapy approaches. At one end of the art therapy spectrum is the use of visual media with focus on the product and artistic aspects. Verbalization in this approach is only secondary, and pertains mainly to instructions about the use of media and socialization. At the other end is emphasis on the process, verbal free association to the images rendered, and insight.

Kramer's (1971, 1979) and Ulman's (1975a, 1975b) work is discussed as representative of art as therapy. Art psychotherapy is subdivided into two viewpoints: humanistic/structural and psychodynamic/psycho-analytical. The work of Betensky (1973a, 1973b, 1977, 1987), Nucho (1987), Tokuda (1973), McNiff (1977, 1981), and Rhyne (1970, 1973, 1987) is discussed as representative of the humanistic/structural viewpoint. Landgarten's (1981), Wadeson's (1980, 1987), and Rubin's (1978, 1984, 1987) approaches constitute a transition between the humanistic/struc-tural and psychodynamic/psychoanalytical viewpoints. The psycho-dynamic/psychoanalytical approach is represented by Naumburg (1953, 1966, 1973), Robbins (Robbins, 1983, 1987; Robbins & Sibley, 1976), and Levick (1983). The divisions between the different approaches are to some degree arbitrary in that the art therapists discussed here use a combination of different approaches.

Art as Therapy

The concept of art as therapy is most extensively covered in the literature by *Kramer* (1958, 1971, 1979) and is based on her work with children. According to Kramer the creative process itself is therapeutic; the art therapist provides conditions to nurture and support the creative process, including technical advice and emotional support. Initially the art therapist may call attention to the perceptual aspects of the client's expression and behavior by commenting on "the effects of the child's initially random or kinesthetically experienced acts" (Kramer, 1979, p. 222). Through the manipulation of art materials the individual im-poses form and structure on the materials and also on his/her own raw emotions. The idea or images for the work may be based on the child's wishes or fantasies, but making an object involves kinesthetic, emotion-al, and intellectual activities under the control of the ego. Ultimately the goal for the child is to produce aesthetic objects with symbolic value for him/her. The child's confrontation with his/her own work as well as its pathology is made easier through the narcissistic gratifications obtained in viewing the work. Defenses are manifested in the child's work through stereotyped and fixed bizarre images, as well as false sentiment displayed through the work.

Art as therapy is "conceived of primarily as a means of supporting the ego, fostering the development of sense of identity, and promoting maturation in general" (Kramer, 1971, p. xiii). In this approach the art therapist functions as an artist and educator who is able to modify the techniques and media used according to the client's pathology. Insight is not emphasized, and the client's unconscious material is not uncovered or interpreted directly to the client. Nevertheless, the therapist interprets the expression in Freudian psychoanalytic terms for his/her own and others' benefit. In her writing Kramer also analyzes the works produced by her clients in terms of formal elements and aesthetic value.

Kramer (1971, 1979) bases her approach of art as therapy primarily on the concept of sublimation. In sublimation, primitive urges and behavior are transformed into ego-syntonic and socially acceptable behavior. Through sublimation the individual arrives at an inner harmony and also harmony in the expression. The latter is achieved in an art work through integration and balance of tensions.

Kramer (1979) states that art as therapy is contraindicated with brain-damaged and borderline children. The first are overwhelmed by the profusion of stimuli and the freedom of creative art; for the second group art is often upsetting and leads to chaotic behavior. However, the use of art in therapy with neurologically handicapped children has been discussed by Uhlin and De Chiara (1984).

Like Kramer, *Ulman* (1975a, 1975b) believes that art therapy and the function of art therapy can be understood only on the basis of sublimation. The artist as therapist is equipped to deal with nonverbal expression through visual images since regression to primitive, preverbal level modes of thought is not alien to the artist's ego. Ulman (1975a) considers that the motivation for integration comes from within the personality through its striving to bring order out of chaos, and establishing a relation between the self and the world: "In the creative process, inner and outer realities are fused into a new entity" (p. 13).

The clients' interaction with the media directly expresses their feelings, which in turn can be translated in words. In contrast, "on the rarer occasions when the artistic process is completed, the artist patient has created a new form which in some way exemplifies a human process or understanding. It can be talked about but cannot be translated in words" (p. 32).

Art Psychotherapy

The following approaches to art therapy are all considered as art psychotherapy. Here, the emphasis is placed upon the *process* of creating the expression, and the client's verbalization about the visual product integrates its different aspects for him/her. The importance of the structural aspects of the visual expression and creativity varies in the different approaches. The reflective distance from the product as opposed to identification with the product also varies between the different approaches, as do the use of free associations to the images produced and the importance placed on defense mechanisms. Different approaches vary also in the extent and variety of media used, and the therapist's structuring the use of the media.

Humanistic/Structural Viewpoint

Betensky (Betensky, 1973a, 1973b, 1977, 1987; Betensky & Nucho, 1982) uses spontaneous expressions in art media as a communication between inner experience and outer or external reality. Betensky (1977) describes her approach as phenomenological dealing with cognitive exploration of the relationship between objective reality and subjective experience of feelings and thoughts.

An important part of exploring this relationship in the context of art therapy is looking at the product. Betensky and Nucho (1982) conceptualize the perception of the expression as proceeding in several steps. First, the act of looking at it separates the object from its creator. The second step is standing back from it to gain objectivity. This is followed by involved gazing at the product during which "the maker becomes the beholder and receiver" (p. 138); the therapist encourages the client to describe what s/he sees (Betensky & Nucho, 1982). This visual processing of the product helps the client to detect personal patterns and communicate feelings experienced while looking at it with the therapist (Betensky, 1973b). The configuration or gestalt of the perception is grasped with all the senses. Betensky (1973a) designates this experience as a "psychological occurrence" which at the same time is physical, rational, and emotional. Physically, the client may be experiencing different sensations, such as increased heartbeat or change in the tone of the voice. Rationally, the client synthesizes the different separate thoughts about self and his/her interaction with others. Emotionally s/he may be experiencing intense feelings touching the inner core of his/her being.

The perception of an art expression by the client is an integral part of the phenomenological approach to art therapy. It consists not only of the perception of its content, but also its structure. Betensky (1973a) suggests that there is a structural relationship between the art expression and the personality balance of its creator. The strengthening or weakening in the structure of the work reflects a shift in the functioning of the personality. The client's verbalization about this structure increases his/her awareness of it. The self-disclosure through perception is seen as a creative act in that it integrates inner experience with its external representation. Different art media used are important in this process of self-disclosure in that media have their own intrinsic qualities. Betensky uses a wide range of media in her work with clients.

Nucho's (1987) psychocybernetic model of art therapy is based on gaining access to and integrating the dual systems of verbal and visual expressions. This model consists of four phases: Unfreezing, Doing, Dialoguing, and Ending.

In the Unfreezing phase, the client is introduced to the visual process of expression and to the art materials. In the Doing phase the client is engaged in the art experience, giving a visual form to imagery. The resulting visual expression is processed in the Dialoguing phase; this involves a distancing from the work, decoding the visual images, and translating them into verbal expression. The Ending phase deals with closure and integration of ideas derived from the visual expression, including review of the work and noting changes.

Tokuda (1973, 1980), in his "Image Art Psychotherapy" (IAPT), emphasizes the importance of action in graphic expression and the objective analysis of the image created as part of the therapeutic process. In this process a three-way communication takes place between the patient, the graphic expression, and the therapist. This communication promotes the patient's image integration and self-integration.

The objective analysis of the image consists of examining the formal elements of the image (Image Form), the reference of the image to either past, present, or future (Time Image), and whether it refers to realistic space, inner space, or imaginary space (Space Image). The analysis of Image Category differentiates between thought image, sensory image, hallucinatory image, dream image, or unconscious image. The objective analysis facilitates an appreciation of the image from different angles.

Tokuda (1973, 1980) emphasizes the integrative and stabilizing rhythm involved in the act of drawing and the reviewing or examination of the drawing. The drawing represents psychosomatic self-expression, including preconceptual emotion, followed by perceptual and verbal cognitive integration.

In the therapy setting the client may be defensive in regard to the visual expression. The therapist's task is to reassure the client and to provoke images by providing stimuli. The themes provided by the therapist can be geometric patterns, or even based on coloring the simplified reproduced expressions of known artists. The themes can also be abstract, psychological, or sociological.

Rhyne (1970, 1973, 1987) also emphasizes the configurational aspects of visual expression in therapy. The focus of her approach is identification with the expression instead of distancing from it. Rhyne uses different materials to evoke images. These become the basis for forming personal gestalts or configurations as they are experienced in the present and also related to the time dimensions of past and future. The art expression may be free and spontaneous, or the therapist may suggest specific themes.

Rhyne (1973) sees images as personal messages which individuals send to themselves. The expression of images through lines and shapes gives the individual an opportunity to contact him/herself through the senses and to create a tangible record of sensations, perceptions, and feelings. The memories of the past are encoded through sensory experiences. Through the expression in art media the individual can reexperience these memories, integrating them into the present. Rhyne (1973) considers the style of expression and the relationship between forms, in addition to the pictorial content.

Rhyne (1970, 1973, 1987) bases her work on the Gestalt psychology approach to art (Arnheim, 1966, 1972) and Gestalt approach to therapy (Perls, 1969). The focus here is on identification with the sensations and perceptions, and their integration in the present context. In her work with clients, Rhyne emphasizes also the use of art expression in problem solving.

McNiff (1977, 1981) emphasizes the structural and integrative aspects of art and art expression. According to McNiff (1981), the arts provide safe expression, emotional focusing, and competency and mastery through the organization of sensory experiences. In his approach McNiff deals with all the expressive modalities: oral and written language, movement, sound, and visual expression. The following summary refers only to the visual expression.

McNiff (1981) sees art as a cognitive form of expression and an organization of perceptual stimuli to produce aesthetic order and balance. McNiff states that "the perception of aesthetic equilibrium can directly affect the functioning of the whole person" (p. xv). The other cognitive aspects of art are motivation and problem solving involving engagement in external reality. In his view the psychotherapeutic use of art focuses on the cognitive efforts to resolve ambiguity in one's emotional life. Emotional crisis fragments the perceptual processes, which can be restored through the concrete enactment in a visual expression involving sensory modalities. In his work with clients McNiff encourages spontaneous expression using different art media. Both the conscious thought processes and the physical manipulation of the media contribute to the sense of control and mastery. Sharing the permanent object of the expression contributes to social interaction and validation by others. The communication between the client and the therapist takes place through the client's own personal language and symbols.

McNiff (1981) bases his approach on the Gestalt theories of perception, especially as represented by Arnheim (1969). These are supplemented by the cognitive and conceptual aspects of motivation (McNiff, 1977), and art as renewing and changing order.

Transitional Viewpoint

Landgarten (1981) considers the visual expressions produced in therapy as the basic agent of change. The art media may be used as a symbolic agent for boundaries and setting limits, as symbolic risk taking, and symbolic expression. The art expression may be free spontaneous expression or the therapist may give specific themes and topical suggestions appropriate to the circumstances. Often the client is asked to provide a written comment to the images depicted through the different media. These comments may be, for example, self-messages, descriptions of feelings, or references to relationships.

Landgarten analyzes the visual expression for content, process, and form. In long term therapy Landgarten (1981) seems to concentrate first on reality oriented topics. Only in later stages of therapy does she focus on spontaneous expressions. The main thematic suggestions by the therapist deal with body image, self-image, ego control and mastery, needs, and references to family. The materials suggested are often either collage or plasticine, both of which lend themselves to concrete representations of objects. These concrete objects can easily be elaborated with specific written messages. The therapist may also suggest using a colored background as a means of integration. Landgarten relates color to feeling.

Landgarten (1981) uses psychodynamic therapeutic principles as the theoretical reference. In addition to the symbolic aspect of the expression and the insight associated with it, she also emphasizes reality orientation and problem solving. The therapist is able to impose a considerable amount of structure on the art expression through the thematic approach and the use of media, enhancing the production of concrete images.

For *Wadeson* (1980) the verbalization about and associations to the expression through art media are as important as the visual expression itself. The therapist considers the language of the client's imagery, style, specific symbols, and moods associated with the expressions. Both the client's selection of the content and the pictorial style contribute to the subjective quality of the expression. The visual expression also has the advantage of producing a permanent tangible record which is not subject to the distortion of memory. The visual expression allows the client to express feelings and also to gain distance from them.

Wadeson feels that, for the therapist, art expressions facilitate understanding of the client's dynamics and current issues. The images also reflect transference to the therapist.

Rubin's (1978, 1984) approach to art therapy. i.e., facilitating expression, is based on her experience as an art therapist with children and her training as a psychoanalyst. Rubin (1987) points out that from the psychoanalytical viewpoint art can greatly enhance experience of insight because of its concrete and visual nature. Rubin emphasizes the use of the creative process in art and the role of art therapy in building integrative capacities and self-esteem. She also uses art to communicate and express feelings, to help with diagnosis, and to facilitate the uncovering of unconscious imagery or to support defenses. Working with children in both the diagnostic interview and the therapy session, Rubin (1978) gives the child free choice of media and uses an unstructured approach.

In the art therapy diagnostic interview the therapist decodes the symbolic messages presented in the expression and the images produced by asking the child open-ended questions, and also by observing the child's nonverbal behavior during the process and interaction with the media. In the supportive environment the child feels free to be spontaneous and express feelings. The formal elements of the expression offer information about the child's developmental level and cognitive functioning. The form and process also convey important information about the child's feelings and ideas when the content of the expression is vague and inarticulate. The art interview helps to assess the child's major conflicts, coping mechanisms, and defenses (Rubin, 1978). The child's ability to reflect on the process and product is indicative of his readiness for an insight oriented approach.

The child's creativity manifests itself in his/her ability to create order out of unstructured media. Art gives form to feeling, and leads to mastery of the tools and processes. According to Rubin (1978) the disguise offered through art may be left undisturbed when the child benefits by the defenses offered through this disguise. Repetitive confrontations with the feared idea and its representation through images help the child eventually to work through the unacceptable feelings and ideas. Rubin states that "in [the] course of art therapy vague, unfocused and fuzzy images and ideas often become more articulated and clear" (1978, p. 98). The expression of symbolic images often precede the verbal associations and insight by several weeks. Rubin (1978) cautions using active interventions and ascribing tasks to the client.

In her theoretical interpretation of the therapy process, Rubin applies the psychoanalytic view: the client reflects the transference reactions to the therapist through his/her interaction with the media (Rubin, 1978, 1987). The art therapist considers not only the verbal and nonverbal behavior of the client during the process of making the products, but also its manifest and latent content. For children the associative content is represented in the title of the product and the stories related to it. The implied latent content manifests itself through the distortions, exaggerations, and omissions in the visual expression, as well as the selection of symbols.

Psychodynamic/Psychoanalytical Viewpoint

Naumburg (1950, 1953, 1966, 1973), as a pioneer of art therapy, has left as marked an influence on art as psychotherapy. Naumburg (1966) states that in the process of dynamically oriented art therapy, unconscious feelings and thoughts are expressed in symbolic images. These images are produced in a spontaneous or "free" expression through art media. The client uses theme images as the basis of his/her free associations, thus translating communication through images into communication through words. The mode of imaginal communication is seen as more primitive than verbal expression, and as originating in the unconscious layers of the psyche. Naumburg's (1953) viewpoint of the clients' spontaneous interpretation of their symbolic images combines aspects of both Freudian and Jungian approaches to fantasy. The Freudian approach is substantiated by the use of symbolic images as an escape from reality; the Jungian interpretation predominates when the images serve a unifying function in regard to the collective past or individual future. These images are produced in a transference context; the latter can be in reference either to the therapist or to the images produced. If the images are produced as a result of transference, the client's resentment against his/her parents is deflected from the therapist to the images. The narcissistic identification with the visual expression helps the client become detached from his/her positive transference to the therapist.

In dynamically oriented art therapy the client is encouraged to make his/her own selection of materials. The meaning of the images produced can also be elicited through the questioning of moods or circumstances that evoked the design, such as the selection of color and that color's relationship to past experiences. Naumburg (1973) emphasizes that "all art therapists should be familiar with the principles and practice of psychoanalysis" (p. ix); nevertheless, in her work she also incorporates Jungian thought.

Naumburg (1950) points out that the visual expression of symbolic images involves the active participation of the conscious personality as compared to the passive stance the client assumes in verbal dream analysis. This active and creative participation may shorten considerably the period necessary for treatment.

Robbins (Robbins, 1983, 1987; Robbins & Sibley, 1976) combines the psychoanalytic perspective, including transference phenomena and object-relations theory, Jungian concepts, and holistic and humanistic viewpoints. The theoretical aspects are implemented through the concrete use of art therapy techniques to facilitate therapeutic and creative change (Robbins & Sibley, 1976). Robbins emphasizes the simultaneous presence of two levels of consciousness during the process of art experience, i.e., the symbolic connection to the depth of the inner being, and the objective observation and evaluation by the synthesizing ego.

In this approach the function of art therapy techniques focuses on three areas of self-development: (1) building out or the development of self-image, communication, and interaction with others; (2) revealing and discovering the inner aspects of self; and (3) the integration of inner and outer worlds. Self-motivated and self-actualizing individuals do not need assistance in the form of particular techniques. Others need more direction in the use of media and specific techniques in that they are afraid to move towards self-discovery and they retreat into a defensive stance (Robbins & Sibley, 1976).

From the object-relations theory viewpoint, Robbins (1987) sees art as a mirroring container that organizes "an array of different impressions coming from many levels of awareness" (p. 73).

Levick (1983), in her approach to art therapy, combines Naumburg's (1966) dynamically oriented approach with the knowledge of normal cognitive and emotional development. According to Levick, understanding of the psychoanalytic theory is essential for the art therapist's training. Her particular expertise and in-depth explorations cover the mechanisms of defense and their adaptive and maladaptive role in human development. Levick compares Piaget's (1962) stages of cognitive development with the Freudian stages of psychosexual development; Levick classifies the different defense mechanisms present at different stages and describes their manifestation in the graphic expression.

In her work Levick (1983) considers the process, form, content and/or associations as reflecting personality development, personality traits, and the unconscious. Art therapy is seen as related to psychoanalysis in that it releases unconscious material. As in psychoanalysis, the transference relation between the therapist and the client plays an important role in art therapy. Both the graphic expressions and the associations are considered in regard to condensation, displacement, symbolism, and secondary elaborations. Levick (1983) also refers to Arnheim (1974) and his concept that pictures reflect a "lower level of abstraction" as compared to symbols which portray higher-level abstractions. Levick (1983, 1984) acknowledges imagery as a style of thinking, and elaborates on it from the developmental standpoint.

LEVELS OF EXPRESSION

The expression and the use of media in art therapy can be seen as taking place on different levels. Kagin and Lusebrink (1978) have formulated a conceptual model of the Expressive Therapies Continuum (ETC), based on Bruner's (1964) and Horowitz's (1970) models, as summarized earlier. The ETC consists of four levels of expression and interaction with media. The first three levels are kinesthetic/sensory, perceptual/affective, and cognitive/symbolic; these levels reflect a developmental sequence in information processing. The fourth level, the creative level, can be present at any of the previous levels and may involve the synthesis of all the other levels.

The kinesthetic level focuses primarily on the release of energy and expression through bodily action and movement. The sensory component of this level refers to the tactile and haptic or any other sensations experienced while interacting with the media. The perceptual level focuses on the formal qualities of the expression; the affective component of this level reflects the emotions expressed and released through the interaction with the media. The cognitive/symbolic level requires the presence of mental images for its operations. The cognitive component of this level deals with logical, analytical thought and problem solving; the symbolic component emphasizes intuitive concept formation, and realization and actualization of symbols. The creative level emphasizes the emergent, synthesizing, and self-actualizing forces within the individual.

Different media enhance different aspects of expression. As with any conceptual model, the ETC creates concrete divisions between the different aspects of expression. The transition between the levels may be quite fluid, and at any instance several levels may be present with one level predominating. The effects of different media on different levels of the ETC are dealt with in more detail in Chapter 5.

DIFFERENT ASPECTS OF CREATIVITY

The different approaches to art therapy acknowledge the role of creativity as an active component of therapy. Imagery plays an active role in creativity, according to many subjective accounts (Forisha, 1978;

Ghiselin, 1952). On the other hand, research linking imagery and creativity has yielded contradictory findings, and the use of imagery in creative thought seems to depend on the sex, personality, and cognitive style of the individual. In regard to the sexual differences of using imagery in creative thought, studies of women show a slight positive correlation between imagery and creativity, but for males this correlation is highly variable and depends on personality factors (Forisha, 1978).

Creativity is a highly complex and multidimensional concept. MacKinnon (1975) considers four major aspects of creativity: (1) the creative person, (2) the creative situation or environment, (3) the creative process, and (4) the creative product.

The following main characteristics describe the *creative personality*. They can be enhanced at different times in the process of art therapy.

1. Internal locus of evaluation, which also requires self-reliance (Rogers, 1971), and strong but flexible ego (Arieti, 1967; MacKinnon, 1975).
2. Openness to inner and outer stimuli (Arnheim, 1974; MacKinnon, 1975); this aspect includes the ability to receive conflicting information without forcing closures, and the ability to withstand the anxiety and tension in the struggle to reconcile opposites (Rogers, 1971).
3. Preference for cognitive complexity, combined with curiosity, and intensive and extensive exploration of stimuli and problematic elements (Getzels & Csikszentmihalyi, 1975).
4. Creation of order out of chaos (Barron, 1953), and reorganization and transformation of external environment in accordance to the individual's view (Taylor, 1975).

A knowledge of the characteristics of a *creative climate* is helpful for a therapist in order to provide a therapeutic climate supportive of the client's creativity. Descriptions of the creative climate vary depending on the school of thought. The humanistic proponents of creativity advocate psychological safety and freedom by accepting the individuals' worth unconditionally. This includes providing a climate in which external evaluation is absent (Rogers, 1971). The proponents of the cognitive school of thought perceive humans as possessing a disposition to seek pleasure through encountering problems and raising the level of stimulation instead of reducing it (Getzels & Csikszentmihalyi, 1975). Thus the creative climate has to provide for many possibilities of stimulation. The creative endeavor is strenuous, and requires a capacity for coping with hardships, anxieties, fears, and failures. Therefore, at times the permissive climate can be self-defeating instead of being creativity-fostering (Maddi, 1975). Situations and role models dealing with these problems are necessary components of the creative and therapeutic climate.

For the therapist using the creative process as part of the therapeutic design, it is necessary to have an understanding of the *psychodynamics of the creative process*. The most commonly known stages of creativity are those proposed by Wallas (1926): preparation, incubation, illumination, and verification. The stage of *preparation* is characterized by openness and exploration of a large amount of objects and ideas. The creative process is enhanced by the intensity and extensiveness of the exploration of stimuli. Inner stimuli, such as thoughts, emotions, and sense impressions, are utilized in order to probe in the deeper and more profound qualities of the outer stimuli (Getzels & Csikszentmihalyi, 1975).

The *incubation* period requires postponement of closures, and acceptance of incongruent and often disturbing elements existing side by side. The preparatory stage and the first part of the incubatory stage are characterized by divergent thinking and temporary relaxation of ego control. During incubation the thinking is nonverbal and prefocal, involving ego diffusion.

The later stages of incubation include bisociation, which operates on more than one plane, as compared with routine skills of thinking which occur in one plane. Bissociation includes transitory states of instability characterized by a disturbance of thought and concurrent with states of anxiety (Koestler, 1964).

The *illumination* stage is characterized by the excitement of "Eureka" or discovery of new ideas. The moral judgment at this stage has to be postponed because the unknown must be recognized as unknowable until it occurs (Rogers, 1971). The depth of investigation and the period of prefocal thinking allow creative individuals to relate to the underlying problem. Less creative people usually relate to the problem's superficially observable manifestations. Taylor (1975) compares this to the difference of relating to the cause and to the symptom in medical terms: the more generic the problem, the more effective or creative the outcome.

The *externalization and verification* stage requires explicit and deductive thinking often associated with depression and sober acceptance of the material. The verification stage uses convergent thinking and selectivity in order to bring out the emerging structure and its essence.

The *creative product* is characterized by transformation or reformulation of a problem or situation. According to Taylor (1975), the creative product transforms the existing perception or the constraints of reality, and has a potential to stimulate and alter the conventional ways of perceiving in others.

Another variation of the different stages of creativity is proposed by Ehrenzweig (1971), in which the first stage is experienced as paranoid or schizoid. During this stage the inadequate old whole is experienced as disintegrating, and the separate elements appear as unrelated, accidental, and persecutory. The paranoid stage is followed by the oceanic stage, where the ego relaxes its hold on reality and accepts the incongruences of the separate parts by using undifferentiated syncretistic vision. Ehrenzweig describes this perceptual mode as "low level scanning" or unfocused attention, which allows one to survey the different possibilities without premature closure. The recombining of parts and the formation of new wholes involves release of energy characterizing the manic stage. The verification stage is characterized by depression and sober acceptance of the limitations of the material.

Arieti (1976) proposes that in the creative process Freud's (1967) primary and secondary processes of functioning are combined forming a tertiary process of thought. Arieti (1976) states that "the primary process offers the artist the imagination" (p. 156) whereby the representations are loosely organized, based on similarities, suggestions, and partial representations. The secondary process screens and/or eliminates the verbal or pictorial partial representations. The tertiary process forms a synthesis between the primary and secondary processes, producing an emerging representation.

CREATIVITY AND ART THERAPY

The healing aspects of creativity in art therapy are used and interpreted in different ways. The concept of sublimation of aggressive and sexual energies through art in therapy is emphasized by Kramer (1971, 1979). This sublimation takes place through the transformation of the emotional content into a pictorial form, thus synthesizing the content and form. Through the art expression the individual makes sense of his/her experience. The process of sublimation uses analogy to establish a symbolic linkage between a primitive need and more complex ideas (Kramer, 1979).

Creativity can be seen as serving the human need to overcome and gain control over anxiety (Grossman, 1981). Creativity and art help to transform the pain experienced in loss and mourning (Fleming, 1983).

The creative act involves a state of consciousness different from everyday consciousness (McNiff, 1981; Robbins & Sibley, 1976). Garai (1978) discusses the similarities of creative art experiences and psychedelic experiences, including those of symbolic death and rebirth. In

Garai's (1976, 1987) view the creative expression of all feelings is one of the main tasks in art therapy. The creative experience and artistic involvement produces a temporary fusion with the work and loss of boundaries, which alternate with heightened awareness of the separate existence of the created object (Rubin, 1984). The role of art expression in the integration of inner and outer experience is emphasized by several art therapists (Garai, 1978; Robbins, 1987; Ulman 1975a).

The integration of sensory and kinesthetic aspects with the verbal, cognitive, and symbolic aspects is a part of the creative process in art therapy (Kagin & Lusebrink, 1978; Rubin, 1984). This integration of several levels opens new views for the individual (McNiff, 1981).

The creative process is enhanced in art therapy through the client's exploration of and involvement with the art media. The therapist lends the client an auxiliary ego in dealing with the anxiety involved in the creative process; the art therapist also has to be able to provide a technical support for the client's creative art expression (Kramer, 1971, 1979; Rubin, 1984).

From the psychoanalytical viewpoint a shift in between levels of consciousness may precipitate the emergence of primitive introjects, which can be frightening and overwhelming, and at the same time also can give energy and inspiration to the creative act. The art therapist's role is to support the generative primary mode of communication. The art therapist also gives support to the client in facing destructive introjects and helps the client in avoiding a narcissistic injury (Robbins & Sibley, 1976). Validation of the client's creative experience is an important aspect of the art therapist's role; therefore, the therapist's knowledge and experience of his/her own artistic creativity is essential (McNiff, 1981; Robbins & Sibley, 1976; Rubin, 1984).

SUMMARY

Imagery is used in different approaches in verbal therapy and art therapy. In art therapy, images, feelings, thoughts, and sensations are expressed through their portrayal in visual media. Different art therapy approaches vary in their emphasis on art as therapy or art as psychotherapy. The main proponents for art as therapy are Kramer and Ulman. In using art as psychotherapy, the following therapists emphasize the use of media and the structural and configurational aspects of the expression: Betensky, Nucho, Tokuda, Rhyne, McNiff, Landgarten, and Wadeson. Rubin, Naumburg, Robbins, and Levick focus mainly on the psychodynamic aspects and the verbal associations to the visual expression.

The use of imagery in verbal therapy and the use of imagery in art therapy have several common characteristics which distinguish them from other verbal therapies. These characteristics are present regardless of the theoretical approaches used in the different imagery therapies. At the same time the visual expressions through art media and art therapy have additional characteristics not present in verbal imagery therapy.

Creativity is an important component of art therapy. Knowledge of the characteristics of the creative personality and climate, as well as of the stages of the creative process is important for the therapist using imagery and especially visual media. Different art therapists emphasize different aspects of creativity in their therapeutic work. Support for the creative process and validation of the creative experience are important aspects of the art therapist's role.

The different components of imagery, symbolism, and visual expression are discussed next before considering the interaction of these component parts in the context of a systems approach to therapy.

CHAPTER 2

Images and Information Processing

INTRODUCTION

The unique role of images in information processing is to provide a counterpart to verbal processing. Images appear to be more intimately linked to the individual experience than the verbal labels naming these experiences. Images may be more directly expressed visually than verbally. The specific characteristics of imagery that enhance their effectiveness in therapy were pointed out previously.

This chapter deals with developmental aspects of imagery, types of imagery, cognitive aspects of imagery, and images present in different states of consciousness. It also considers structures involved in forming visual imagery and the processes associated with imagery. Lastly, the chapter covers the levels of imagery and their function and enhancement.

An image can be an internal or external mental representation of a feeling or a mood, a scheme, an abstract concept, or a representation of an object, scene, or person. Regardless of their internal or external origin and visual or verbal description, images are experienced internally, and therefore this chapter focuses on internal images.

Images and perceptions seem to share the same channels for processing the basic visual elements. Internally formed images may interfere with the perception of external stimuli, especially if these stimuli are subliminal or not clearly defined (Marks, 1983; Segal, 1972). In the absence of external stimuli, images can be experienced as quasi-sensory or quasi-perceptual representations of perceptual, sensory, or other experiential states (Richardson, 1969). Images are considered one of the modes of thought and knowledge (Paivio, 1971).

Images can be simple or complex, concrete or fleeting, symbolic or abstract; they also can create an internal environment in which the individual becomes a participant. As representatives of nonlinear, right-hemispheric thinking, images provide information for the individual about the self, or his/her physical, emotional, mental, and spiritual experiences and needs. Thus images have an internal origin, and as dynamic, emerging entities they express the different levels and aspects of an individual's internal functioning.

The symbolic qualities and the formal qualities of imagery will be discussed later. The present chapter explores the different aspects of internal imagery itself.

MODALITIES OF IMAGERY

Usually the images dealt with in therapy are visual images. Nevertheless, images can be experienced in all the sensory modalities: visual, audio, kinesthetic, olfactory, gustatory, tactile, and also somatosensory. The three main imaginal modalities are visual, audio, and kinesthetic. The other modalities often elaborate on the above and assist in recalling complex images, especially those involving affect.

An individual may have a preferred modality for experiencing and expressing internal images. The preferred modality and the vividness of imagery in the different modalities can be assessed through self-reported tests on imagery.

In the therapeutic setting, images can be described by using words or, more directly, by using modality-specific expressive means. Thus, visual images can be delineated through two-dimensional and three-dimensional art media. Images in the kinesthetic modality can be expressed through movement and dance, and in the audio modality through rhythm and melody conveyed on musical instruments. Expressions in each modality have their advantages and disadvantages. The visual expressions incorporate gesture and provide a concrete record, which can be looked at objectively. On the other side, visual expressions can provide too much reflective distance on internal imagery, as well as intellectualization about the image. Expressions in the audio modality have much more direct feedback on the individual than visual modality expressions, including rhythm and moods; these may influence the individual's level of arousal more directly than the visual modality. Similarly, kinesthetic expressions involve gross motor movement, directly engaging the whole body in the expression. Both audio and kinesthetic expressions require a permanent record for detailed recall and reexamination of the experience.

Vividness and Control of Imagery

Assessing the vividness of visual imagery, as well as the preferred modality of client expression, is important for the art therapist. There are discernible differences between individuals in their preference for verbalization or visualization, as well as their ability to form and control images. Individuals who have extensive use of verbal information processing are designated as verbalizers. Visualizers are assumed to process information on the basis of visual imagery (Richardson, 1969). According to the verbalizer-visualizer dichotomy, a specific processing style may produce vulnerability to specific tasks, especially in the experimental settings. In the clinical setting the deficiency in imagery ability is presumed to be minimized through increased verbal elaborations. It appears that this dichotomy is one of degree, with most individuals having both visual and auditory imagery (Strosahl & Ascough, 1981).

Imagery tests can be divided into two large groups (1) performance tests investigating the visual-spatial ability; and (2) verbal questionnaires measuring the individually reported differences in the vividness of imagery (Paivio, 1971). The latter are of more importance in the clinical setting. The best-known verbal questionnaire of differences in the individual abilities to form imagery in the different sensory modalities is Sheehan's (1967) modified Betts Questionnaire of Mental Imagery Vividness Scale (Betts QMIV). This test measures the subjective evaluations of images in the following sensory modalities: visual, auditory, tactile, kinesthetic, taste, olfactory, and somato-sensory.

Another test used to determine the individual differences in vividness of imagery is Marks' (1973b) Vividness of Visual Imagery Questionnaire (VVIQ), which concentrates only on imagery experienced in the visual modality.

These tests have a limited reliability in comparing ratings by different subjects because the reference points for vividness of imagery may be different for each subject.

The perception and encoding of visual information internally depends on whether the individual is a good visualizer or, vice versa, the manner of encoding external visual information influences whether the individual has vivid internal images. Good visualizers have more consistent scan-path in perceiving pictures externally and they make fewer eye movements than poor visualizers in forming images. Good visualizers can generate more complex images in a single focus; they may have eye movements present in forming highly complex and unfamiliar images or in differentiating specific details or features in the images. Good visualizers experience more hypnagogic imagery and have higher recall of dreams than poor visualizers (Marks, 1983).

In addition, vividness of images varies, depending upon the type of imagery; thus memory images are less vivid than imagination imagery. The latter is characterized by its novelty, substantiality and color, and withdrawal from the word, as pointed out earlier.

Control of imagery is another individual dimension which varies with each person. Awareness of imagery and attention to internal stimuli are necessary for an individual to hold an image in mind and to bring the image into consciousness (Richardson, 1983). The individual difference in the ability to control imagery can be assessed using the Gordon's (1950) test of Visual Imagery Control. Control of imagery is an important factor in therapy, especially for individuals who are low visualizers and therefore have little awareness of the influence of images on emotions. Lack of awareness and control over imagery may evoke strong feelings or anxiety without the individual's being aware of their source. Singer (1974) points out that awareness of one's own imaginal processes increases to some extent control over these processes, and the affect and behavior associated with them.

Some individuals feel uncomfortable and at a loss to express themselves through visual imagery, especially those who feel much more at home with verbal expressions. This difficulty can be surmounted either by expressing the images in the individual's preferred modality, or by training the client to become aware of visual images. The latter approach will be discussed later in this chapter. Following the cognitive developmental sequence of mental imagery, as next discussed, is another way to increase the awareness and expression of internal images.

COGNITIVE DEVELOPMENTAL ASPECTS OF IMAGERY

The presence of stable mental imagery is a prerequisite for internal experiences using images; a stable mental image is usually present in children by the end of the sensory-motor period, ages 18–24 months. According to Piaget (Piaget, 1962; Piaget & Inhelder, 1971) the preliminary steps are images of significant others and the development of imitation through sensory-motor activities using both objects and self-body.

At the end of the sensory-motor stage deferred imitation becomes the basis of internalized mental images.

In the preconceptual stage, ages 2–4, the child has arrived at object permanency; symbolic play is used to assimilate external information. The play during this stage serves as the representation of formal images through concrete objects as their external counterparts, whereas the images themselves have a static quality.

In the preoperational stage, ages 4–7, the representational imagery continues to have a static quality and, therefore, concrete objects and concrete expressions are necessary for handling dynamic imagery. Around the ages 5–7 the verbal and imaginal systems become integrated. During the period of concrete operations, ages 8–12, imagery achieves a dynamic and also anticipatory quality. In this stage the child can manipulate the images internally, but the expression through concrete means is more effective and graphic expression is often recommended.

In the developmental stage of formal operations, from age 12 on, the adolescent is able to "think about thought"; daydreaming is at its peak at this time. Daydreaming has an action-based quality from ages 10–13, but it becomes increasingly future oriented, as well as exploratory of socially different roles (Singer, 1975a).

Piaget and Inhelder (1971) consider four procedures to obtain information about mental imagery: (1) verbal description based on introspection, (2) drawing by the subject, (3) choice by the subject from prepared drawings, and (4) reproduction by gesture. With children, the last three methods are recommended. Since Piaget and Inhelder regard the mental image as an active and internalized imitation, they postulate a close relationship among mental image, imitative gesture, and graphic image. The concrete representation of a mental image requires its representation through the latter two forms of expressions, both of which include motor factors. Gesture image is simpler than mental image, whereas drawing is more complex than mental image.

Thus images are a mode of information-processing in addition to the verbal modality. Images are initially based on kinesthetic imitation using gestures and the self-body. In the course of development, images become more and more internalized and require less external objects as a support for their dynamic manipulation. Graphic images or drawings nevertheless retain the developmental component of imagery in that they start with a kinesthetic gesture. Thus the visual expression has an added advantage of representing images over the verbal representation of images.

TYPES AND LEVELS OF IMAGERY

Since images are dynamic and emergent events, it is important to be familiar with the different types of imagery and the structures and levels of consciousness involved in their formation.

Internal images differ in their quality and function. They can be considered along the following three dimensions, which all interact:

1. Types of imagery
2. Cognitive levels of imagery
3. Imagery associated with different states of consciousness

In order to define the three dimensions clearly, each will be discussed separately.

Types of Imagery

Types of imagery can be ordered on several levels, starting from images originating in perception to those of internal origin. Thus, the different types of imagery cover a spectrum: afterimages, eidectic images, voluntary thought images, spontaneous images, and imagination images. The last three types of imagery are important in therapy and are discussed first. Illusions, pseudohallucinations, hallucinations, and dreams will be discussed under state-dependent imagery.

Thought or *memory images* are likely to have a hazy character and to dissolve under fixed attention. Voluntary thought images are formed as a result of an individual instructing him/herself to imagine something or of receiving instructions to do so. The vividness and controllability of voluntary thought images vary from individual to individual. They can be present in any of the modalities and can have present specific somatic activity. For example, the instructions "imagine lemon juice in your mouth" may produce salivation (Richardson, 1983).

Spontaneous thought imagery emerges into awareness of itself whenever goal-directed verbal thought is blocked or becomes confused or uncertain. Similarly, the inability to recall something may produce spontaneous thought imagery which helps one to understand and reconstruct the situation. This type of thought imagery is a constantly changing phenomenon that occurs spontaneously concurrently with functioning in external reality.

If attention is withdrawn from the external reality or under conditions where the input from the external reality is reduced, as in sensory isolation, spontaneous thought imagery may change over to imagination imagery, as characterized by its novelty, substantiality, and color (Richardson, 1983).

Imagination imagery represents the inner world. These images are often unconnected to direct memories, but they may have an absorbing quality for the individual. Relaxation enhances imagination imagery, and a certain amount of relaxed awareness needs to be present for experiencing this imagery. Guided imagery, such as Leuner's (1978) Guided Affective Imagery, exhibits similar qualities to imagination imagery. Insight, especially creative insight, and understanding are often facilitated by imagination imagery; on the other hand, imagination imagery can play tricks on individuals in monotonous or isolated conditions by creating illusions in the perception of external reality. The creation of illusions may be partially explained by the observations that imagery and perception seem to share the same channels for processing basic visual elements, as was mentioned earlier.

Both imagination and thought images can be emotionally colored and may be experienced as emotionally pleasant or unpleasant. The unpleasant memory or imagination images may be repressed from consciousness or disassociated from their unpleasant affect. Both spontaneous thought images and imagination images may be symbolic and may also represent psychic or somatic phenomena. Thus an image of a rose can represent the perceptual experience of a rose, or the image of a rose can stand for inner centeredness, or the petals of a rose can form the image of a womblike protective structure. Ultimately, the inner psychic or physical or emotional experiences elude representation through images or words. Thus an image of a knife penetrating a body can portray aggression or a stabbing pain. Either of these experiences cannot be portrayed in their entirety through images or words; the representations only approximate the experience.

Cognitive Levels of Imagery

Cognitive levels of imagery can be conceptualized as ranging from sensory experiences to concrete images to abstract concepts. This approach to imagery is based on cognitive psychology, which considers the role of imagery in information processing.

On a *sensory level*, an image may be experienced as a sensory configuration without cognitive meaning. The sensory level is transitory and is evoked by the reactivation of a sensory trace representing such features as lines, angles, etc. (Paivio, 1971). The next step in the sequence of imagery formation is the formation of *concrete representational* images. Even though these images may be based on previous perceptions, they are not stored in picture representations. The images presumably have emergent qualities in that they are brought forth or constructed in the visual sensory medium, i.e., visual cortex, from parts or "chunks" of information. Their parallel mode of processing information points to their right-hemispheric origin (Paivio, 1971). These images fade over a period of time, and they have to be reinstated in the visual medium. Images as such may represent a "deeper" knowledge (Kosslyn, 1980).

The next cognitive level of imagery involves images with *referential meaning* formed in response to concrete words (Paivio, 1971). This level involves interaction between the two hemispheres or both parallel and sequential processing. On this level images are anticipatory. The anticipatory function may involve (1) the structure of images, such as rotation of an image in space and seeing it from a different point of view (Shepard & Cooper, 1982), or (2) the meaning of images in that the images anticipate the individual's actions in the future.

On a more complex cognitive level images may have *associative meaning* in that they provide the imaginal counterpart to abstract words and concepts. This may involve other modalities such as kinesthetic, tactile, audio, and olfactory (Paivio, 1971). The images on this level may also represent the figurative aspect of a symbol (Piaget, 1962) as discussed in the next chapter.

From the cognitive standpoint, knowledge is presumed to be *propositional* in nature: abstract, nonverbal, and nonimaginal. This assumption is based on the interaction of the two representational processes, imaginal and verbal, which require a common propositional basis. Propositions, from the cognitive viewpoint, have truth value and are abstract representations of the essential features and the underlying structures of knowledge (Anderson, 1978).

To summarize, from the cognitive viewpoint, images are spatial representations possibly generated from abstract representations of underlying structures and content in long-term memory. Images as representations generated in the visual cortex have quasi-pictorial qualities, such as size, orientation, and spatial extent; they depict knowledge instead of describing it (Kosslyn, 1980). The level on which an image is experienced depends not only on the information it represents, but also on the awareness and attention directed towards it: (1) a focused awareness may elaborate on the differential and detailed aspects of an image; (2) a more global and associative awareness may elaborate on the context of the image and its meaning; and (3) a more cognitive awareness may emphasize the abstract aspects of images representing the underlying structures. For example, in imagining a chair, an individual can focus on the image of a particular favorite easy chair, and in the mind's eye see its shape, or the pattern of the printed material covering it. An associative approach will bring up the feelings and experiences associated with sitting in the chair. A more abstract image would provide either a schema for the structure of the chair, or an abstraction of the support a chair gives the person sitting in it.

In general, memory retains modality-specific information, and the experiential and perceptual events are remembered in modality-specific areas (Kieras, 1978). Perceptual events are reconstructed as images through specific modalities, or combinations thereof. Even though images can represent concrete objects, they are not concrete "pictures in our heads." Images have an emergent quality and they can be described as dynamic and changing (Bugelski, 1983; Kosslyn, 1980; Neisser, 1978).

Imagery Associated with Different States of Consciousness

The third dimension of images ordered on several levels is the state of consciousness. What are the different states of consciousness, and what are the characteristics of images in these? In the normal awake state, consciousness may be regarded as related to the awareness, especially the focal awareness, of internal or external phenomena. People attend to sights, sounds, and smells in their external environment. They are aware, to a greater or lesser degree, of their thoughts, images, and feelings (Marks, 1983). As discussed before, attention directed to a particular image may activate the sensory level where the encoding consists of the sensory features such as shapes, colors, and textures, producing a quasi-sensory perceptual imagery experience. This image may be elaborated through input from other sensory modalities and associations from previous experiences.

In altered states of consciousness, awareness changes, and so does the quality of images experienced. Changes can be produced by drowsiness and sleep or through meditation or sensory deprivation, which may cause withdrawal from external reality. Emotional exhaustion and upheavals, shifts in metabolism, serious illnesses (either physical or mental), and the use of drugs, especially psychedelic drugs, are all circumstances under which people may experience altered states of consciousness.

Altered states differ from the normal states of consciousness either through hyperarousal, hypoarousal, or a combination of both. Hyperarousal, characterized by a high rate of information processing, is present in emotional upheavals and acute psychosis. This arousal can be limited predominately to the visual system, such as that present in LSD and mescaline intoxication. Altered states of consciousness are associated also with hypoarousal, as in meditation and sensory deprivation. Rapid eye movement (REM) sleep is a combination of hypo- and hyperarousal where gross motor movement is inhibited yet the autonomic nervous system, eye movement, and brain activity are increased. All of these are known to produce vivid images, over which the individual lacks control.

The visual phenomena and images experienced in the different states of consciousness can be ordered on several levels, ranging from sensory images to complex imagery to mystical experiences beyond images and words.

The simplest images on the sensory level are *entoptic images*, which arise from stimulation within the optic structures of the eye or in the optic tract. A well-known entoptic experience is that of seeing stars after a blow to the eye or head. Similarly, vague luminescent shapes, dancing lines, and geometric figures are entoptic phenomena, as are experiences of shadows cast by the blood vessels upon the retina (Horowitz, 1970). Entoptic images might possibly contribute to pseudohallucinations and hallucinations (Horowitz, 1983).

Hypnagogic images and *hypnopompic images* occur in the transition stages between waking and sleep. Hypnagogic images are series of images present in between being awake and falling asleep. Hypnopompic images are similar images occurring while waking up. Hypnagogic and hypnopompic images can be entoptic. However, they can also originate by repeated stimulation of the visual system during the day, as in recurrent images. Hypnagogic and hypnopompic images are not under voluntary control and they tend to progress from reality-oriented images towards fantasy images (Horowitz, 1970).

The content of *dream images* changes during the night. Earlier dreams are more reality oriented and deal with the previous day's residues. As the REM periods proceed during the night, the dreams become more complex and bizarre and incorporate earlier emotionally colored visual experiences and memories (Molinari & Foulkes, 1969). On the other hand, left-hemispheric activity increases during the night. Lucid dreaming, as experienced towards the morning hours, has lifelike quality and the dreamer is aware that he has some control over the dreams (LaBerge, 1980).

Drug-induced images are pseudohallucinations, since these experiences lack the delusional component that they exist in reality. Pseudohallucinations range from those based on entoptic phenomena and perceptual distortions to fantastic complex images experienced with larger amount of drugs and later in the drug "trip." The stages experienced are influenced by the individual differences in response to the drug.

The types of imagery present under the influence of drugs can be placed on three to four general levels (Grof, 1976; Klüver, 1966; Masters & Houston, 1968).

1. At the beginning of the intoxication, sensory experiences are enhanced. On the sensory level, the images have a simple ornamental or geometrical pattern which undergoes constant changes and lacks continuity. The images can be described as "form constants," such as grating, lattice, honeycomb, tunnel, funnel, spiral (Kluver, 1966; Siegel & Jarvik, 1975). Objects, in turn, may appear as multiples, as in polypsia. There may be a large variation in color tones. Symmetry is the most outstanding feature of colors, forms, and configurations (Klüver, 1966). Sensory level images are the result of the chemical stimulation of the perceptive visual analyzers on a very basic level (Ey, 1973; Grof, 1976).

2. The next stage of intoxication is characterized by the presence of complex abstract or scenic images. These images are recollective in nature and reflect emotionally charged personal experiences in the form of metaphors. Through images, parts of the body, such as muscles, the cardiovascular system, the bowels, and urogenital apparatus release the tensions accumulated in response to traumatic situations (Grof, 1976). Images associated with paranoia may also be present at this stage. This recollective-analytical level of psychedelic drug intoxication is referred to as the "Freudian" level of consciousness.

3. The next deeper level present in the intoxication involves the individual's participation with all senses and profound emotions. This level is referred to as the symbolic level (Masters & Houston, 1968) or perinatal level (Grof, 1976). The symbolic level may involve images of birth or death and dying, evolutionary and historical themes, and images of an archetypal character. Archetypal images may include identification with galaxies and the solar system, sacrificial ceremonies, devils and wrathful deities, and beautiful rainbows. The images produced on this level are most likely to be communicated through graphic means, such as painting. The images to be drawn or painted are described as already present on the canvas. The images experienced in this stage are also likened to dream images. The most frequent imaginal form expressed is that of the mandala, which represents the basic tenet of spiritual harmony with the universe (Masters & Houston, 1968).

4. The last level is defined as the transpersonal level of illumination or integration often associated with self-integration. This level is experienced as basically uncommunicable, and may involve religious or mysti-

cal experiences. Ego boundaries are experienced as dissolved beyond the limitations of space and time.

In *psychosis* and *schizophrenia* the images and hallucinations experienced fall predominantly on levels 1 and 3, as described: the geometric and ornamental, and the archetypal symbolic images. Images of geometrical patterns are predominantly experienced by paranoid schizophrenics and the images of the symbolic stage are experienced by chronic schizophrenics and by acute psychotics. Similarly to psychedelic drug users, psychotics and schizophrenics need to express their images through visual means. The schizophrenic may experience the transpersonal level through psychotic delusions, such as of being in heaven. The more personal or "Freudian" images may appear in the later stages of reconstitution.

In summary, the levels of consciousness and the concomitant images experienced in psychosis, schizophrenia, and psychedelic drug intoxication range from superficial-sensory, to intensively personal, to archetypal-symbolic, and lastly to transpersonal-illuminative. The experiences of these stages depend on the depth of psychosis or intoxication, and the individual differences in openness to these experiences.

HEMISPHERIC DIFFERENCES AND PSYCHOPHYSIOLOGICAL COMPONENTS OF IMAGERY

Openness to different stimuli, and different modes of processing the stimuli are structually based on hemispheric differences in information processing. The two ways of processing information, the imaginal mode and the verbal mode, are associated with the differences in the functioning of the two hemispheres. Verbal processing is predominantly associated with the left-hemispheric functioning, whereas imagery is associated with that of the right hemisphere.

The right hemisphere is significantly faster in visual coding, whereas the left hemisphere is significantly faster in verbal coding of information (Seamon & Gazzaniga, 1973). The two hemispheres respond differentially to imagery and verbal-inner speech tasks. Alpha activity is suppressed more in the right hemisphere with visual imagery than with verbal-inner speech tasks (Dumas & Morgan, 1975; Robbins & McAdam, 1974).

Right-hemispheric functions involve the processing of visuo-spatial information, visual imagery, and visual memory, as well as the discrimination of hue and color (Davidoff, 1976; Pennal, 1977). The right hemisphere is predominant in perceiving faces (Levy, Treverthen, & Sperry,

1972), including processing the emotional expression of faces (Ley, 1983). Affective imagery activates right-hemispheric functioning relatively more than left-hemispheric functioning (Ehrlichman & Wiener, 1980; Ley, 1983). Dream images are also associated with right-hemispheric activity, including strong emotions, the prominence of objects, space, and hearing music (Cohen, 1977). The function of the right hemisphere is impaired in depression, as is the ability to form internal images (Tucker, Stenslie, Roth, & Shearer, 1981).

Electroencephalographic (EEG) studies show that imagery is a predominant right-hemisphere process. Alpha activity in the occipital, temporal, and parietal areas of the brain shows desynchronization concurrent with imagery tasks (alpha activity desynchronization in an area indicates active involvement in the information processing) (Dumas & Morgan, 1975; Ehrlichman & Wiener, 1980; Morgan, McDonald, & Hilgard, 1974; Morgan, McDonald, & McDonald, 1971; Robbins & McAdam, 1974). However, this right-hemispheric advantage in visualization and perception of visual stimuli may be sex-determined. In visualization studies, males show more right-hemispheric laterization in visual and imagery tasks. Females do not display hemispheric differentiation in these tasks (Ray, Morell, Frediana, & Tucker, 1976; Tucker, 1976).

The right hemisphere, especially the right anterior frontal cortex, appears to be primarily responsible for arts and crafts (Ornstein, 1972), and for the ability to form internal representations of body image (Achterberg & Lawlis, 1980).

Right-hemispheric activity may also contribute to creativity in dreams and to cognitive associative functioning (Dimond & Beaumont, 1974). The two hemispheres are complementary to each other in that the left hemisphere processes information sequentially and the right hemisphere processes information in a parallel manner. The interaction between these two modes of information processing increases the possibility of creative solutions. In the cases where the two hemispheres do not fully communicate with each other, the differences in the information processing can contribute to conflict. Each hemisphere may arrive at a different solution and the solutions are incompatible with each other (Bogen & Bogen, 1969). The hemispheric predominance for different types of information processing is relative. In normal individuals both hemispheres are fully active and integrated with each other, whereby with increasing complexity in tasks, the lateral perferences are replaced by increasing bilateral participation.

The presence of imagery can also be detected and differentiated by the psychophysiological components of the imagery (eye movements, alpha activity in the visual and parietal cortex, and covert muscular responses), including changes in autonomic nervous system activity (heart rate and respiration rate). The pattern of the psychophysiological components of imagery varies depending on the task and the level of information processing.

Imagery associated with cognitive tasks and visual recall imagery generally have more concomitant eye movements and desynchronization of alpha activity in the visual cortex than imagination imagery and daydreaming. There also seem to be differences in eye movements associated with short- and long-term memory. Long-term memory is associated with ocular quiescence, or the absence of eye movements. Image processing in the short-term memory has concomitant eye movements (Gale, Morris, Lucas, & Richardson, 1972; Hall, 1974; Singer, Greenberg & Antrobus, 1971). Long-term memory and prolonged imagination imagery are associated with a relative ocular quiescence and presence of alpha activity in the occipital area. Even simple tasks, such as imagining the letter *P*, *pencil*, and *pasture*, have different physiological concomitants: more eye movements were associated with the images of letter *P* and *pencil* than with the image of *pasture*. It appears that the subjects' eyes were following the outlines of the letter and the object as they were imagining them, whereas the image of a pasture was a long-term memory image from the past involving different sensory modalities (Lusebrink, 1986–87). The vividness of imagery and whether the individual is a visualizer or nonvisualizer influence brain activity. High visualizers generally have greater alpha amplitude than low visualizers. Low visualizers experience greater difficulty in producing images (Marks, 1973a).

Imagination of voluntary movement is associated with covert muscle contractions in the corresponding muscle groups (Jacobson, 1930). Images associated with negative emotional value have concomitant increase in heart and respiration rate. Heart and respiration rate also increase with the complexity, difficulty, novelty, and activity level of the tasks (Jones & Johnson, 1980).

In summary, the right-hemispheric activity is predominantly associated with the processing of visuo-spatial information, both in perception and in imagery. The left hemisphere processes predominantly verbal and propositional information. In addition to imagery, the right hemisphere processes more subjective emotions and information related to body image than the left hemisphere.

Art expression enhances right-hemispheric functioning and imagery formation, and right-hemispheric functioning affects expression. Images are expressed externally through representations in visual media, and the perception of external visual images in turn activates right hemispheric activity. Different types and tasks of imagery have different psychophysiological components.

IMAGERY AND EMOTIONS

In considering the relationship between imagery and emotions, it is necessary to differentiate between objective visuo-spatial imagery and subjective imagery, which is intimately linked to emotions.

Silberman and Weingarten (1986), in their literature review of lateralization of emotions, conclude that both hemispheres process emotional information, but show differences in the manner of processing and the type of emotions processed. The right hemisphere integrates information across modalities more readily than the left hemisphere. The left hemisphere has an important role in verbally mediated emotional information and mood states. The two hemispheres differ in their preference for the type of emotions they process—the right hemisphere is involved in negative emotions, the left hemisphere in positive emotions. This specialization is present most strongly for the anterior positions.

The differential processing of negative and positive emotions in the two hemispheres is explained by reciprocal inhibition or differential activation and arousal of the structures involved in processing emotional information (Miller, 1988). Tucker (1981) differentiates between the activation of the left hemisphere involving emotions associated with alert expectations, such as those that are happy, anticipatory, or anxious, and the arousal of the right hemisphere involving emotion associated with a reflective awareness and depression.

Emotional imagery activates the right hemisphere, whereas the latter is deactivated following an intensive expression of emotion. The right hemisphere is closely involved with bodily processes and syncretistic thinking. It integrates analog data from sensory and visceral channels with a more expansive emotional response than the left hemisphere's differential and sequential processing, which attenuates the emotional arousal process (Tucker, 1981). Each hemispheric activity may be primed or activated to increase its functioning with input that evokes processes specific to the particular hemisphere. Thus right hemispheric functioning can be activated with high-imagery words and words high in affective value. Left hemispheric functioning can be enhanced through verbal analytical evaluation of the images.

Emotional imagery incorporates sensory/somatic, perceptual/schematic, and cognitive/conceptual or meaning levels. According to Lang's (1979) bio-informational theory of emotional imagery, the pattern of the physiological components is a significant part of the emotional image. This pattern in turn influences important changes in the cognitive structure. Emotional image in this context is defined as "a conceptual network in the brain, integrating perceptual, meaning and somato visceral propositions" (Lang, Levin, Miller, & Kozak, 1983, p. 279). For example, the pattern of heart rate and blood pressure responses differentiate between anger and fear imagery scenes. Both anger and fear scenes increase heart rate and systolic blood pressure, whereas anger but not fear scenes also increase the diastolic blood pressure (Lang, 1979; Schwartz, Weinberger, & Singer, 1981). The physiological components of the imagery response can be significantly increased if the subjects are exposed to detailed descriptions of bodily sensations, such as the fear response descriptions "your heart races" or "you perspire heavily." Physiological increases were not present when the image stimulus was described in color and form (Lang, 1979). Therefore, it appears that there are not only differences in the sensory/somatic responses to different emotional imagery, but also that the responses differ depending on which aspect of the imagery is emphasized. Thus the emphasis on the perceptual/schematic aspect of imagery, such as color and form, does not increase the physiological components of the emotional response. It appears that the emphasis on the formal aspects of imagery promotes a shift towards more cognitive processing as compared to the emphasis on the sensory aspects of the experience, where the emotional arousal of the individual is increased. The different components of emotions are further elaborated upon in Chapter 10.

CHARACTERISTICS OF IMAGERY ON DIFFERENT LEVELS

The different levels of imagery discussed in this chapter relate to perception, emotion, cognition, and imagination, as well as to different states of consciousness, structural locations, and physiological concomitants. The above information seems to affirm the statement that imagery is a dynamic and emergent concept with several different levels, and not a stable and concrete representation of "pictures in the head."

Images on each level have different qualities in regard to their complexity, structural basis, level of arousal, elaborations contributed by other sensory modalities, as well as function and possibilities for emotional coloring, as seen in Table 2.1.

The simplest imagery level is purely visual and is characterized by the elemental components of imagery and perception, such as lines, angles, spirals, and their various combinations. This level is shared with perception; perceptual overstimulation or irritative lesions in the visual pathways and visual cortex may lead to the production of elemental images. Where the external perceptual stimuli are ambiguous, the information provided by internal channels on the sensory and on the level of concrete representations will produce perception of internal images as

Table 2.1
Levels of Imagery

Level	Types of images	Function
Sensory	Hallucinatory constants, Simple visual elements Lines, angles, spirals	Visual synthesis, short-term memory
Concrete representation	Images of objects	Recognition of objects and their meaning
Associative	Memory images, with images from other sensory modalities	Memory, associative elaboration Personal symbolic representations
Propositional/abstract and symbolic/archetypal	Abstract and imagination images	Abstractions of underlying symbolic representations of knowledge relating to self

superimposed by the external field. The early stage of the sensory level does not have direct interaction with the left hemisphere and does not have direct access to the verbal counterparts. The information from the elemental visual level proceeds to the next level of concrete objects with meaning. At the same time information from the elemental visual level can also be forwarded to the frontal eye fields, in the frontal lobes, where more creative and complex information can take place and affective enhancement and elaboration of the images may occur.

On the concrete representation level the simple visual elements are combined into gestalts of objects, places, and people, and obtain meaning partially through the contribution of past experiences and anticipated actions. On this second level some interaction takes place between the hemispheres where the verbal modality contributes to the meaning of the imagery.

The associative level is more complex than the previous two. On this level the images are elaborated with associations provided from other modalities in the associative area of the brain. Here the imagery may pursue either a cognitive course towards the associative imaginal representation of abstract concepts or a subjective, self-experiential course, such as imagination imagery with the contribution of sensory experiences from other modalities. The imagination imagery may lead to the experiences of symbolic images associated with archetypal symbolism. Images have affective value on the symbolic level.

Images become more ephemeral as well as more abstract as the conceptual, propositional aspect is emphasized. Images involving the subjective, experiential aspect become more complex and vivid where the individual may have experiences of being an active participant in the imagery through the sensory, kinesthetic, and affective involvement. Imagery originating on this level may be based on physical sensations translated into images. For example, the sensation of pain or inflammation in a certain area may be represented in the visual medium as metaphorical images.

Knowledge, either objective or subjective, or a combination of both, is ultimately amodal, nonverbal, and nonimaginal. Knowledge possesses a propositional or truth value on the objective level. On the subjective level, knowledge may be the experience of losing ego boundaries and of merging with the universe.

In the therapeutic setting, images can be described by using words (i.e., translated in the verbal modality) or they can be portrayed more directly using modality-specific expressive means. Acknowledging the imagery level of the client is important because each level is associated with a different level of arousal and different states of consciousness. For example, the client may be introspective and symbolic, or logical and cognitive, or even just involved in making geometrical designs on the elemental imagery level.

FUNCTION OF IMAGERY

Developmentally, imagery is important in information processing prior to verbal and imaginal system integration. The different positive aspects of imagery for young children are reviewed by Tower (1983).

In young children imaginal representation dominates thought, determines affect, influences behavior, and promotes assimilation and integration of external information before the integration of the two systems takes place. Imagery contributes to cognition in that it increases attention and concentration in children, provides for quicker processing of information, and increases reflective distance and cognitive tempo. As discussed previously, for the young child visual strategies for rehearsing and encoding information predominate. This is enhanced through imaginative play where external objects provide a concrete means for manipulating and supporting the imagery. Imagery also promotes original thinking, including divergent thinking. Imagery also has affective benefits, such as increased self-identity and self-control, increased resources in dealing with stress, increased frustration tolerance, and decreased aggression levels.

Imagery and visual expression facilitate the development of cognitive skills in handicapped and nonverbal children (Silver, 1978). Imagery as a style of thinking and as an integral part of the creative process can be used as an early intervention with children having emotional and learning disabilities (Levick, 1984). Images are important in daydreaming in a positive-constructive context, as well as in dealing with guilt and failure, especially during adolescence (Gold & Henderson, 1984; Singer, 1975a).

At any age, imagery as associated with the holistic mode of experiencing is a means par excellence for the individual to express subjective experiences and to process information relating to self. Images not only provide insight into personal functioning and problem solving, but also are facilitators of creative understanding and insights, especially in the discovery stage (Kaufman, 1984).

ENHANCEMENT OF IMAGERY

What enhances image formation? Can the ability to become aware of images be improved? First, reduction of external stimuli and relaxation, especially in a recumbent position, facilitate the emergence of images in consciousness. Relaxed alertness and attention to internal stimuli are two basic conditions for formation of imagination imagery.

Second, one has to increase the ability to observe external objects in detail to learn to become a good visualizer. Third, in imaging, one has to be aware that the image may not be "a picture in the mind's eye," but only fleeting images at first.

Samuels and Samuels (1975) give useful suggestions on how to increase both vividness and control of imagery through step-by-step exercises. The first step involves looking at a small uncomplicated form, such as a triangle drawn on a sheet of paper, and then recalling it and internally inspecting the image. The next step is concentrating on a three-dimensional object, such as an apple, by staring at and experiencing it with all senses. The final step is experiencing an apple in imagination from different vantage points, including "zooming in and zooming out." Control and transformation of images in visualization can be achieved through imagining a balloon and changing its movement and color. Distant memory images are brought to awareness by visualizing a childhood room and giving the individual a chance to explore the image as he/she moves within the room. The state of imagination imagery can be deepened first by using the image of an escalator or elevator going down and counting backwards from 10 to 1, and then imagining coming into a room with a comfortable chair that faces a screen. Finally, in seeking to find an answer to a question, the individual may experience an image on the inner screen that may provide information about the question. This image, though, may be presented not as a direct answer to the question, but as an unexpected metaphor to be explored.

Becoming aware of and involving all the sensory modalities enriches the visualization experience and the imagery present. The exercises noted were selected to emphasize the characteristics of imagery on different levels: the elementary visual images, elaborated images of objects, and complex scenes involving affect and input from different modalities.

Since imagery is associated with the right-hemispheric activity, exercises providing predominantly right-hemispheric activity prepare one for receptivity to images. First, the ongoing left-hemispheric activity can be relegated to the background of one's awareness through meditation coupled with a relaxed awareness of thoughts coming and going through one's mind without following them, and letting them pass as birds flying by (Samuels & Samuels, 1975).

An openness to nature, including a peaceful walk in the country; being aware of a multitude of sights, smells, textures (Edwards, 1979); or enjoying the immenseness and timelessness of a starry night sky—all these enhance right-hemispheric activity. Listening to melodious music in a relaxed setting also helps to activate the right hemisphere, as does sensing textures with the eyes closed and without verbal interferences.

Finally, drawing, painting, and sculpting are all right-hemispheric activities. Art therapy not only caters to a modality-specific depiction of images, but it also reinforces the emergent qualities of imagery. Thus art therapy reinforces the process of image formation. First, in visual expression the images are constructed using kinesthetic gestures and simple visual elements that parallel the developmental sequence of images on a basic visual imagery level. Second, through depiction of images, one has the opportunity to become aware of details and elaborations, either in imagery or in elaboration of the depicted image. By encouraging the client to elaborate on the image, to inspect it, and to describe the perception of the image, the art therapist not only enhances the client's awareness of the image but also improves the client's visualizing ability. The use of color reinforces the right-hemisphere activity and adds to the emotional quality of the images. Third, in naming and discussing the images, the right-hemispheric activity is supplemented and elaborated by the interaction with the left hemisphere.

The sensory qualities of an image are enhanced by depicting it in clay with eyes closed. Allowing the hands to form the object and feel its surfaces without the visual feedback often activates the sensory and emotional aspects of imagery. The audio modality may be added to the art expression by painting to music and letting the hand move over the surface of the paper with the music. This approach involves other aspects which are predominantly experienced by the right hemisphere—color and melody. Luthe's (1976) Creativity Mobilization Technique activates the right hemisphere by requiring the individual to do multiple kinesthetic "mess paintings" within a short period of time, which suspends the judgmental qualities of the left hemisphere.

SUMMARY

Imagery enhances ideation fluency and cognitive flexibility, including generation of novel information which may contribute to a novel solution. Images are used in problem solving when the information is too complex to be processed sequentially (Kaufman, 1984). Images function as a mentally, emotionally, and physically self-regulatory mechanism. Images may enhance healing and relieve stress, and, in contrast, "any blockage of the ability to image disrupts self-regulatory abilities" (Sheikh & Kunzendorf, 1984, p. 115).

In summary, images are dynamic, emerging entities, ranging from percept-like pictures to metaphorical complex images or abstract representations of concepts. Images are associated with right-brain activity. Formation and vividness of imagery can be enhanced through activities which enhance right-brain functioning, including drawing and painting of internal images. Images facilitate access to information about self, including the level of physical functioning.

Images increase in complexity with the changing levels of information processing. Similarly, images on different levels of consciousness have different qualities and functions. Perception images are simple visual forms that can progress either to abstracted cognitions or to elaborate symbols through the input from other modalities. The function of imagery includes information processing related to right-brain activities, information processing related to the self, and information processing related to problem solving, creating, and healing.

To use imagery in therapy it is necessary to be familiar with images as representations of symbols and symbolic experiences. This aspect of imagery is discussed in the following chapter.

CHAPTER 3

Levels and Functions
of Symbolism

"I am a space ship which has in it also the scary presence of a 'blob.' It is floating around till I proceed to spray it with silver paint."

Joan, an art therapy student, had recorded and drawn the dream as part of self-exploration. She associated this dream with fear; the space ship presented for her a protection, but the blob did not have any particular references. Subsequently she proceeded to paint the blob, elaborating on it in the process.

A couple of nights later she had the following dream: "I am in a lighted tent, camping at night. A black bear approaches the tent; I am scared, but I feel also protected."

By painting the dream images again, Joan realized that the bear was related to the blob; as a bear it was more differentiated in form, and more down to earth, literally, than the blob. A few nights later, Joan had another dream which she felt was a resolution of the earlier two.

"I am going down the steps to the basement. I am concerned since I do not know what I will encounter, but I open the door. My friend comes from the basement to meet me."

The painting of this dream now has the dark form in a human shape and it is familiar. Curiously, a dark object is still lying on the floor, but it does not have fearful references, nor does it arouse a particular interest at this time.

In the example, the dream images are associated with strong feelings. In giving the images a concrete form in reality through painting, the images and feelings are transformed and personalized. The fearful aspects of the images are transformed into something known, and therefore not threatening. The unknown quality is relegated to a less threatening object than the original image. What is common to these images? They all have a form, they are associated with feelings, and they possess aspects which are not fully known, but are represented symbolically.

COMPONENTS AND DEVELOPMENTAL ASPECTS OF SYMBOLS

A symbol stands as a visible sign of something else, to which it may be related through association or convention; a symbol especially stands "as a visible sign for something invisible," (Webster's, 1976, p. 1180) as an idea, a quality. In Piaget's terms, a symbol is "a material event (signifier) that signifies for the person who uses the symbol another event which he knows (significate)" (Furth, 1969, p. 25). A symbol is considered a form of representation of a mental image used to evoke absent realities (Piaget, 1962). These absent realities can range from something known to the senses but not present, to something unknown. A symbol is the best approximation available at the present time to represent the unknown aspect. In the psychoanalytic view, a symbol can be an object, image, or act representing in disguised form a latent thought or a repressed desire of which the individual is unconscious (Freud, 1967). According to Jung, a true symbol represents and expresses an intuitive idea or it has a meaning "that cannot yet be formulated in any other or better way" (Jung cited in Jacobi, 1959, p. 89). The unknown aspects represented by the symbol may have more profound meaning than the visible image of the symbol; the contents of these images for the most part transcend consciousness (Jacobi, 1959).

The level on which a symbol and its meaning is experienced depends mainly on the attitude of the observing consciousness. If the content of the symbol has been consciously apprehended, the symbol representing it may be regarded as unambiguous and unipolar, and therefore personal and concretistic, causally explicable. True symbols are ambiguous and bipolar; as psychic factors they cannot be causally apprehended (Jacobi, 1959).

The positive role of visual symbolism in thought and creative expression and its relationship to art therapy has been eloquently discussed by Naumburg (1966). Image making served as a form of communication to primitive man; at the same time images also represented his relation to the cosmos and his search for the meaning of existence. According to Naumburg, the unconscious of modern man as represented through images "is the source of that generative power which makes it possible for art to become a means of integration and renewal to the human psyche" (1966, p. 42). In comparing the visual images from prehistoric times to those encountered in art in more recent times, Naumburg states, "The archaic patterns projected from the unconscious imagery of man today are rooted in the same human responses as those which motivated man in primitive times, for age-old patterns of symbolic response remain active and observable today" (1966, p. 45).

Symbols are represented and made accessible through images. Both images and symbols contribute to information processing; in addition, universal symbols guide the unfolding of inherent patterns of meaning, which is seen as a basic process of life (Progoff, 1963).

In order to facilitate the expression of symbols and sustain their unfolding, it is necessary to be familiar with the following aspects of symbolic experience:

1. Components inherent in symbols
2. Developmental aspects of symbol formation
3. Conditions contributing to the emergence of symbols
4. Function and meaning of symbols
5. Levels of symbols
6. Symbolic unfolding of the psyche and the neurotic distortion of this process

Each of these aspects is discussed and elaborated separately and each aspect is considered from the cognitive or Piagetian, psychoanalytic, and Werner and Kaplan's (1963) developmental organismic viewpoints. The analytic psychology or Jungian viewpoint is discussed in reference to the levels of symbolism.

Components Inherent in Symbols

The following components contribute to the experience of a symbol: (1) imaginal/structural, (2) affective, (3) sensory, and (4) kinesthetic. The interaction of these components contains the unknown meaning of the symbol and leads to a goal-directed action, and eventually to the resolution of the symbol in personal terms.

The image representing the symbol has an inherent structure which remains stable through the different variations of a particular manifest figurative content. According to Piaget, a symbol has an external, figurative aspect, and an internal operative structure (Furth, 1969). In Werner and Kaplan's (1963) view, *symbol* designates "a pattern or configuration in some medium (sounds, lines, body movements) insofar as this pattern is taken to refer to some content" (p. 15); at the same time, symbol emphasizes "a fusion or indissolubility of form and meaning" (p. 15).

According to the psychoanalyatic view of Holt (1967), the stable recurrence of symbols is due to their structural nature. The operative structure of a symbolic image is related to its meaning.

Symbol as represented by an image also contains drive energy and affect. This aspect is emphasized in the psychoanalytical approach to symbol in which objects, events, and phenomena are organized in relation to drives and needs. These are processed in the primary process mode associated with self-oriented categories and the assimilation of new experiences in self (Noy, 1979).

From the Jungian viewpoint of analytical psychology, a symbol possesses numinosity or energy charge. A symbol also is a transformer of energy from its biological form to the differentiated cultural form. This transformation is due to the bipolar character of symbols, and the synthesis of unconscious and conscious material: The emergence of a symbol gives a form and progressive direction to a part of the energy present in the unconscious. The symbol arrests the regressive pull towards the unconscious (Jung cited in Jacobi, 1959). The Piagetian approach is concerned with cognitive functioning associated with lowered drive activity (Greenspan, 1979). Nevertheless, Piaget (1962) states that a symbol can be used also as "affective language" or as depicting feelings; thus a symbol at the same time can be conscious and unconscious. Piaget used the term *secondary symbolism* to refer to unconscious symbolism. The accommodative aspects of a symbol are generally conscious and the assimilative aspects are usually unconscious.

The sensory aspects associated with the symbolic image are related to the original physiognomic qualities of perception (Werner & Kaplan, 1963). The latter is based on "sensing" or feeling the stimuli as contrasted to perceiving them. This gives the symbol a dynamic, primitive quality "in which the external and the internal, the motoric, affective, sensual, and imaginal elements are all intermingled prior to their differentiation" (Kreitler & Kreitler, 1972, p. 117). Another holdover of the primary unity of senses encountered in symbolic images is synesthesia or the response "to a stimulus of one sensory modality with sensations which belong to another sense modality" (Kreitler & Kreitler, 1972, p. 70).

Symbols also have a kinesthetic component, represented by bodily expression and movement (Kreitler & Kreitler, 1972). This component can be seen as a residue from earlier developmental stages of symbol formation. The early developmental aspects of mental image and symbol formation are based on deferred imitation (Piaget, 1962) and on acts of depiction by external sensorimotor patterns (Barten, 1980). These different components contribute to the multilevel character of symbols (Kreitler & Kreitler, 1972) and their unfolding over a period of time.

Developmental Aspects of Symbol Formation

The knowledge of the developmental aspects of symbol formation is helpful in understanding the different components of symbols. The cognitive, psychoanalytic, and developmental organismic schools of thought agree that the basic condition for symbol formation is the ability to form a stable mental image or representation. The psychoanalytic view specifies that mental representation of an affective object comes before that of a nonaffective object (Bell, 1970). This is important from the viewpoint of secondary repression, in that in order to repress a mental representation one needs to form a mental image in the first place. Greenspan (1979) states that the inability to recall memories from the first years of life does not represent a repression, but "the lack of adequate cognitive structures in the sensory-motor period" (p. 102).

The emergence of symbolic function occurs at the end of the sensorimotor stage and is dependent on the child's ability to form deferred imitations and mental representations (Piaget, 1962). Deferred imitations produce images through the internalization of accommodated external actions. Images facilitate the differentiation between the signifier and the significate necessary for symbol formation. Symbols are based on the individual's actions, and this aspect contributes to the child's egocentrical view in the earlier stages of symbol formation. According to Piaget, the symbol has a figurative aspect and an operative aspect. The figurative aspect is based on the deferred imitation and its internalized representation, and the operative aspect refers to the meaning or knowing components of the symbol.

In the earlier stages symbols serve predominantly an assimilative function, as is evident in symbolic play. Two aspects of symbolic play are noteworthy in regard to the developmental aspect of symbols. One is that an object has to be defined through its conventional use before it can become part of the symbolic process (Sinclair, 1970). The other is the observation that the internal image is static between ages 2–4 and requires concurrent overt manipulation of concrete objects. It is transformed into a dynamic anticipatory image by age 7; at this time, the concomitant overt gesture duplicating the form of the perceptual response becomes internalized (Wolff & Levin, 1972). Both of these aspects involve accommodative and maturational factors. The exploration of objects and their qualities in reality and the ability to differentiate and internalize these qualities provide information about the object.

In the psychoanalytical view, symbolic thinking may be taken as synonymous with the primary process. This process is characterized by highly mobile drive associations, condensation, or representation of several images by a single image. Representation of a whole by a part and displacement, or the substitution of one idea or image through another connected to it through association, are also part of the primary process. Symbolism itself can be seen as an instance of displacement (Holt, 1967). Primary process is differentiated from secondary process, which is associated with reality orientation and conceptual thinking. Originally Freud assumed that the primary process remains in the unconsciousness without change and that the secondary process evolves with maturation. The more recent psychoanalytic approach (Holt, 1967; Noy, 1979) proposes that each of these processes undergoes maturation and serves a different function. In the primary process, the objects, events, and phenomena are organized in relation to drives and needs. In the secondary process, objects, events, and phenomena are organized as knowledge. Developmentally drive-controlled needs facilitate sensorimotor schemes representing the needed objects. The transition from sensorimotor schemes to internalized symbolic representation is presumed to occur in either of two ways: (1) the gradual emergence of internal images during dreams and transitional states of consciousness, during which the motor action is inhibited and external stimulation absent (Holt, 1967); or (2) the formation of stable body image and the transformation of body sensations, especially those associated with the alimentary and genital tract into symbolic images (Galenson, Miller, & Roiphe, 1976). Secondary repression, or repression of mental images and symbols formed in the early stages, occurs at the oedipal stage.

In Werner and Kaplan's (1963) view, development proceeds from a state of relative globality and undifferentiation towards increasing differentiation and hierarchical integration. In this approach the central notion of symbol formation is dynamic schematization. Initially in infancy the world is perceived in terms of sensorimotor patterns or as "things of action." The manipulation of objects leads to awareness of their characteristics and internalization of the sensorimotor patterns. The dynamic-physiognomic activity of the organism involving postural, sensory, affective, and imaginal components forms an internal representation of the object. These components give the object its form, structure, and meaning for the individual. Barten (1980) points out that in the early stages of internalization and transformation the symbolic vehicle is undifferentiated from its referent or the content it symbolizes. With the increased distance between the symbolic vehicle and its content, the symbolic vehicle gains autonomy and follows its own rules. Developmentally, the physiognomic perception is replaced by an advanced conceptual-objective one.

CONDITIONS CONTRIBUTING TO THE EMERGENCE OF SYMBOLS

The components of the symbolic image and experience are developmentally based. This facilitates the understanding of symbols, and their unfolding and transformation as experienced by adults. The structural component of the symbolic image may be enhanced by providing related concrete experiences involving motoric and sensory components. The motoric and sensory experiences increase operational knowledge. The activation of innate structures might also be facilitated through a physiognomic experience that allows the individual to get in touch with the original dynamic mode of perception. The physiognomic experience can then be evaluated from an objective conceptual viewpoint.

Symbol formation can also be enhanced by inhibiting the motor component and external stimulation, as in dreams and relaxation. The affective component of symbolic image may be augmented through expressive means which allow the emergence of the primary process. The expression in media with emphasis on sensory modalities is associated with increased affect. The same holds true for increasing the sensory component of a symbol. The use of tactile media, such as finger paints or clay, especially taps into both the affective and sensory components of symbols. A medium having its own inherent structure, such as clay, contributes not only to the sensory component, but also to the structural component of symbols in that it promotes sublimation. The creative merging of primary and secondary processes into a new mode of expression is termed tertiary by Arieti (1976).

Because media promoting affective expression tap into the primary process, they also may promote expression of developmentally more regressed symbols. This is also enhanced by the fact that affective images are internalized prior to nonaffective images, which in turn contributes to an earlier symbol formation.

Both sensory and kinesthetic components predominate in early memories and experiences. Expression in modalities or media involving sensory and kinesthetic components may facilitate the expression of these memories. Such an expression brings the kinesthetic and sensory memories to the level of consciousness or gives a mental representation which in turn can contribute to the formation of a symbol. On the other hand, the media favoring sensory and kinesthetic expression may lead to regression to a pre-symbolic state, like the media that promote the affective component of symbols.

Symbolic perception arises in conditions where the external stimuli are ambiguous or disordered. The individual through dynamic perception tries to organize the field and impose his own structure and meaning on it. Similarly, conditions of psychic disorientation and dissociation lead to symbol formation. The spontaneous emergence of the ordered structure of a mandala or a circle with a center is known to compensate for the disorder and confusion. The central point of a mandala may provide a focus around which everything is ordered; or the concentric arrangement allows contradictory and irreconcilable elements to coexist (Jung, 1972).

FUNCTION AND MEANING OF SYMBOLS

Two of the basic functions of symbols are abstraction and representation of meaning. The meaning may be unknown because a direct expression is not yet possible, and the symbol provides the best and most descriptive way to represent this meaning (Jung, 1956). On the other hand, the symbolic process may be associated with repression and the symbols are disguised representations of latent thoughts (Freud, 1967), and a disguise for the unacceptable (Levick, 1983). Symbols also contribute to the sublimation of unacceptable material to a culturally acceptable level. In Jungian theory, however, symbols are mediators and transformers of energy, as was pointed out earlier. Thus the functions of symbols may be to reveal, to disguise, to mediate.

Symbols contribute to abstraction and concept formation. According to Kreitler and Kreitler (1972):

> Abstraction is generally viewed as a high-level cognitive process which consists in the removal of features that characterize only the individual or particular phenomenon. Its product is a concept that includes those features which are common to a class of particular objects or events. (p. 302)

In abstraction, the specific features are removed to reveal the central and salient ones. Thus abstract symbolic images, such as a circle, are devoid of conventional references, but at the same time can evoke many references to specific objects (Kreitler & Kreitler, 1972). Another example of the symbol as an abstraction is the representation of bodily processes. This function of a symbol was discussed by Freud (1967). In the contemporary use of imagery, images and symbols become the mediators between the body and psyche assisting in healing somatic illnesses.

Through the process of abstraction, symbols allow us to perceive a concrete personal experience in a larger, universal context. The opposite effect is achieved with concretization and amplification with personal experiences and associations which endow the abstraction with personal meaning (Kreitler & Kreitler, 1972). Expression through art media concretizes the symbolic images, giving them a specific form which has a structural, imaginal, and affective component. The affective aspect may be portrayed through color choice because colors are considered as symbols of feelings.

In the example of a dream at the beginning of this chapter, the image of a blob is concretized through the painting of the dream images. The individual's personal associations to the specific image or color are important. In this instance, the color black is associated with fear, impurity. The concretization of the dream images facilitates its transformation, in this case concretization, literally, in terms of "down-to-earth." The blob becomes a bear in the subsequent dream, and the dreamer is protected in a tent which is lighted with yellow light. Light in universal terms usually refers to intellect, as may the color symbolism of yellow. For the dream the image of light contributes the feeling of security. The bear is still black, but its form is changed from a blob to that of an animal which stands upright, thus approaching the human form. The painting again emphasizes the supportive elements and neutralizes some of the fearful components. In the last dream, the main element is a friend in a basement. The friend is portrayed in dark colors, but now he is a known entity with which one can interact. The basement itself still contains some unknown elements, but these do not seem to be threatening nor do they compel the immediate attention of the dreamer.

This dream sequence illustrates how the threatening affective component presented by the symbol is concretized and revealed on personal terms. The dream images and painted images interact in that the dream images are expressed in paint and, in turn, the painted images are incorporated and transformed in dreams. This sequence of dreams presents opposites: black blob and silver paint, black bear and lighted tent, male and female. The transformation of the blob represents the effects of the sequential symbolic mediation between the opposites.

From a Freudian viewpoint, this same dream could be considered as disguising strong feelings associated with phallic and/or sexual concerns, since the form of the blob and its transformation may be seen as phallic. Again, the dreamer's own association would shed more light on the meaning of the dream.

In looking at a symbol, one has to consider the functions of the four components of the symbol: kinesthetic, sensory, affective, and imaginal/structural. It seems that any of these components may predominate at a given time. The predominant component of the symbol may influence the others. Thus, strong emotions may color the image; this may manifest itself as change in the image to some variation of the original one, or it may also distort the basic structure of the image. On the other hand, as the emotion inherent in the symbol is worked through, the image may clarify itself, as in the example of the dream images. Any of the components may be used as a part of a whole to discover the meaning of the symbol at a particular time.

The meaning of the symbol may change to a different level, or the symbol may have several levels of meanings, hence symbols are considered to be multileveled. Art media and art expressions provide means to portray multileveledness, and this quality makes them well suited for the expression of symbols. According to Kreitler and Kreitler (1972):

> Multileveledness is the capacity of a work of art to be grasped, elaborated, and experienced in several systems of connected potential meanings, each of which allows a meaningful, clear, comprehensive, and sometimes even autonomous organization of all major constituents of the work of art. Each system of meanings is called a level. (pp. 294–295)

This "multileveledness" is made possible not only by the work itself, but also by the capacity of the observer to grasp the expression at several levels, and to be able to shift the point of view without losing a grasp of the totality of the expression.

Levels of Symbols

Symbols may be experienced and interpreted on different levels of psychic depth as reflected by the images present, their complexity, and their meaningfulness, feelings of personal involvement and/or awe.

The unfolding of the sensory and symbolic images under the influence of the psychedelic drugs gives one perspective on the different levels of symbolic experience (Grof, 1976; Masters and Houston, 1968). The experience proceeds in a pattern or progression through the following levels of increasingly complex awareness.

1. The beginning of the experience is on the sensory level with an increased awareness of patterning. Images on this level lack continuity, or do not have personal reference.
2. On the next level, the recollective-analytical level, exploration of one's own mental space takes place, with the concomitant self-analysis and exploration of personal problems and values. The

recollective-analytical level of the psychedelic experience is referred to also as the "Freudian" level of consciousness.

3. The symbolic level involves experiences of rituals on archetypal levels, and evolutionary and historical themes. In painting this level, one of the most frequent and interesting forms encountered is the mandala.

4. The last level is the integral level, which seems to be religious or mystical experience. This is the level of psychological integration, "illumination," and a sense of self-transformation. This level is rarely reached and it is experienced as basically uncommunicable.

In everyday functioning, the state of consciousness of the individual, and the affective value that a particular image has for the individual determines whether the image will be seen as a concrete representation or as a symbol. If a rational, cognitive state of mind predominates, images will be seen as representations of concrete objects. The images will carry personal symbolism if they are associated with previous traumatic experience or strong emotions. Images on the universal, archetypal level of symbolism are likely to manifest themselves during major traumatic experiences, in major transitions in life, in the individuation process, and also in major mental diseases such as psychosis.

The universal archetypal basis of the symbols provides a structure and an integrative viewpoint in periods of upheaval when the individual's regular modes of functioning are not sufficient. The awareness of individual limitations and the acceptance of a larger consciousness than one's own ego consciousness lead to a renewed contact with the archetypal core and its content. The archetypal roots of symbolism are discussed later in the context of Jungian symbolism.

The continuum from images as concrete representations to images as personal and, finally, as universal symbols manifests itself in most individuals and appropriately to particular circumstances. Each aspect of this continuum has its advantages and disadvantages. The images as representations of concrete objects and specific instances are reality-oriented. Concrete images are limiting, however, in that they do not refer to generalizations, nor do they have multileveled meanings which offer the possibility to perceive a particular image from multiple vantage points. Personal symbolism defines an individual's view in the context of his/her life experience. Personal symbolism is limited in that it is mainly regressive instead of being progressive or future-oriented. Universal symbolism has multileveled meanings which are at the same time potentials for future actions. The danger in dealing with universal symbolism is that it may remain in the realm of potentials without a concrete realization. The state of consciousness in which universal symbolism is experienced is global in its character in that there is a lack of attention to specific references in reality and to specific increments of time. The archetypal content of the psyche can overwhelm the consciousness, e.g., in psychosis, when the archetypal symbolic experience is imposed on reality.

Personal or Freudian Symbolism

According to Freud (1967), different objects or ideas are cathected or charged with psychic energy for an individual in different degrees of intensity, depending on the individual's life experiences. If the affect associated with the internal representation of these ideas of objects is too intense or threatening, a symbolic representation is used. Symbols are formed through displacement and condensation. In displacement the libido associated with originally intensely colored emotional ideas and experiences is transferred to less intense ideas and images that then are able to emerge into consciousness as substitutes for the more intense ones (Freud, 1967).

Freud applied the term "condensation" originally to dream interpretation. According to Freud (1967), "Dreams are brief, meagre and laconic in comparison with the range and wealth of dream thoughts" (p. 313). In condensation several thoughts or images are represented by a single word or image. Similarly to displacement, condensation contributes to symbolism, except that condensed images do not display the psychic energy as displacement. According to Freud, symbolism consists of both condensation and displacement, especially in dream symbolism. In condensed images the emotional intensity is toned down through displacement. In dealing with symbolism, and especially dream symbolism, Freud advises combining the client's free associations with the interpreter's knowledge of symbols. The correct interpretation in each instance is decided by the context. In Freud's observations certain elements in different patients' dreams had similar meanings.

According to Freud (1967), the meaning of dreams is rather limited. It encompasses the body, its parts and orifices, with a special emphasis on sexual and eliminatory organs. Other meanings refer to immediate family and basic life experiences such as birth and death. Brenner (1955) points out that these meanings of symbols emphasize the interests of a small child who relies on primary process thinking.

Jung's Approach to Universal Symbolism

According to Jung, symbols are the essence and the images of psychic energy. The symbol has an objective, visible meaning behind which is hidden an invisible and more profound meaning. Symbols act as mediators between consciousness and the unconscious. Symbols transcend consciousness and act as releasers and transformers of psychic energy. Symbols provide a means to gain distance from the immediate, concrete bodily experience and to transform it into an event in "the realm of the psychic" that is symbolically real. As a result of this transformation, the symbol bridges the concrete reality with the psychic real. The innate human ability to function in both areas offers a cure of "crucial psychic disorders" (Jacobi, 1959, p. 92). Each symbol can be seen in the personal and the collective sense.

The collective unconscious or archetypal psyche consists of the fundamental psychic conditions accumulated over millions of years. The collective unconscious is objective in that it does not have moral judgments. The collective psyche acquires moral values only through the confrontation with the conscious (Jacobi, 1959).

The collective unconscious contains the archetypal core or the structual determinants of the psyche. Archetypes are potentials or inherent possibilities of representation, which are represented through archetypal images or symbols. Archetypes are a system for action and, at the same time, image and emotion. Psychologically, an archetype can be understood as an image of the instinct, and also as a spiritual goal towards which the instinct evolves. One part of the archetypal symbol points upwards toward the spiritual realm, and the other part points downwards towards the biological processes. An archetype manifests itself as an experience of fundamental importance carrying a numinous charge. Archetypes closest to our consciousness have the least richness of meaning and numinosity or energy charge (Jacobi, 1959).

Archetypes can be described by their dynamic and formal aspects. The dynamic aspects of archetypes are manifested as energy and its expression through actions, emotions, and behavior. The formal aspects are represented through images, e.g., dream or fantasy images. The formal aspects also can be represented as percepts through auditory or other sensory experiences. The content of the archetypal manifestations can be seen as corresponding to mythological themes (Whitmont, 1973). The more universal strata are revealed by the symbols, the more global and forceful are the images.

According to Jung (1968), symbols are living components of the psyche, and they have to be experienced. They cannot be created only intellectually. Symbols involve wholeness and they resonate through the whole being. The following methods can be used to resolve and integrate archetypal symbolism in individual terms:

1. Expression of the archetypal image through visual and tactile media provides a means to actualize the structural component of the archetypal image. Verbalization at this stage is often vague or difficult because of the global nature of the symbolic image. The meaning of the archetypal structure may still be unconscious at this point and an explanation of the image may not be possible. Contemplating and interacting with the visual or tactile expression of the symbolic image facilitates the emergence of the meaning on a conscious level (Lyddiatt, 1971).

2. Circumambulation or concentric elaboration of the symbolic images with personal references and association provides personal clarification of the meaning of the symbol (Jung, 1968).

3. Amplification or introduction of related mythological or mythic themes and images by the therapist at times helps to clarify the context of the archetypal symbolism. Personal responses by the therapist or other individuals to the images produced can be used in the method of amplification, but the individual's own affect and experience is the most important factor in determining the personal resolution of the symbolic image.

4. Active imagination is a technique facilitating symbolic unfolding of the psyche. Active imagination requires a passive concentration on the inner images, whereby the images assume a life of their own and the symbolic events develop according to their own logic. According to Jung (1970), "when you concentrate on a mental picture, it begins to stir, the image becomes enriched by details, it moves and develop(s). . . . When we concentrate on an inner picture and when we are careful not to interrupt the natural flow of events, our unconscious will produce a series of images which make a complete story" (p. 193).

5. Contemplation of an archetypal image, its characteristics, and its structure activates the archetype within. Tibetan tankas and Navaho Indian sandpaintings are culturally based examples of archetypal visual images used for spiritual insight and healing. In art therapy the method of the Sun Wheel (Rhinehart & Englehorn, 1987) provides another example of the use of archetypal structure to integrate opposites and to bridge the conscious and unconscious. The Sun Wheel incorporates the circular

form of the mandala with a rainbow color spectrum and the numbers 1, 4, and 12.

Levels of Universal Symbols

Images representing universal symbols can be classified on the following levels, depending on the objects or ideas they represent (Assagioli, 1965).

1. Nature symbols, e.g., earth, fire, sky, sun, river, flower, etc.
2. Animal symbols, e.g., lion, snake, bear, bull, fish, worm-chrysalis-butterfly (transformation), egg, etc.
3. Human symbols, e.g., mother, father, child, old wise man, king, queen, human heart, human eye, birth, death, resurrection, etc.
4. Man-made symbols, e.g., bridge, channel, flag, fountain, house, mirror, sword, etc.
5. Religious and mythological symbols, e.g., God, Christ, Shiva, Buddha; Apollo, Venus, Valhalla, Siegfried, etc.
6. Abstract symbols, e.g., numbers, geometrical symbols—dot, circle, square, sphere, cone, spiral, etc.
7. Individual or spontaneous symbols which emerge during treatment or in dreams, daydreams, etc.

The natural symbolism can be seen as related to organismic functions, and the animal symbolism as related to drives and functions of drives. Animals possess human characteristics in fairy tales and mythology. Developmentally, animal images are frequently present in small children's dreams. Human symbolism originates in childhood and becomes richer through life experiences. Man-made symbols are based on images of and experiences with man-made objects. These symbols are used to represent emotional and psychological experiences. For example, a bridge can stand for uniting two opposite opinions, and a fountain can represent a contained flow of psychic energy. The objects themselves have to be known in reality and internalized as images before they can assume a symbolic valence. The use and meaning of man-made symbols are to a certain extent dependent on the cultural background of the individual.

Religious symbols represent the transcendent and spiritual aspects of the psyche. They may carry certain cultural or particular religious connotations, such as Christ as a symbol of self-sacrifice for Christians. Abstract symbols require a considerable emotional distance and the ability to abstract. Abstract symbols are least likely to have readily accessible personal references. In their formation abstract symbols have undergone multiple condensations before arriving at their final representation through a simplified abstract image.

The last category of individual symbols is qualitatively different from the previous categories in that any image can have an idiosyncratic meaning based on the person's life experience.

The categories of universal symbolism differ in the relative accessibility of their affective, sensory, and kinesthetic component. The images representing nature and animal symbolism have an easy access to their affective, sensory, and kinesthetic components. By identifying with the images, the individual can clarify the symbolic meaning of the images. Man-made symbols and especially abstract symbols are less likely to have readily accessible affective components as compared to nature and animal symbolism. Mythological symbols, such as the image of Aphrodite or Apollo, may become resolved through successive ascriptions of human qualities to the mythological image (Bolen, 1984, 1989).

Some of the levels are more easily accessible to consciousness and their meaning because they are at least partially resolved through life experiences; examples in this group would especially be human and man-made symbols, and possibly animal symbols. Because a symbol can have different meanings at different levels, one cannot say "this is that," equating a symbol with a concrete object or occurrence. "This may be that for me at the present time" might be a more acceptable statement than a concrete interpretation. Once a symbol is lived through on one level, it may reappear with a different meaning on another level.

In the dream example discussed in this chapter, the image of the blob is abstract and alive, i.e., blob and animal at the same time; it changes to animal and then to a human form, becoming less scary through this transformation.

SYMBOLIC UNFOLDING OF THE PSYCHE AND THE NEUROTIC DISTORTION OF THIS PROCESS

Symbols as archetypal images seem to have an instinctive direction which supports the purposeful development of the personality (Hillman, 1983; Progoff, 1963). Symbols as archetypal images facilitate the psychic growth alternating between alienation and identification with the Self (Edinger, 1973). Similarly, the individuation process unfolds itself through symbolic images (von Franz, 1968). The images related to Self and individuation are present in dreams and active imagination. The psyche has its own inner rhythm which presents itself through the symbols. According to Progoff (1963), psychic growth begins with the image of its goal, and the pattern of growth unfolds itself as the image acts itself out. The representation of the images through art expression gives a concrete form to the process taking place within an individual. This process of unfolding through symbolic images requires sensitivity to its flow, and openness to the symbolic experience, instead of analytical interpretation (Hillman, 1977, 1983; Progoff, 1963; Watkins, 1984). Portraying the experiences through art media, writing, and movement carries the process of the psyche forward. Elaborations of the imaginal, sensory, affective, and kinesthetic components of the symbol facilitates and deepens the imaginal symbolic experience. Art embodies or gives a body to the archetypal image (McConeghey, 1980). Part of this symbolic unfolding reflects the goal-directed, purposeful differentiation of the original unity of the psyche.

In the process of unfolding, differentiating, and forming the symbols, the different components of the symbol may become dissociated. Instead of perceiving a purposeful unfolding process, a neurotic distortion manifests itself. According to Kubie (1961), this dissociation may be manifested as affect separated from its image or action; similarly, the action can be segregated from its image or affect, and the image from its action or affect. The symbols involved in this dissociation have a stereotyped and rigid repetitiveness. The repressed conflict is relegated to the personal unconscious, which is experienced as chaotic and confused.

In the psychoanalytical view and in the view of Kubie's (1961) schema of the neurotic process, it appears that the unconscious (referring to the personal one) is to be mistrusted. As a result the symbols are perceived as disguising this unconscious repressed content.

The goal of therapy is the appropriate unification of the different components of the symbols, which in turn allows reaching for the universal, healing level and activating the symbolic unfolding of the psyche.

In the Jungian (1968) approach, the symbolic image becomes the center or nodal point around which the personal elaborations converge. In the archetypal psychology approach (Hillman, 1983), the flow of archetypal images comes from a deeper source, involving all the components of the symbol and is goal-directed toward the development of personality.

SUMMARY

A symbol is a mental image representing either an absent reality, something only partially known, or something unknown. Symbols representing previously consciously apprehended content are concrete, unipolar, and causally explicable. A true symbol as a psychic factor is ambiguous and bipolar, and cannot be causally apprehended (Jacobi, 1959).

Symbols have imaginal/structural, affective, sensory, and kinesthetic components. The development of symbol formation can be based on deferred imitation and internalization of external actions through mental images (Piaget, 1962). From the psychoanalytic viewpoint, the development of symbol formation can occur through gradual emergence of internal images in states of inhibited motor actions, such as dreaming, and of transitional states of consciousness (Holt, 1967). Symbol formation also occurs through the formation of stable body image and transformation of bodily sensations (Galenson et al., 1976). Secondary repression of the mental images formed at early stages occurs at the oedipal stage. Symbols may contribute to concept formation, abstraction, and sublimation, as well as to disguise unacceptable thoughts. The dissociation of the different components of the symbol leads to a neurotic distortion of the personality. From the Jungian viewpoint, symbols as archetypes are mediators of psychic energy and support a purposeful development of personality.

Imagery and especially images as symbols are multidimensional and represent different levels of the psyche. Diverse theoretical approaches, e.g., cognitive, Freudian, and Jungian, are valid and necessary in dealing with the different levels of symbolic images.

CHAPTER 4

Depicting and Integrating Images

A middle-aged woman, in supportive counseling after the breakup of a relationship, complained of vague fears of "things falling apart" and that "something bad may happen." She represented this experience in the session with a drawing titled "Fear" (Fig. 4.1). As her feelings were discussed, the therapist asked her to do some free movement or scribble with a felt tip marker on a piece of paper to release some of her tension. At the next session the woman brought in a doodle (Fig. 4.2) which she had done at home when her anxiety started to increase again. She described the process of creating the doodle as starting out with a scribble reflecting her anxiety. While doing this activity she felt somewhat relieved. In looking at the scribble, she became involved in a perseverative filling in of the spaces between the lines created by the scribble. Ultimately the area was defined as a circle with a couple of sharp protrusions pointing clockwise. The client felt a sense of being centered and experiencing deep cutting pain "as a sharp metal disc cutting through me."

When asked by the therapist to create another viewpoint of the drawing, the client produced another drawing, which she titled "Burning of the Old Grass" (Fig. 4.3). She explained that the middle part of this drawing was a vertical cross section of a "converter" where the line of the "old grass" was sucked in and burned to produce a flame and to produce directed energy. After discussing the meaning of this drawing, the woman experienced a spontaneous image of "a unicorn lying on fallen leaves" (Fig. 4.4). The horn of the unicorn represented directed energy and was also an antenna for sensitivity to environment. She felt calm and composed, yet alert, not unlike the feeling she tried to convey through portraying the unicorn.

INTRODUCTION

In writing, letters form words and sentences that convey meaning. What are the equivalents for words in art therapy and image representa-

67

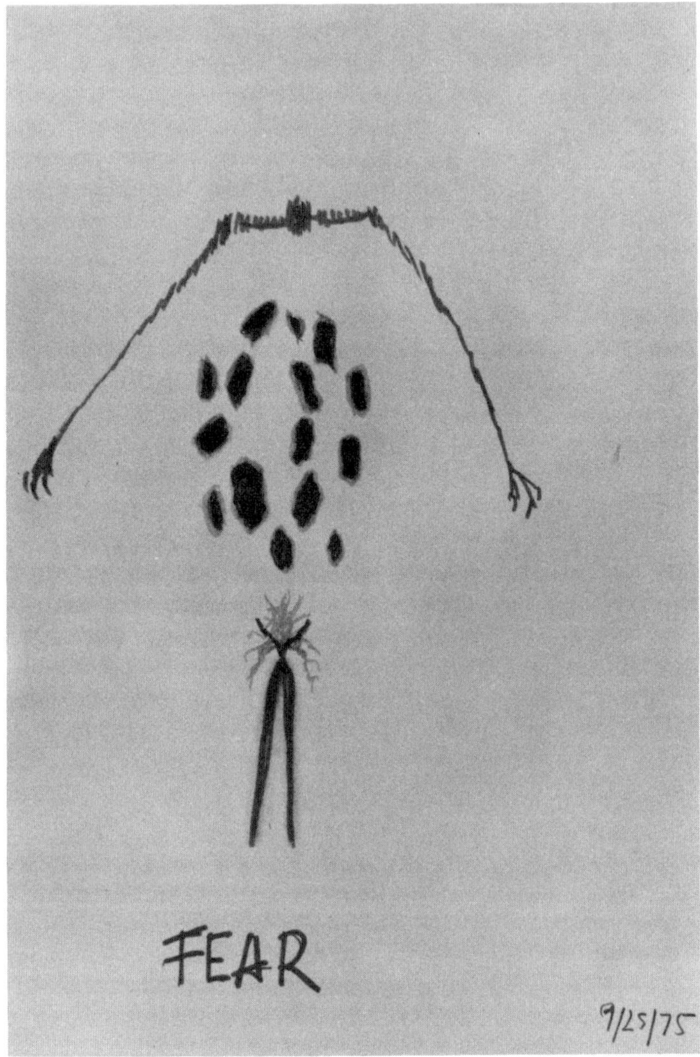

Figure 4.1. "Fear."

tions? What is the syntax of visual forms conveying a meaning? As with internal images, externally expressed images have emergent qualities and are generated on different levels of increased complexity. From the perspective of formal elements, the means of visual expression can be placed on the following levels:

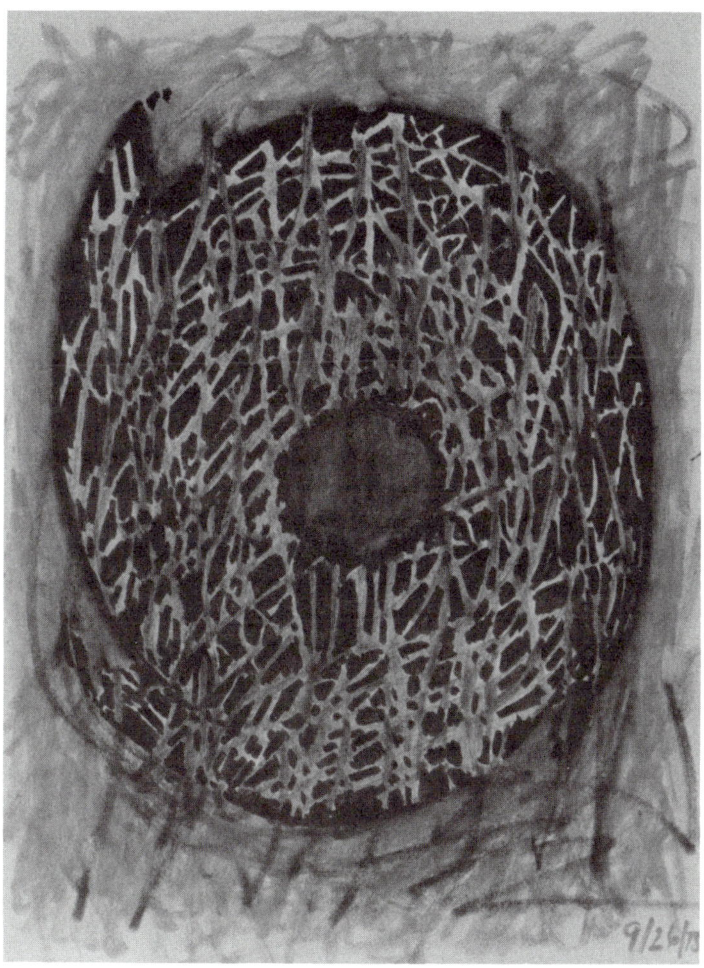

Figure 4.2. Doodle and elaboration.

1. The level of simple visual elements consists of line, shape, textures, and detail.
2. The level of individual forms includes the size, shape, directionality, and color conveying the content of the form.
3. The level of spatial context combines the formal elements in a statement of interrelationships either two-dimensionally or three-dimensionally, constituting a visual syntax.

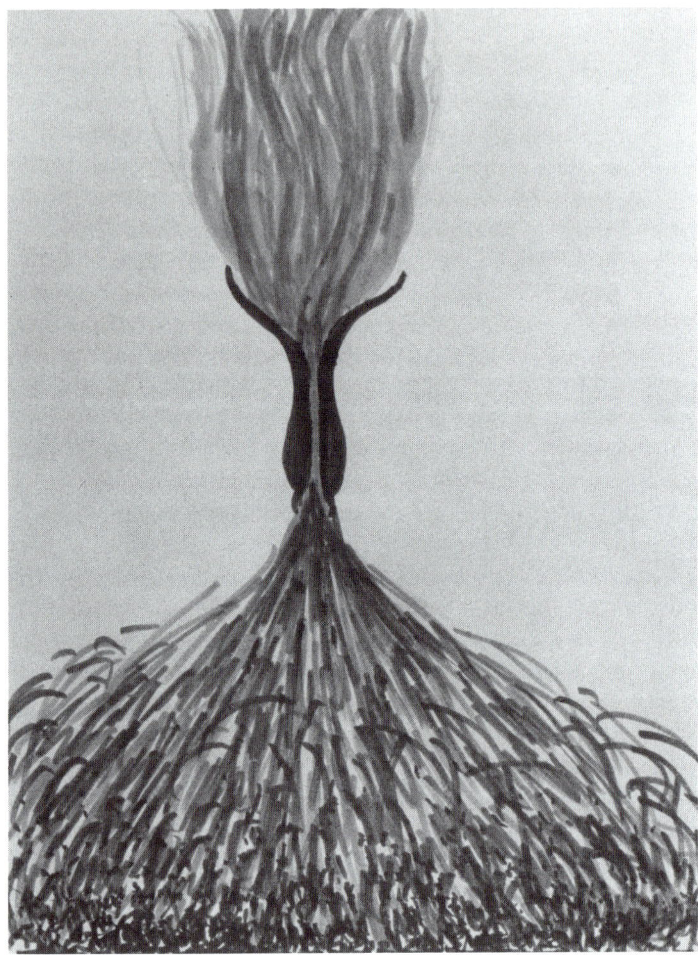

Figure 4.3. "Burning of the Old Grass."

The use of different media and different expressive styles interact with each other in reinforcing the expression on different levels.

This chapter first addresses the basic elements of the two-dimensional visual expression: line, form and the shape it takes, space articulation through form, visual syntax, form as content, and color. Secondly, it covers the influence of the medium on the expression and on the different levels of expression. The discussion of different media properties and different expressive styles concludes this chapter.

Figure 4.4. "A Unicorn Lying on Fallen Leaves."

LINE AND FORM

Line

A line is defined by its length, the pressure used, and the energy exerted in creating it. Following a line with the eyes reveals its direction to the perceiver. Lines can move horizontally, vertically, diagonally, or can be curvilinear or circular. Lines interact with each other, creating angles and crossings. They meander around getting lost in each other, or may flow along one another, reinforcing the movement. Lines may skip, creating interruptions in their flow that have to be filled by the perceiver where the perceiver becomes an active participant in the creation of a line.

The length of the line, a short stroke or a line traveling across the page, elaborates on the energy level, commitment, and intent present in creating the line. The width and the intensity of the line reflect the pressure exerted and the control used. A dynamic line, applied fast, reveals its landing and take-off from the page in the variation in the width of the line. The energy portrayed in a dynamic line is different from the steady but sluggish continuous line. For the dynamic line the paper is a field to land onto and to lift off from, whereas the continuous line is created through the traction against the paper and may be experienced as a stable ground.

Different strokes tell different stories. Light, wispy strokes may be noncommital in their intent or reflect a fear of commitment; the same strokes for another individual may reflect a search for the right form or expression, which eventually reveals itself. The heavy line may reflect the creator's assertion, or the continuous heavy line may form an external barrier to protect a precarious balance within.

The relationship between the line and the space on which it is depicted creates a scale determining the size of the line. The paper acts as a field which in turn influences the size of the line. A very large paper can be intimidating and reduce the expression to a short line in a corner, or a large surface can be stimulating and inviting to travel across its entire surface in one stroke. The paper also provides definite boundaries and most people respect these boundaries. Very small children and regressed psychotics often go past the boundaries of the paper.

Another function of a line is to divide and to differentiate a homogeneous field; here the line serves the role of a pathway. For example, in a field of finger paint, a line drawn with a finger defines a pathway and divides the field. When the line meets itself, the line may become a boundary and changes into a contour differentiating the figure/ground relationship and defining a form (Kagin, 1978).

A blank sheet of paper can also be considered as a homogeneous field, and a line drawn with a pencil makes a pathway in this field. The resistance to the first step in visual expression at times may be based on the resistance to violating the homogeneity of the field. By suggesting that the client make a pathway, the therapist may help the client by providing a frame of reference to the initial action of dividing the field.

The meaning of lines is created through the isomorphic experience in perceiving the line. The concept of isomorphism is based on "the relationship between the physical forces in the observed object and the physical dynamics in the observer" where the "processes that take place in different media may be nevertheless similar in their structural organization" (Arnheim, 1972, p. 58). Isomorphic resonance may apply to a kinesthetic experience, or it may create various related psychological and emotional experiences (Arnheim, 1972).

The vertical line may be associated with ascent and upright position, whereas the horizontal line may imply passivity or calmness. The diagonal line portrays a dynamic quality and it may suggest instability or loss of balance. The curved and circular lines are fluid, complex, and suggest motion of natural phenomena (Feldman, 1972). The right angle may suggest stability, and two lines crossing at right angles to each other may imply conflict and strife. Acute angles are often perceived as aggressive. Obtuse or wide angles may imply openness and balance if the two sides of the angle form a mirror image in respect to a vertical axis.

Lines also serve the function of expressing abstraction either by combining with other lines or by defining forms through outlines. Thus an arrow is formed by a straight line and the angle of it demarks a direction, or a circle with two dots can be seen as a face. As compared with the dynamic line reflecting isomorphically psychological and emotional experiences, line as an abstraction is not tied to a specific instance, but reflects the general features common to several instances. Abstraction represents concepts whereby "the specific features disappear, while the essential and central ones become salient and distinct" (Kreitler & Kreitler, 1972, p. 307). Lines as abstractions may become pictographs, or pictures representing an idea, similar to hieroglyphs.

The drawings represented in Figures 4.1–4.4 reflect different expressive aspects of line. Movement and expression of emotion seem to be the predominant meaning of the lines.

Form

A line surrounding an area or a color covering an area defines a form on a flat two-dimensional surface. A form is characterized by its contour, shape, size, directional arrangement or major axis, and the elaboration by any structures or details present. The creation of a form is influenced by the mood and level of consciousness of its creator, by the creator's degree of introspection or extroversion, and by the amount of spontaneity or control exercised in creating the form.

The contour or the edge quality of a form can be influenced by any of the above factors. Forms can be defined by well-controlled outlines or forms can have diffuse contour quality. Forms can be represented by hard-edged shapes, or have undefined or disintegrated contours with an undifferentiated transition between line and area and between the forms themselves.

The solidity of the form and its contour may reflect the intent of the creator or may reflect the ego functioning of the creator. Thus vague forms with diffuse contours may either reflect introspection or the tentativeness and lack of ego differentiation of the creator. Hard-edge forms may be forceful, deliberate statements or they may be encapsulated by an outline, protecting and defending the vulnerability of the individual.

The shape of a form is described by its contour. Forms can take many shapes, which in general can be classified either as geometrical or as organic-biomorphic. Geometric shapes are characterized by their straightness and regular curvature and possess cerebral qualities of the intellect. Biomorphic shapes are irregular and curvilinear, reflecting the pattern of organic growth (Feldman, 1972).

The size of the form depends upon the scale established by the form in relationship to its surroundings and other forms. The size of the form may reflect the amount of energy available to the individual or it may reflect the individual's self-evaluation. Thus, in a Kinetic Family Drawing (Burns & Kaufman, 1970), children may depict themselves as either large or small depending on their self-perception in the context of the family. Egocentricity, either developmental or pathological, may be expressed through the rendering of large forms. Small forms may represent depression and/or low self-concept.

The scale or the size relationship of a form to its surroundings also determines the emotional distance between the spectator and the expression. A form that fills the whole page or flows over the boundaries of the paper has an immediate, at times even looming, presence. Forms of intermediate size have a comfortable distance and portray an everyday quality in reference to the viewer. Thus, individuals keep a "perspective" on the forms or objects they portray, and are able to establish a relationship to their environment. Small forms tend to disappear in the distance, hence are assumed to be of less importance.

The directional disposition of a form is determined by the direction of the major axis of its shape. Horizontal, oblong forms are experienced as stable, and vertical placement of the forms conveys an upward thrust. Diagonal placement of a form has a dynamic quality, or it can also be perceived as unstable.

The textures and details of the form add surface qualities and elaborate on differentiation. The surface textures convey and evoke sensory qualities associated with the form. Smooth surfaces may reflect sensuality or care as contrasted to rough surfaces, which possibly reflect emotions, such as frustration or anger.

Details elaborate on the individuality of the form, differentiating its aspects. Perseverative concentration on details may be a means to avoid emotional involvement. For example, the drawings of obsessive-compulsives are filled with repeated details. Detailed designs can fill a whole page, as in the decorative schizophrenic drawings, without ever arriving at a unifying statement (Plokker, 1965; Prinzhorn, 1972). Detailed meandering designs may also be seen in the visual expressions of psychedelic substance users (Master & Houston, 1968). The perseverative quality of details may reflect an avoidance of dealing with the meaning of the form or an inability to form a "gestalt" of an experience and to pursue its evolution into a theme.

Through the elaboration of a form, details may become a first step in changing the form, or increasing attention to the details may have a regressive quality that contributes to splitting the form into several separate entities, which ultimately leads to disorganization.

GESTALTS OR CONFIGURATIONS

Forms can be abstract or refer to reality and external objects. An abstract form can be a form that does not have an external object reference and/or it can represent the end product of abstraction. Abstraction refers to high-level cognitive processes as well as to perceptual representation of internal processes. Perceptual expression of internal processes represent abstractions of a multitude of sensory experiences. Thus, internal experiences may be represented more adequately through abstract forms than through specific object references.

The given example consists of a variety of forms, ranging from small forms depicting encapsulated abstractions to a medium-sized form—the unicorn—and relatively large forms—the disk and the tree.

A whole gestalt is more than the sum of its component parts and survives and remains recognizable regardless of the changes of its parts or the media through which the gestalt is expressed. Thus a square remains a square regardless of its size, color, or whether it is drawn on a piece of paper or made of sticks (Kreitler & Kreitler, 1972). Good gestalts are defined as "the best organizations of the stimuli in the given circumstances" and they are "usually characterized by regularity, symmetry, inclusiveness, unity, harmony, maximal simplicity and conciseness" (Kreitler & Kreitler, 1972, p. 83). Gestalt perception is innate, especially the tendency to organize stimuli in simple good gestalts, seems to be universal, and varies but little across cultures. Learning and experience play a more important part in regard to more complex gestalts. Thus a circle or a simple mandala form is encountered in many cultures, but elaborations on the circle, such as those present in Tibetan mandalas, are culturally determined.

Good gestalts are associated with the presence of a relatively low level of tension and homeostatic tendency of the organism. Bad gestalts are tension-laden. Complex gestalts, on the other hand, while more tension-evoking than simple gestalts, may be perceived as stimulating and inviting exploration (Kreitler & Kreitler, 1972). A simple good gestalt may be elaborated through the addition of details and thus create a complex gestalt. An individual's preference for simple or complex gestalts depends on the level of his/her intellectual development and energy level. The ability to form gestalts is different for a mentally retarded individual who becomes frustrated and irritated if confronted with complex stimuli as compared to a creative adolescent who delights in the challenge of the complex stimuli.

Since simple good gestalts represent a homeostasis, there may be a reluctance to face the tension present in breaking up good gestalts. In the therapy session this resistance may be conteracted by a change in medium. Similarly, the frustration of not being able to achieve a good gestalt in a particular medium may be counteracted by asking or suggesting that the client choose another more appropriate medium.

The concept of gestalt or structural configuration is an essential part of art therapy. It relates directly to the use of art media, and the particular structural qualities inherent in a medium. The therapeutic importance of the latter has been emphasized by several authors (Kagin, 1969; Kagin & Lusebrink, 1978; Lusebrink et al., 1983; Rubin, 1978, 1984).

In the process of dialoguing with the material and discovering its inherent structural qualities, individuals seem to define their own particular structural configurations or good gestalts. The simultaneous discovery of the medium potential and the individual's inner potential is experienced as a creative act by the individual (Kagin & Lusebrink, 1978).

The influence of the media properties or the gestalt inherent in the medium may be exemplified in the work with clay. Most individuals initally will form a ball [or a square] when first starting to work with clay. This form seems to be a good gestalt for clay and also for satisfying the individual. In further working, the ball may be differentiated or elaborated in more complex gestalts—the most obvious being a flattened ball with indentation, an "ashtray." In the case where the individual has a preconceived idea for the form to be modeled, the specific structural

qualities of the clay will soon impose limitations and require accommodation.

The drawings presented in Figures 4.1 and 4.2 used predominantly circular good gestalts, and in Figure 4.4, an implied circular gestalt in the area covered by the leaves.

DIFFERENTIATION OF SPACE

Forms play an important role in differentiating the space surrounding them. In visual representation space is defined by the two-dimensional surface on which the forms are represented. It is important for the therapist to note how much of the space is utilized, as it may reflect the nature of the client's interaction with the environment.

The location of the forms and their directional disposition may give some indication of the individual's functioning. Most individuals place forms in the central area or slightly to the left. More extreme shifting to the left may refer to preoccupation with the past and shifting to the right may indicate future-oriented functioning. Hammer (1958) reports that location in the upper area of the page may be associated with aloofness, fantasy, and intellectual concerns or striving. Location in the lower part of the page may be associated with either insecurity or concrete operations. Left placement may also be indicative of impulsiveness and immedate satisfaction of needs and right placement may be associated with controlled actions.

The horizontal disposition of forms may be seen as stable or passive and the vertical disposition as ascending and active. Diagonal direction in the placement of forms may be seen as dynamic, or even unstable, while a circular pattern may be seen as stabilizing. A radial pattern is dynamic and exuberant, and in more forceful depiction may stand for disintegration, such as explosion.

Bordering of the page is another pattern which may have reference to the functioning of the individual. This pattern may be indicative of the need for containment, either as a guard against internal disintegration or the need for protection from environmental forces which are perceived as threatening. Psychotic individuals not having internal limits may disregard the natural limit or border imposed by the edge of the page. The edges of the page may become the supporting ground line, as in pre-schematic drawings by children. The edges of the page may also be violated where the forms extend past the boundaries of the paper, possibly indicating constriction by the environment.

The location of forms in Figure 4.1 is predominantly in the middle area with only a part of the space covered. The opposite is true in Figure 4.2, where all the space is covered, and the large circular form has an implied left-to-right movement created through the directional sharp protrusions.

VISUAL SYNTAX

The utilization of the page through the placement of forms and lines, considered together with the dynamic character of these forms and lines, becomes part of the visual syntax.

The relationship between size, shape, and location of forms creates movement and/or tensions in the visual field. The movement can be created by the directional arrangement of forms. Movement can also be implied by rhythmical repetition of forms and brush strokes or lines. Another implied movement is created through the overlapping of forms; overlapping and penetration between forms may create depth effect. Tension can be created through a dynamic balance of forms, whereas symmetry produces a stable or even static effect. An overemphasis on symmetry may be indicative of a need for stability counteracting inner instability. The visual field may be experienced by the perceiver along a continuum from being disorganized and lacking unity to possessing a sense of oneness and a high degree of unity. Ultimately the organization also depends on the organization in the eye of the beholder. The same visual expression can be perceived as chaotic by one individual while another will be able to perceive organization through the implied forces and counterforces present in the expression (Lusebrink, 1975). In visual perception the viewer's eyes move over the surface of an expression, and meanings form through the integration of the different perceptions separated in time (Yarbus, 1967). This integration of the different perceptions in the visual field is referred to as a funded perception (Feldman, 1972).

Visual syntax and form as a content were investigated by Rhyne (1979a, 1983). Subjects were asked to draw abstract representations of experiences of emotionally laden mind states. These drawings in turn were related to personal constructs. Visual forms expressing similar verbal concepts used highly cogent visual elements. "Sad," "melancholy," "dead" were expressed with downward curving lines, whereas "happy," "joyous," "cheerful" expressions were curvilinear and had implied upward movement. "Raging," "angry," "furious," "agitated" were also represented with an upward movement but with a sharp angularity predominating. "Tranquil," "quiet," "serene," "lazy," were expressed

with undulating curves implying slow movement. The visual representation of "fearful" was located around the edges or pulling inward, or
also represented as a small figure or dot in the lower half of the page,
often in the left corner. "Depressed" had a downward movement, but
"excited" had movement which was outward, loosely upward. "Passive" was associated with static qualities where the space predominated.
In contrast, "aggressive" was characterized by constructs such as angular, diagonal, pushing outward. The representation of "serene" was associated with a horizontal, balanced, harmonious relationship between
parts. "Hoping" was vertically oriented, with upward and reaching out
movement, open to space. In contrast, "threatened" was diagonally
oriented, unstable, pulling inward, discordant, and off balance. In "hostile," representation drawing dominated the space and the predominant
movement was angular. The drawing of "guilty" was characterized by
being closed off from space, downward movement, and distinctive
qualities of boundaries in many forms. On the other hand, "innocent"
was represented by a dominant circular movement on a blank background or by being undifferentiated. The constructs associated with
"going crazy" were descriptions of loose drawing with the dominant
movement pushing outward. The constructs related to "being sane" had
balance and orderly structure (Rhyne, 1979a, pp. 85–158).

Rhyne (1979a) emphasizes that lines are "plurisignificant" and do
not represent one-to-one relationship to the constructs associated with
them. Similarly, Kreitler and Kreitler (1972) point out the presence of
"multileveledness" in works of art, in that the work can be "grasped,
elaborated and experienced in several systems of connected meanings"
(p. 294), whereby each of these systems is called a level. The capacity of
the observer to experience "multileveledness" depends on the ability to
shift points of view perceptually, conceptually, and experientially. Along
with the shifting from level to level, the various levels may coexist. This
shifting required in integration may be designated as "integrative grasp"
as opposed to "reductive grasp" which concentrates on one level.

The visual expressions produced in art therapy sessions most likely
will not be works of arts, but will reflect a process. Nevertheless, "multileveledness" is present in many art therapy expressions. It is a part of
the therapist's role to explore the levels and their integrative and reductive meaning.

All four drawings in the case study convey a sense of symmetry and
display a good sense of organization. The "forms as content" in the first
drawing indicate the emotions of sadness through the downward lines
and of fearfulness through the forms pulling inward (Fig. 4.1). In Figure
4.2 angry and agitated feelings are implied through the angularity of the

lines and the upward movement of the sharp edges. In Figure 4.3 happy and joyful feelings are displayed through the curvilinear implied movement upward, and hope is displayed through vertically oriented movement reaching out and upward. In the last drawing (Fig. 4.4) feelings of serenity are conveyed with horizontal forms and through the harmonious relationship between the two lower forms. Hope is symbolized through the upward and reaching out movement of the tree.

Before proceeding to the exploration of the different levels involved in visual expression, it is important to be familiar at least with some perceptual, somatic, and conceptual aspects of a very important component of visual expression—color.

COLOR

For the art therapist, "color is an important window in the client's inner life" (Levy, 1980, p. 2). Color facilitates the discrimination of different forms. At the same time color creates moods. Moods and feeling states can be expressed through color designation, such as "I am blue" or "I see red."

Colors can be pure hues or they can be diluted with white, such as pastels. Or colors can be grayed shades through admixture of several colors or black. Each of these colors evokes different reactions or different levels in the perceiver. Saturated complementary colors, such as bright blue and bright yellow, or bright red and bright green, are experienced generally as more tension-laden than pastel colors or grayed shades. The energy expended and the disruption of balance experienced are lessened in perceiving grays and pastel shades than in perceiving bright colors (Kreitler & Kreitler, 1972).

Color hues are first differentiated in the central part of the retina by the excitation of the cones. Grays and blacks are perceived by the rods in the periphery of the retina. There are three types of cones, responding to blue, green, and red colors. Each color has a predominant wavelength; the red hue has the longest wavelength, followed by yellow, green, and blue (with the shortest wavelength). The highest response peak is in the foveal or central area of the iris for all the four colors, but the height and the width of the excitability curve varies. The retinal excitation for yellow covers the greatest area and red the smallest; blue and green retinal excitation areas are intermediate in size. Blue excitation decreases more slowly at the periphery; green falls off most rapidly. In the peripheral area red appears orange, green as yellowish green, yellow as gray, and blue as dark gray (Motokawa, 1970).

It may be questioned whether this knowledge is at all informative and necessary for art therapists. Lacking empirical studies and proof, one can make only conjectures, based on clinical observations of color preferences by individuals with certain presenting problems. Depressed people usually describe the world as gray and use black or graying colors in their visual expressions. Yellowish green in folklore is associated with guilt and jealousy. Does this mean that these individuals use their peripheral vision instead of the central part of the fovea? In behavioral terms, people do not look at the object directly or have difficulty establishing and maintaining eye contact, which is true for most individuals experiencing jealousy.

Colors are experienced not only in the retina but also further down the optical tract in the lateral geniculate nucleus located in the thalamus which acts as a relay station between the retina and the visual cortex. Here colors are differentiated on the basis of three complementary pairs: red/green, blue/yellow, and black/white. Each of these pairs operate on an "on/off" basis. For example, the excitation caused by the red wavelength will turn off the perception of green. Similar chromatic opponent responses are experienced in the visual cortex (Uttal, 1973). The on/off character of the color information processing at this level may explain the tension experienced in looking at saturated complementary color. There are also differences in color processing among the two hemispheres. The right hemisphere was found to be superior in discriminating both hue and saturation (Davidoff, 1976).

The physiological response to color may involve the whole organism. Thus, red color patches were found significantly more arousing than blue and yellow, and green more than blue, as measured by using the galvanic skin response (Jacobs & Hustmyer, 1974). In general, the following intense colors have high arousal value: red, orange and yellow. Green, blue, purple, and brown have moderate arousal value, whereas white, gray, and black have low arousal value (Hooke, Youell, & Etkin, 1975). Color not only affects an individual's level of arousal, but the individual's typical arousal level also influences his/her color preference. Similarly, different meanings associated with color reflect its physiological influence.

These examples address the physiological effects color perception has on the human organism. Therefore it is important for the art therapist to be aware of the physiological components of color response.

The meaning of color is associated not only with arousal level, but also with mood and feeling states. Individuals may have their personal color meanings and associations. Some meanings have a cultural basis. Nevertheless, there is striking similarity of the general meanings of colors crossculturally (Kreitler & Kreitler, 1972). Robbins, Lusebrink, and Rhyne (1979) investigated the color constructs related to different colors in sets of life-stage drawings. Red was related to movement and energy; both orange and yellow were related to energy, but yellow also was related to roundness. Green was associated predominantly with growth and with verticality and flow. Associations to blue were horizontal and calm. Purple had several different meanings: movement, energy, horizontal, centered, and balanced. Brown was related to horizontal lines and dwindling energy, and black to depression, to the painful, still, and contained feelings.

Levy (1980) investigated mood states associated with the viewing of eight color samples. He found that intense yellow arouses feelings of vigor, liveliness, and vitality, whereas responses to light, slightly grayed bluish violet were associated with a sense of sadness, quiescence, and inactivity. Reaction to intense green with slight blue admixture was assertive yet, at the same time, was quiet and inactive. Intense red-orange aroused feelings of vigor, anger, tension, and energy, as contrasted to light bluish green which was reacted to with feelings of relaxation and self-effacement. Dark mustard greenish-yellow evoked a sense of slowness, quietness, some sadness, lack of vigor. Levy (1980) points out that only six largely negative emotions were sampled. A more detailed elaboration on the psychological meaning of color is presented by Birren (1961).

The basic universal meanings of color are similar to those found in all these studies (Kreitler & Kreitler, 1972). As can be seen, the prominent dimensions of color meanings are in terms of bodily expressions, sensations, and feelings. Some other dimensions as reported by Kreitler and Kreitler (1972) are discussed in reference to levels of information processing.

MULTILEVELEDNESS OF VISUAL EXPRESSION

Multileveledness of visual and symbolic expression requires that the art therapist consider the different levels of information processing that may contribute to or help to understand the meaning of the expression.

In addressing the question of whether an image is more expressive than a logically formulated message, Kreitler and Kreitler (1972) affirm that images are more expressive, "possibly because an image taps large reservoirs of prelogical, primitive or personal, sensed, felt, and imagined meanings which have never been quite integrated into formal language" (p. 321). How can an art therapist relate to and use in therapy this "large reservoir" of personal, sensed, felt, and imagined meanings? How can the therapist help the client unravel the physiognomic component of perception, which combines "the external and internal, motoric, affective, sensual, and imaginal elements . . . all intermingled prior to their differentiation" (Kreitler & Kreitler, 1972, p. 117)? The simplest answer seems to be to explore and emphasize each of these components individually. Several authors have attempted to investigate and/or order these components hierarchically.

Kreitler and Kreitler (1972) refer to their study which investigated the dimensions of meaning of color. They found at least five dimensions: (1) meaning in terms of bodily expression; (2) sensations and feelings; (3) metaphors based on resemblance; (4) general abstract interpretation; and (5) a true symbol representing a contrast and its solution. In another study the same authors investigated the means used for communicating the meaning of symbols. Among the categories, meaning was represented through (1) bodily expression and movement; (2) sensation and feeling; (3) metaphor; (4) the symbol proper, as well as (5) exemplifying instances and situations. The organization of the image representation is similar to that already discussed earlier in Chapter 2 in regard to internal imagery.

MEDIA PROPERTIES, MEDIATORS, AND REFLECTIVE DISTANCE

Given a choice of many materials, an individual may respond differently depending on his/her awareness of stimuli in the environment, curiosity, energy level, and the motivation to explore and get involved with a particular medium. This selection process alone can serve as an evaluative tool (Rubin, 1978).

The responses to the media available could be placed on a continuum, at one end of which is a chance of taking the nearest medium available to the individual. At the other extreme of this continuum is a multileveled response to a particular medium which can fulfill the individual's needs for expression at that particular time. Most likely, the individual will choose a material that is familiar and with which the individual feels most comfortable. Another factor to be considered in the choice of the medium is the need for *control*; if an individual needs to have control over the medium and his/her expression, it is most likely that a material will be chosen that will provide this control.

Barlow, Shupe, and Niswander (1977) propose that control of the media reflects control of oneself and the environment. The media also extend and increase sensory and integrative experiences of the client and provide a learning experience of imposing order on complex information. The use of different media increases options for experiences and expression for the client in the following area: variety of in-depth art experiences, self-expression, alternate forms of communication, decision making, and release of emotional energies. Barlow (1983) points out that the interaction with the media involving sensory overload reflects environmental overload, and the client may have difficulties dealing with it.

At times the self-election of media can be counterproductive, as with the obsessive-compulsive client choosing a medium that reinforces his/her need for control and perseveration. An opposite example would be the hyperactive child, who is fascinated with finger paint, but ends up making muddy puddles of paint, going with ever-increasing speed until all the paint is used up.

This leads to the question which has been controversial in art therapy—is it valid for the therapist to choose a medium for the client? Can the therapist enhance the expression, insight, emotional release, or creativity of the client by suggesting or providing specific media? On what criteria should this selection be based?

In order to make intelligent choices, the therapist has to be familiar with the expressive qualities of the media, and also he/she has to be able to make some generalizations across the media, abstracting the qualities that different media have in common, and the qualities that separate them.

The most common divisions in the use of art media are graphic arts, painting, sculpture, ceramics, and fibers, with different variations and interactions between the different components.

Since the focus in art therapy is on the process instead of the product, a classification of the media in reference to their influence on the process is more appropriate. Media dimensions, a classification proposed by Kagin (1969), differentiate media into fluid versus resistive, simple versus complex, and structured versus unstructured. Each of these pairs constitutes a continuum along which different media may be approximately placed. A particular quality of a medium depends also on the individual's interactive style, and level of development or regression. Thus, for example, clay may be used as a resistive and structured medium by an experienced potter, while a young child may proceed to add more water to it till the clay becomes a puddle of mud, namely, it obtains a very fluid and unstructured quality. Figure 4.5 presents some examples of general qualities of two-dimensional media, whereas Figure 4.6 does the same for three-dimensional media. As mentioned above,

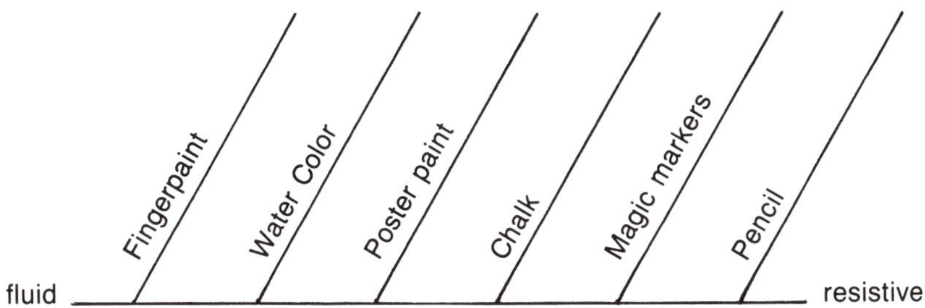

Figure 4.5. Approximate media properties for some two-dimensional media.

these are only approximations, and different individuals may experience the media differently.

The continuum from fluid to resistive refers to the particular structural qualities inherent in the material. The therapeutic aspect of these qualities is cogent for art therapy and is emphasized by several authors (Betensky, 1983; Graves (Kagin), 1983; Kagin, 1969; Kagin & Lusebrink, 1978; Rubin, 1978, 1983, 1984). The theoretical implications of the structural qualities inherent in the media were discussed earlier in this chapter in reference to gestalts.

The second category falls along the continuum from simple to complex. This refers to the number of steps or physical and mental operations required to use a particular medium. Thus, for example, a felt-tip marker is a simple medium, since it requires only one step to make a line on paper. A wood construction can be a complex experience, in that it requires selection of right sizes of wood, planning, using hammer and nails, finishing, etc. This differentiation of media into simple and complex is particularly important in working with small children and developmentally impaired and handicapped individuals. An art experience that is complex may frustrate the individual in that he either refuses to cooperate or destroys the expression.

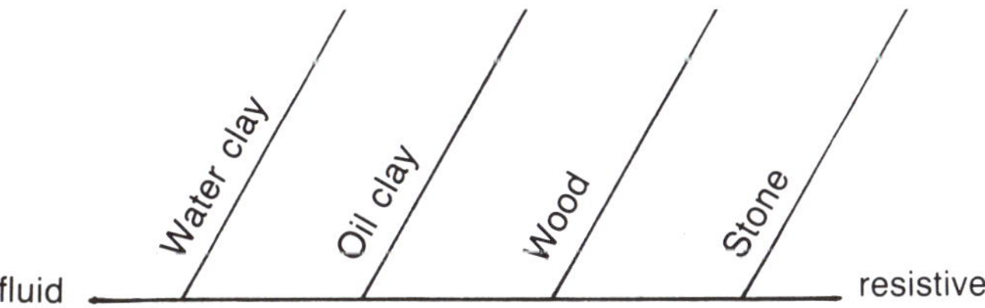

Figure 4.6. Approximate media properties for some three-dimensional media.

The third category, structured versus unstructured, refers to whether the art experience is directed or nondirected, i.e., does the therapist give particular directions for it. This category again can be seen as a continuum, from the client doing free expression with the medium of his/her choice, to the therapist asking the client to paint or draw how they are feeling today, to the therapist structuring a task in several steps for a mentally retarded or handicapped child.

Some examples of the use and misuse of different media have been mentioned throughout this chapter, including the influence of media on the different levels of expression. Specific examples of art experiences used in therapy sessions will be discussed in Chapter 6.

Another variable to be considered in choosing media in the therapeutic setting is whether the media selected are mediated or unmediated (Kagin & Lusebrink, 1978). A mediator is essentially a tool introducing a distance between the individual and the material used. For example, fingerpaint is applied to the paper directly with the fingers and the individual responds to the sensory qualities of the paint. Poster paint, on the other hand, is applied with a brush, which provides more cognitive control and distance for the use of the medium. The mediator inhibits direct involvement with the medium, at the same providing opportunity to differentiate the expression from the proximal tactile sensations, while emphasizing the more distal visual perception and eye/motor coordination. Mediators also increase the reflective distance, the cognitive distance between the art experience and the individual's reflection upon it (Kagin & Lusebrink, 1978).

Reflective distance is another variable to consider also in regard to the different levels of expression along the Expressive Therapies Continuum (Kagin & Lusebrink, 1978). The reflective distance is minimal on the Kinesthetic/Sensory level, and increases on the Perceptual and especially on the Cognitive level. The affective component may decrease the reflective distance. On the symbolic level the reflective distance may be either minimal (e.g., in regression) or considerable (e.g., with the use of abstract symbols). The understanding of the general principle of reflective distance is useful for the art therapist in planning sessions and the use of media.

EXPRESSIVE STYLES

So far we have considered many variables involved in an expression through art media: formal elements, including the influence of color, form as content and visual syntax, levels of information representation and expression, media properties and choices, mediators and reflective distance. How do all these variables add up to an individual expression?

Each individual has a characteristic style or mode of expression which combines all the variables forming the unique qualities or traits that identify or separate his/her expression from others. The expressive style of an individual may be rather consistent over a period of time, or it may undergo some changes as s/he discovers new ways of beholding the environment, or reacts to changes in the environment. The individual in therapy may exhibit rapid changes in times of inner turmoil (Pickford, 1971; Simon, 1970, 1974).

Are there any similarities between the different styles of individuals? In art an expressive style may emerge over a period of time and may be practiced by a considerable group of artists. The artistic styles may be thus classified as realistic, impressionistic, expressionistic, surrealistic, etc. Another classification of artistic styles reflects the underlying expressive messages, such as the style of objective accuracy, of formal order or emotions, and of fantasy (Feldman, 1972).

Based on Feldman's above classification, Lusebrink (1983) describes six expressive styles encountered in art therapy. These styles are aligned along the Expressive Therapies Continuum (ETC) (Kagin & Lusebrink, 1978), namely, kinesthetic, sensory, formal-perceptual, affective, cognitive, and symbolic. The first two styles presented are not specific to Feldman's classification. The kinesthetic style emphasizes expression through gross motor movement, such as dynamic and/or rhythmic strokes, splashes, drips and scribbles. Expressions in the sensory style are characterized by the sensory and tactile qualities of surfaces, such as a whole surface covered with texture, or mixing of colors. The formal-perceptual style places emphasis on well-defined forms, without specific content or emotional significance. The emotional involvement characterizes the affective style through distortion and exaggeration of forms. This style may invoke also the sensory style, in that the whole surface may be activated by textures and/or color mixtures. The cognitive style emphasizes analytical, logical, and structural relationships, reality presentation and also abstraction, including letters, words, and numbers. The symbolic style is characterized by metaphorical or multileveled meaning of forms and their relationships, subjective color symbolism, and possible figure/ground reversal.

Determining a client's predominant style is advantageous for the therapist in that it facilitates the understanding of clients' expression, and detection of changes in their information processing. For example, in one instance what looked like a psychotic scribble, after retrospective discussion with the client, turned out to be a highly abstract communication. Knowing this particular psychotic client's expressive style helped to discuss the meaning of different lines in following sessions. In another instance a psychotic client presented a paper with numbers from 1 to 5 written in the upper part of the sheet. A few days later the same client painted with fast sketchy strokes covering different areas of the paper; both expressions had symbolic meaning to the client. Relating the two expressive styles to the levels of information processing involved in both instances, the therapist could appreciate the switch from the more abstract and cognitive left-brain functioning to the more emotional right brain thought processes of the client.

The different styles present in the four drawings given as examples in this chapter cover the different levels of expression as defined by the ETC (Kagin & Lusebrink, 1978). Figure 4.1 is executed in a perceptual style with affect possibly influencing the shape and placement of the forms; the small size of the forms and the disconnection between them imply a fair reflective distance. The oppposite is true in Figure 4.2, where there is a lack of reflective distance in the large presence of the form executed predominantly in a kinesthetic style with some overlay of organization in a perceptual manner. Figure 4.3 through the rhythmical repetition of lines creates an expression in a style where the perceptual and affective elements both are present and yet balanced between the two. The texturelike lower part of the drawing has some implied sensory qualities. The last drawing is created in cognitive/symbolic style with a comfortable reflective distance.

Awareness of the formal elements, visual syntax, and expressive styles contributes to the understanding of the emotions and content expressed, and the commonalities and changes manifested over a period of time in series of drawings. Thus the four drawings discussed here convey a strong sense of form and organization; the circular motif and the arrangement of using three forms seems to be carried through all drawings. Both line quality and forms and their placement express different emotions experienced and portrayed. The arrangement of forms changes from symmetrical balance to more dynamic balance and rendering of depth. The movement changes from centripetal through centrifugal to an upward one, implying hope.

SUMMARY

The material discussed in this chapter breaks down into components the different aspects specific to art therapy. These aspects become part of the art therapist's therapeutic skills either by their background as artists or art teachers, and/or by their training as art therapists. The media variables may enter into planning a session, and the therapist may consider the formal elements as these emerge during the rendering of the visual expression. The particular emphasis used in therapy, such as whether the session is structured or unstructured, depends on the needs of the client and the therapeutic style of the therapist.

The examples given in this chapter portray different stages of imagery: first, a cognitive attempt to express sensations and emotions associated with fear and anxiety; second, a motoric expression of anxiety leading to the emergent form of a disc. The third drawing portrays a cognitive symbolic transformation of this image through the motoric portrayal of the sensation of pulling together. The last drawing is a spontaneous imagination image with symbolic meaning. The sequence exemplifies the process of portraying and relating the different aspects of imagery, thus facilitating integration of the experience and discovery of new avenues of action for the individual.

The different formal and expressive aspects discussed in this chapter can be ordered on different levels of increasing complexity, similar to those described in reference to visual imagery. The external expression of visual images is generated through the use of simple visual elements, similarly to images being generated internally on a hypothetical "visual screen." The shape of a line and form in themselves acquire meaning either through external or internal reference. The forms and other visual elements combine into a complex expression, reflecting input from other modalities, similar to complex internal images. The knowledge of formal elements, visual syntax, and levels of expression and use of media will provide a source of alternatives for the therapist as questions may arise related specifically to the visual expressions and the use of media in the therapy sessions.

The last three chapters have discussed different aspects of images, symbol formation and symbolism, and elements of expression and understanding or reading the expression. The next chapter introduces the systems approach to imagery and art therapy.

CHAPTER 5

Levels of Expression and Systems Approach to Therapy

Imagery, symbols, and visual expression *all* are multidimensional and multileveled. The outstanding components of imagery, symbols, and visual expression, as discussed in detail in previous chapters, are the kinesthetic/sensory, perceptual or structural, affective, and cognitive. In addition, images, symbols, and visual expression can have a metaphorical or symbolic meaning. The relationship between these different components on a developmental basis was conceptualized by Bruner (1964), who proposed three modes of representation: the enactive, the iconic, and the symbolic. The enactive mode reflects events through an appropriate motor response; the iconic mode selectively organizes individual perceptions and images; and the symbolic mode designates and transforms experience into abstract and complex methods of representation.

Horowitz (1970, 1978, 1983) elaborated on Bruner's model by proposing the following three modes of representation of thought: enactive, image, and lexical. In Horowitz's model, the enactive and image modes represent thought based on perceptions, memories, and fantasies, and the lexical mode serves abstraction and conceptualization.

THE EXPRESSIVE THERAPIES CONTINUUM (ETC)

Kagin and Lusebrink (1978) formulated a conceptual model of expression and interaction with media on different levels constituting the Expressive Therapies Continuum (ETC). This model consists of four levels organized in a developmental sequence of image formation and information processing. The first three levels reflect the developmental sequence and increasing abstraction in information processing in the following sequence: kinesthetic/sensory level (K/S), perceptual/affective level (P/A), and cognitive/symbolic level (C/Sy). The fourth level, the creative level (CR), can be present at any of the previous levels and may involve synthesis of all the other levels (Fig. 5.1). These same levels of organization can be applied to expression in other modalities, such as movement or expression through sound and rhythm.

The *kinesthetic* level focuses primarily on release of energy and expression through bodily action and movement. Art media serve on this level as passive facilitators of the kinesthetic action; for example, pounding clay. The *sensory* component of this level refers to the tactile and haptic or any other sensation experienced by interacting with art media. For example, fingerpaint facilitates expression on the sensory level through individuals' experiencing the paint as smooth and pleasant or as slimy and unpleasant, depending on the user. The kinesthetic and sensory components of expression and interaction with media are conceptualized as two poles of the same level in that as the action component increases, the sensory awareness decreases and vice versa.

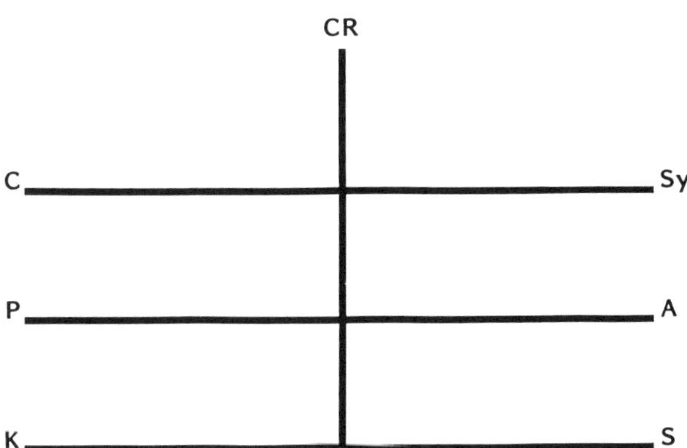

Fig. 5.1. Schematic representation of Expressive Therapies Continuum.

The K/S level is characterized by a minimal reflective distance (Rusch, 1970) between the stimulus and an involvement in the action or sensation. An activity on the kinesthetic level gives individuals the opportunity to let go of inhibitions and control. Expression and interaction with the media on the K/S level can lead to an awareness of the rhythm created through the coordinated action of the organism. The rhythm itself becomes a unifying and healing experience as the whole organism is involved in the rhythmical action (Rubin, 1984). The rhythm created by the motoric and affective aspects accompanying the act of drawing produces a sense of relaxation and stability (Tokuda, 1973). Interaction with the media on the K/S level may lead to the next or P/A level in that the individual may become aware of the form or the affect associated with the expression.

The *perceptual/affective or P/A* level represents the interaction between the perceptual and affective aspects of expression and the influence of different media upon that interaction. The perceptual pole of this level focuses on the form or structural qualities of the expression, such as defining boundaries, differentiating form, and striving to achieve an appropriate representation for an inner or external experience. On this level a dialogue exists between the individual and the medium that creates an isomorphic interaction (Arnheim, 1969) between the two. Media with high structural qualities (e.g., wood or mosaic) are more likely to evoke an inner organization in the individual than fluid media (e.g., watercolor) where the individual has to impose a structure upon the medium.

The *affective* component of this level modifies the form, and the form in turn gives a structure to affect. The innate striving for good gestalts may be countered by emotional expression and distortion of the form created or perceived. Extreme examples of this interaction can be seen either in the distortion of form in angry expressions or in the containment of anger in a geometrization of form. The use of intense colors and fluid media, such as poster paint, facilitates the expression of affect. Identification with the forms facilitates the expression of affect and the internalization of structure (Rhyne, 1973).

The reflective distance varies on the P/A level from a considerable reflective distance when the perceptual aspects of the expression are overemphasized to a minimal reflective distance in an overwhelming experience of affect. The internalization and abstraction of perceptual and affective schemata lead to the following C/Sy level.

The *cognitive/symbolic* level is qualitatively different from the previous levels in that it encompasses conceptual and anticipatory operations with images and the corresponding verbalizations describing these operations. The *cognitive* component of this level focuses on analytical, sequential operations; logical thought; and problem solving. The exploration of media properties and internalization contribute to the understanding of the actions necessary to manipulate media; for example, to build a wood construction using hammer and nails. Abstractions and concept representation through visual forms are part of cognitive operations. Resistive and structured media, such as pencils or construction paper, enhance operations on the cognitive level. Naming the product, verbalization of the procedure, and internalization of verbal commands constitute part of the cognitive level.

The reflective distance is considerably larger on the cognitive level as compared to the previous levels. The increased reflective distance contributes to the ability to plan and postpone actions on this level.

The *symbolic* component of this level focuses on intuitive concept formation, realization and actualization of symbols, and the symbolic expression of meaning. As discussed in Chapter 3, symbols are multi-leveled and multidimensional and encompass a kinesthetic or dynamic component as well as affect, structure and form, and meaning. The meaning can be either repressed or displaced, or it may not yet be known. Symbols on this level can be either regressive or progressive. Regressive symbols refer to developmentally earlier experiences and use earlier forms of information processing. Progressive symbols refer to future occurrences and anticipations.

Media that produce ambiguous forms, such as sponge prints, facilitate symbolic perception. On the other hand, symbol resolution is enhanced through media that help to concretize and personalize the different components of the symbolic experience. The reflective distance on the symbolic level depends on the type of symbol and symbolic experience present. The reflective distance diminishes in regressive identification with the symbol and is characterized by regressive behavior and primitive representation of images. The reflective distance increases if the symbol carries emotionally threatening charges, or if the symbol is progressive and points to future possibilities. The reflective distance can be too large if very abstract or universal symbols are used. The more abstract the symbol, the longer it will take to be resolved.

The resolution of both regressive and progressive symbols leads to insight and emotional growth. The symbol formation per se may lead to the sublimation of more basic drives into culturally acceptable expression, thus leading to the next or creative level.

The *creative* level emphasizes the synthesizing and self-actualizing forces of the ego and self. As mentioned earlier, the creative experience may take place on any of the levels of the ETC. The sublimation is an example of a creative act. On the creative level a synthesis may take place between the inner experience and outer reality (Ulman, 1975a), between the individual's expression and the media, or the individual's experiences on the different levels of the ETC. The creative act culminates in an affective experience of closure and a sense of unity between the medium and the message.

The reflective distance in the creative interaction with the media alternates between an individual's total involvement while maintaining some awareness of the interaction and total involvement with subsequent reflection upon the interaction. In the creative transformation (Taylor, 1975) the individual may experience a high degree of intense arousal while creating and a sense of self-fulfillment while reflecting upon the end product as an independent unit. The creative actualization (Maslow, 1971) involves the whole individual and therefore has a healing influence.

Questions posed to the client can be primarily directed at expression on different levels of the ETC in the following manner:

1. "What are you doing?" "What do you want to do?" "Can you act it out?" are directed to responses on the kinesthetic level.
2. "What do you sense?" brings the focus of attention to sensation.
3. "What do you see or perceive?" directs attention of the perceptual aspects of the expression.
4. "How do you feel?" focuses on affect.
5. "How do different parts relate to each other?" "What are the necessary steps to solve the problem?" and similar questions address cognitive operations.
6. "What does it mean to you?" or "What associations do you have with it?" elicit elaborations on the symbolic aspects of the expression.

It is best to avoid questions using *why* because they tend to lead to rationalizations.

A creative expression usually does not need verbal reflection because it stands as a statement by itself. The feelings of completion and satisfaction that accompany a creative expression should be acknowledged by the therapist as well as by the client. This acknowledgment is important for the client for two reasons. First, it helps the client remember and identify creative achievement and feelings in the future. Second, the acknowledgment of the creative experience reinforces the closure at that particular time. This is important because at times clients have a tendency to identify with the creative excitement and accelerate their activity rather than to appreciate the satisfaction of completing a creative act.

THE FUNCTION OF IMAGERY ON DIFFERENT LEVELS OF THE ETC

Imagery can be seen from two perspectives in regard to the different levels of information processing and expression as represented by the ETC. The first is a developmental perspective (Piaget, 1962), and the second is based on modality specific images.

In earlier discussion of the physiological components of imagery, the *kinesthetic and sensory* components were identified as an integral part of images. From the developmental viewpoint, a mental image is based on internalized imitation (Piaget, 1962), and imitation itself is a kinesthetic action. The same holds true for mental images of objects: They have to be explored kinesthetically before a child forms an internal representation which then can be operated upon internally.

The second perspective is on images specifically in the kinesthetic modality. These images can be covert, below the level of awareness, and are manifested through acting them out kinesthetically. The kinesthetic images become the basis for further transformation and representation either verbally or visually. The process of transformation in another modality involves the ability to reflect upon one's experience, or to pause between physical tensions and reaction to them.

Kinesthetic acting out can be also employed as an immature defense mechanism (A. Freud, 1942; Vaillant, 1976). In this case kinesthetic tensions are acted out by the individual without the benefit of gaining insight from the action.

A *sensory* image can be either tactile or visceral. Like kinesthetic images, sensory images can be covert and below the level of awareness, or they can have an emotional, verbal, or visual component that lends itself to representation through other modalities. Sensory images may have a strong emotional component and may become the building blocks for emotionally charged visual images. Ahsen (1982, 1984) conceptualizes the sensory component as one of the tripartite constituents of images. Usually, sensory images are experienced in a state of withdrawal from external stimuli and in a state of physical relaxation and quietness. In extreme cases, either in sensory deprivation or psychosis, the internal sensory images are experienced as hallucinatory, or as having an external origin.

In therapy the sensory component is used for covert conditioning

(Cautela, 1979; Cautela & McCullough, 1978) either to decrease the undesired behavior or increase the desired behavior.

The formation of the image itself is the focus on the *perceptual* level. A visual image is conceptualized as being formed from its constituent parts in the internal visual medium or visual cortex. The image can be experienced as close by, overflowing the visual field, or at a distance (Kosslyn, 1980). The focus on the image may concern just the elements forming the image, such as lines, angles, and areas, and pattern formed through their interaction. The focus also may be on representation of concrete objects and their spatial relationships.

Images have an *affective* component that has psychophysiologic comcomitants (Jones & Johnson, 1980). Affect bestows the formal structures of the images with a dynamic character and endows them with personal qualities based on the individual experiences under which the images were encoded. The intensity of affect associated with specific images may mark them for recall or repression. Dissimilar images with the same intensity of affect may be recalled or repressed at the same time. Lack or inability to experience affect, as in alexithymia, may go hand in hand with inability to experience images.

Overwhelming affect associated with images may lead to repression of the images or to regression in observable behavior including visual expression. Hierarchical ordering of images from the least threatening to the most fear-evoking is used in systematic desensitization (Wolpe, 1958, 1973). One of the bases for systematic desensitization is the assumption that relaxation is incompatible with fearful images. Thus, the threatening images are gradually presented to the client in a relaxed condition.

On the *cognitive* level of the ETC, images are used for mental operations, such as sequencing or problem solving, as well as representing concepts, abstractions, and general categories. The ability to form concepts and symbols is developmentally dependent. Young children and mentally retarded individuals may not have the capacity to free their mental processes from the concrete basis of imagery. The degree of concreteness or abstraction of imagery depends also on the individual style of information processing.

On the cognitive level of the ETC, images are used as mental maps (Sheikh & Jordan, 1983) and mnemonic devices (Bower, 1970). This level encompasses not only representational images but also anticipatory images (Piaget, 1962), such as mental rotations and transformations of images. The cognitive level corresponds to Freud's secondary process thinking, with stable object cathexis.

Emotionally charged images on the cognitive level may be used to represent the personal value system. From a neo-Freudian viewpoint

(Noy, 1979), images as representatives of primary process relate to the information concerning the self. Verbal processing of these self-related images establishes them in the context of external reality.

Images are used in intellectualization as part of defenses. Images as defenses on the cognitive level of the ETC either can be abstract and lacking in personal values, or they can represent elaborate logical solutions (Levick, 1983).

On the *symbolic* level of the ETC, part of the meaning of the image is not known, in that the image, through its structure and as a metaphor, represents an unknown quality or entity. Image as a symbolic metaphor can stand for a somatic experience; or it can be a disguise for threatening affect and displacement for emotionally overwhelming experiences. Images also can symbolize spiritual experiences that cannot be represented with known and concrete expressions. Images as symbols also can have a prospective aspect in that they provide archetypal context for self-development. Dreams as a visual language are rich in symbolic images.

Symbolic images as defenses have a manifest and a latent content. They may manifest themselves only within certain emotional contexts; or they may pervade the whole information processing in imposing a symbolic view on the external reality. Symbolic images may be present under the influence of drugs (Masters & Houston, 1968), or in times of stress.

On the *creative* level of the ETC, images, along with verbal processing, provide an alternate view, and thus enhance a creative synthesis. On this level the component parts of the images, be they kinesthetic or sensory, affective or perceptual, cognitive or symbolic, all play an important role in enriching the images in their different aspects. The fluidity between the component parts and the ability to experience images in their multidimensionality provide many avenues for novel solutions and expressions involving the total personality.

MEDIA USE AT THE DIFFERENT LEVELS OF THE ETC

Different media and art experiences serve specific functions at the different levels of the ETC.

Kinesthetic Level

Media on the ETC kinesthetic level are used predominantly for kinesthetic expression and warm-up. Any of the art materials can be explored on a kinesthetic and sensory level. Kinesthetic explorations involve motor movement, such as actions and gestures—pressing, floating, scratching, rubbing, turning, etc. (McNiff, 1981). Movements may be specific to the material; for example, clay can be explored by pounding, hitting, squeezing, throwing, pinching, twisting (Kagin & Lusebrink, 1978). Exploration of materials is especially valuable for young children (Kramer, 1971), because they need to handle objects and materials physically to internalize images.

A scribble with a pencil or a marker is another warm-up activity that uses the kinesthetic modality. Scribble can be performed in a dyad, as a scribble chase, with the two participants taking turns in leading and following. Both scribble and scribble chase as a warm-up can be elaborated on other levels of the ETC. Finding forms in the scribble and portraying the different forms in a united expression involve first the perceptual level and then the cognitive/symbolic level of the ETC. This sequence, starting with a body movement and then finding images, may lead to a completed creative work (Kramer, 1971).

Rhythmical prolonged activity leads to the emergence of images (Kagin & Lusebrink, 1978; Sheikh & Jordan, 1983). Rhythmic music also leads to rhythmic kinesthetic activity, which may be expressed through paint and elaborated into images. Splash painting is another form of kinesthetic expression through art media. Splash paintings, like scribbles, can be elaborated into visual images (Redden, 1979), or into abstractions (Landgarten, 1981). Action paintings reactivate encoded kinesthetic perceptions, which are then acted out through the painting (Naumburg, 1966).

Kinesthetic activity may lead to experiencing and expressing feelings. Thus, for example, hitting and pounding clay may be an expression of negative feelings; these can be transformed by subsequently making forms out of the clay (Betensky, 1973b). The propensity of kinesthetic expression to be associated with negative feelings can be used therapeutically in enactment of inner fears and anger through battles on paper (Griffis, 1978; McNiff, 1981; Weiss, 1981), or battles with clay and clay figures (Popkin, 1980; Weiss, 1981). Kinesthetic activity involving clay most often leads to expression of negative feelings, but sensory exploration of clay, especially with the eyes closed, is more likely to release sad feelings. Perceptual feedback on the kinesthetically handled material may lead to the emergence of form. For example, pounding clay may produce a form which becomes visually intriguing and is elaborated upon.

Kinesthetic activities also may lead to a chaotic discharge, such as spilling, splashing, or pounding, indicating that "impulses have ascendency over the controlling forces" (Kramer, 1971, p. 78). The therapist may direct this discharge towards a developmentally higher level of expression. For example, after a client created a chaotic picture in "wild" colors, Kramer introduced form through suggesting that the colored areas be delineated as mountains in the fall.

Destruction of artwork is another activity that takes place kinesthetically. Dynamically, destruction of a picture by the client indicates that the anger present is turned towards the work instead of self (Naumburg, 1966). The desruction of artwork can also incorporate the element of making it over. For example, once the client has started to destroy a visual expression, the therapist can encourage the client to rip the paper into small pieces, which are then used for papier-mâché construction. In doing so, the levels of the ETC are changed from the kinesthetic level to the sensory level, followed by construction involving the perceptual and cognitive levels; a corresponding change in affect may take place simultaneously (Lusebrink, 1982). Thus, in the course of art therapy, the client first transfers the emotional conflicts onto the artwork and then, through interaction with the media, arrives at a resolution (Naumburg, 1950).

Sensory Level

On the sensory level of the ETC, warm-up involves exploration of the media predominantly through touch and haptic sense. Touch provides a feedback about surface qualities, such as the texture and temperature of an object or material. The weight and configuration of the object or material are experienced through the haptic sense by the configuration of joints and pressure sensed (Gibson, 1966). Both touch and haptic sense are enhanced by closing one's eyes. Explorations through the touch and haptic sense also improve perceptions of inner sensations. A slow movement of the hand over a paper surface with the eyes closed establishes a contact with the sensory level of experience. When followed through with a brush full of paint, this movement, coupled with sensation, may lead to the experience of affect or expression of affective images.

Colors as visual sensations may have a regressive effect through their emotional component. Colors also influence each other in that they overstep rigid boundaries and establish interrelationships with surrounding colors (Kramer, 1979). At the same time colors have a structural aspect in that they define a form. Explorations in color mixtures provide warm-up exercises that involve external visual stimuli. For example, both finger paint and poster paint lend themselves easily to color explorations. Finger paint offers the more direct tactile experience in being manipulated directly by hand; therefore, finger paint can be an agent of regression. Poster paint, as manipulated by a brush, lends itself to more differentiated exploration and mixtures. Both finger paint and poster paint also enhance figure/ground differentiation (Betensky, 1973b). Finger paint has the additional advantage of lending itself to creating pathways in a homogenous field through parting the paint with a finger and exposing the ground (Kagin, 1978). If the activity using finger paint becomes too regressive, form may be introduced by the therapist's suggesting that the client write his name or make a palm print on the surface. This in itself is a kinesthetic/sensory experience, but it gives the client an opportunity to create a form that enhances self-image.

Like the kinesthetic, sensory activities require that individuals let go of conscious controls and immerse themselves in "unpredictable sensory activities" (McNiff, 1981, p. 51). The integrative function of the sensory level is the grounding in concrete reality through touch and in establishing configurations of objects. Tactile exploration of forms, textures, and weight provide grounding for schizophrenic patients (Denner, 1967; Kramer, 1971). Both finger paint and clay have regressive qualities and constructive qualities. A clay object can be smashed down and constructed many times, as images can be erased and reformulated by finger paint (Rubin, 1978).

Sensory explorations of external objects also enhance imagery formation. Vivid sensory experiences lead to more vivid memory, and training in sensory perceptions, as well as pleasant memories, increases vividness of imagery (Cautela & McCullough, 1978; Sheikh & Jordan, 1983). The sensory level provides a route for image formation developmentally in that "hallucinatory images" in infancy are based on primitive sensations (Holt, 1967).

Perceptual Level

On the perceptual level of the ETC, warm-up exercises involve training in perception. Description of formal elements present in a visual expression, such as forms, colors, lines, also can serve as warm-up exercises. These responses may include the feelings evoked by observing the visual expression (McNiff, 1981; Rubin, 1984). Describing verbally one's perceptions in concrete terms increases the possibility of experiencing images (Sheikh & Jordan, 1983). Perceptual focusing on an external object enhances interaction with the external environment. The objects observed can be close by or distant, and the observer may maintain continuity of concentration while changing perceptual focus (McNiff, 1981). Exercises using art media on the perceptual level may involve changing points of view. Distant objects may be brought close in by enlarging details, and nearby objects may be placed at a distance by elaborating on the environment around them.

On the perceptual level of the ETC, media can function as symbolic agents for limit setting; for example, trays can be used to mark off space (Landgarten, 1981). Limits may be set by reinforcing the perceptual clues of boundaries. Some clients may reinforce their own limits by demarcating the boundaries of the paper or taking a small piece of paper or small amount of clay. Similarly, expansion can be indicated symbolically through the transitions from using small muscle coordination to gross muscle coordination.

The integrative function of the perceptual level of the ETC is the establishment of formal and aesthetic order, which, through the principle of isomorphism, enhances the functional balance of behavior (McNiff, 1981). The creation of regular configurations, either representational or patterned, also helps children to develop schemata that can be used to describe the real world (Kramer, 1979). Internally, in the course of art therapy, unfocused and vague images often become articulate and clear. Creating order from unstructured media is in itself a creative activity. (Rubin, 1978).

Visual expressions can be processed from the viewpoint of content and formal elements, which can be parallel to each other, or diametrically opposed. In either case, the formal elements have to be considered in terms of developmental stages, personality style, coping, and strategies used (Rubin, 1984). With resistive clients (e.g., teenagers), descriptions of the art expression in terms of formal elements give the clients opportunity to share themselves without giving away the "secrets" of the content (Riley, 1979). In art therapy, awareness does not need to be translated into words, it also can be effective by remaining on the perceptual-emotional level (Rhyne, 1973).

On the perceptual level of the ETC, images are used as defenses if they are conventional and stereotypical, indicating that departure from conventional form arouses anxiety (Kramer, 1971). In a similar vein, geometrical drawings emphasize perceptual and kinesthetic control, and may be indications either of anxiety or repressed anger. In general, strengthening or weakening in the structure of the artwork corresponds to a shift in the personality balance (Betensky, 1973a).

The tempo of the expression, either internally or externally influenced, has an effect on the form. Acceleration or deceleration of tempo beyond a certain range can be tension-provoking (Kreitler & Kreitler,

1972). Acceleration of an externally monitored tempo from 80 beats/minute (b/m) to 160 b/m increased the form qualities of the visual expression in clay, while the following deceleration to 40 b/m showed a decrease of refinement of form (Rosal & Lehder, 1983).

Affective Level

The function of expression on the affective level is the expression of feelings. Expression on the affective level can be enhanced with warm-up exercises using media, such as fluid paints and pastel chalk in many colors, that foster expression of feelings and moods.

Another warm-up exercise with emphasis on the affective level of the ETC is painting with music expressive of different moods. A suggestion not to draw consciously but to catch a mood through the visual expression also helps to focus on the affect (Naumburg, 1966). Color is closely involved with emotions, and the fluidity and ease of mixing the media emphasize the emotional quality of color. The use or lack of use of color reflects the feeling states present. The background color of a painting may express an all-pervasive mood or preoccupation. Similarly, lines, through their depiction of movement, may convey a mood (Kramer, 1979).

If the affect appears to be threatening or overwhelming, a more cognitive approach may be recommended. For example, starting on the cognitive level of the ETC, the client is asked to portray through abstract drawings different feeling states or moods, such as love, anger, fear, sadness. Instead of using fluid media like paint, a more resistive medium (e.g., a marker) is recommended to increase control over the expression. The representation of affect itself can range from a kinesthetic expression through dynamic lines to a cognitive schematic representation, such as a circle with two dots for eyes and a curved line for a mouth with a smile or frown. This expression can be either congruous or incongruous with the feelings experienced. In either case, the visual expression is beneficial in itself by differentiating the feelings and giving them a cognitive structure. If further differentiation is indicated, questions relating to when, where, and how the feeling was experienced can be explored.

Interaction with either fluid or resistive media depends on the personal style of the individual. Children who rely predominantly on their intellect for control may draw very well but regress when handling paint. This usually occurs when affect is repressed, and therefore experienced as a threat. Other children may handle color very well, but are unable to impart form or structure on their visual expressions. These individuals are aware of their feelings but have difficulties organizing their lives (Kramer, 1971).

Form and feeling, or perception and affect, influence each other. Form gives structure to a feeling, and feeling makes form alive. Insistence on rigid forms, on the other hand, is indicative of avoidance of feelings. Strong affect distorts perception of forms.

Overwhelming feelings lead to regression, which is also reflected in regressive forms of the expression, both visually and verbally (Rubin, 1978). Art expression can be a harmless outlet for pent-up anger and the regression to more primitive and crude expressions may be beneficial in that it frees the individual from crippling inhibition. Angry explosions followed by lasting disorganization or distress, though, indicate a collapse of important coping and defense mechanisms (Kramer, 1971). A repetitive drawing or playing a feared theme or idea also leads to resolving it (Rubin, 1978), often in a different context.

As discussed in the context of the kinesthetic level, destruction of art work can be seen as anger turned towards the work instead of self. This destruction can be modified at times with a cognitive stance by suggesting that the client save the artwork for marking progress in expression (Naumburg, 1966). An emphasis on the kinesthetic component of the expression enhances the externalization of anger, which, in turn, can be directed towards constructive ends. For example, pounding nails in a board can create a design or become the basis for a string design.

Arousal and the rate at which stimuli are presented have an effect on the affective state of the individual. Fear or dread is experienced when radically new stimuli are presented at too rapid a rate. Anger is produced by high levels of material which cannot be assimilated by the individual, while somewhat more moderate but persistently difficult material produces sadness and weeping. If the material is presented at a moderate pace and has some points of reference to previously assimilated material, the individual responds with surprise and exploration. Joy or smiling is experienced if the novel material arouses interest and can be resolved with matching previously assimilated material (Tomkins, 1962).

Different pictorial themes identify emotions characterizing different presenting problems. For example, suicidal ideation is characterized by themes of hopelessness, helplessness, being harmful to others, anger, and self-hate. Similarly, the differential use of formal elements can be characteristic of a particular mood and/or presenting problem. Thus, increased depression is associated with decrease in color use, decrease in completeness of the expression, increase in empty space, and a trend towards constriction (Wadeson, 1980).

Cognitive Level

The cognitive level of the ETC deals with concept formation, sequencing, spatial relationships and mental maps, and abstraction, as well as the reciprocal interaction of verbalization and image formation. The content and meaning of the expression on the cognitive level emphasizes the logical and reality-directed aspects, as compared with the content and meaning on the symbolic level which emphasizes the metaphorical and inner, self-related aspects. Most contributions to art therapy in working with art media on the cognitive level have been made by Silver (1978). Silver worked predominately with children with communication disorders and learning disabilities.

On the cognitive level, warm-up may focus on observing and depicting relationships among objects in external reality, such as left/right, above/below, front/back (Silver, 1978). Instructions on how to use art media (Kramer, 1971) is a cognitive task. Constructing a topic-directed collage and identifying the images with words or elaborating on the images with verbal messages (Landgarten, 1981) is another activity on the cognitive level. Collages that require comparisons, e.g., depicting one's strengths and weaknesses, involve a cognitive task.

Visual expression on the cognitive level can be used in problem solving; for example, different aspects of a problem can be represented through the choice of different simple shapes (Rhyne, 1979b). Both motivation and decision making are cognitive functions (McNiff, 1981), and art experiences dealing with these aspects involve the cognitive level of the ETC.

Structuring is the main characteristic of art media used on the cognitive level of the ETC. In the structured approach clients are asked to perform certain tasks, to select particular stimuli from the multitude of external stimuli, and to direct their focus on a particular aspect of their reactions and experiences (Silver, 1978). Structuring has a potential drawback of counteracting spontaneity; a way to overcome this potential danger is to leave a structured task open-ended with several correct solutions. For example, selecting two stimulus cards from a group of cards representing humans, animals, and objects, and then drawing a picture incorporating the two, reflect the child's ability to select and to combine them. The selection and combination of these stimulus drawings also reflect the stage of cognitive development at which the child is operating. Silver suggests that highly structured tasks with children should not last too long and should be followed by a free drawing (Silver, 1978).

The cognitive approach to art expression and emphasis on the cognitive level of the ETC are indicated for children with learning disabilities and communication disorders to develop concepts of space, order, and class (Silver, 1978). Focus on observation from reality and cognitive processing is also indicated with chronic schizophrenics (Denner, 1967; Young, 1975).

Individuals who rely predominantly on rationalization and intellectualization as coping devices and defenses may start out expressing themselves on the cognitive level in the therapeutic setting. The therapist is advised gradually to introduce to the client means of expression on other levels of the ETC.

Symbolic Level

The symbolic level of the ETC predominates in processing novel or ambiguous information, or in situations of information overload—perceptual, emotional, or cognitive. The information on the symbolic level is processed using metaphors and intuitive concept formation. Compared to the sequential and analytical mode of processing on the cognitive level of the ETC, information processing on the symbolic level is global in nature. Relaxation and lack of external stimuli enhance symbol formation, as do altered states of consciousness, such as dreaming or drug intoxication.

The client's symbolic experience is enhanced by the therapist's receptiveness to the symbolic mode of information processing. Art experiences exposing the client to either ambiguous stimuli or perceptually overwhelming stimuli can be used as warm-up exercises on the symbolic level. Directions to define forms and structure in a sponge print or to make a collage of a multitude of emotionally significant cutouts are both examples of such warm-up exercises. An exercise using relaxation with eyes closed followed by a fantasy trip directed by the therapist also enhances the symbolic level of information processing. Such guided fantasy trips are discussed in Chapter 7 in the context of guided affective daydreams (Leuner, 1984).

Information processing on the symbolic level of the ETC pertains predominantly to the self. This information can refer to emotions, bodily sensations, or ideational and spiritual strivings. All of these experiences are complex and none of them can be completely defined. Naumburg (1966) refers to Gideon's statement that symbolization arose from the need to give form to the imperceptible. Symbols can have a futuristic component, especially symbols with archetypal content (Jacobi, 1959).

On the symbolic level, fluid media enhance expression because symbols are multidimensional and not rigidly defined. Expressions through fluid media (poster paint or watercolor) lend themselves more readily to figure/ground reversal than expressions in more resistive media (marker or pencil). The ambiguity created by the possibility of figure/ground reversal contributes to the symbolic experience of the expression.

The meaning of symbols needs to be resolved in personal terms and experienced as a frame of reference in reality. Expressions and experiences on the previous levels of the ETC—action on the kinesthetic level, sensations on the sensory level, perceptual images on the perceptual level, and the emotions on the affective level—all contribute to the resolution of the symbol on personal terms.

Action opposite to resolution of symbols is indicated in cases where the client perceives all experiences in a concrete and personal manner and is not able to generalize them. In these instances experiences that introduce the symbolic manner of processing information may be helpful. Amplifying the client's concrete interpretation of personal experiences through myths, folk and fairy tales, or exposure to different artwork and literary work with symbolic overtones may resonate with the client's original experience and place it in a larger, more global and therefore symbolic context. Fairy tales and folk tales are especially helpful in this context in that they speak to children who are developmentally using the symbolic mode of information processing, i.e., ages three to five. Most adults, when asked to relate their favorite fairy tale and to draw a few scenes illustrating it, can gain insight on at least a partially symbolic level.

Symbols serve as defenses through displacement and condensation to disguise the unacceptable (Freud, 1967). Symbols as defense mechanisms are manifested in drawings through subjective graphic representations of specific objects or thoughts (Levick, 1983). A repetitive symbol which appears without changes may indicate a defensive fixation (Leuner, 1984). The "working through" of symbolic defenses can be enhanced through a repetitive confrontation with the same symbolic image, such as a monster, leading to a change of its emotional value to the opposite duality (e.g., good/bad) (Betensky, 1973b).

Symbolic experience as a defense mechanism may promote either withdrawal from reality or misinterpretation of reality in symbolic terms, e.g., in psychosis. The role of symbolism in reconstitution in psychosis is discussed in Chapter 9 in the context of the relation to self.

Creative Level

Enhancement of creativity on the creative level of the ETC may be different for different individuals and for different stages of the creative process. As was discussed in Chapter 1, creativity is fostered by diverse means. The use of imagery in creative thought depends on the sex, personality, and cognitive style of the individual (Forisha, 1978). In the therapy setting, the therapist also has to consider the client's developmental level and ego strength. An individual can be creative within the limits of his/her capacities in a supportive environment. This is particularly true in using art media which lend themselves to a creative expression involving the whole person. In art expression creativity is manifested through the ability to create order out of unstructured media, especially if the product conveys an emotional impact (Rubin, 1978).

The therapeutic environment may provide means of developing creative aspects of the individual. The availability of diverse art media to be explored fosters curiosity as well as perceptual openness and receptiveness to environmental stimuli with all the senses. Exploration of diverse media and their properties on a kinesthetic/sensory level allows the client to process diverse information without premature closures.

Motivation and focusing of the creative effort are other characteristics of the creative personality. In the therapy setting these aspects are important for two reasons. First, many clients have difficulty with motivation due to many previous failures. Second, the client, such as a hyperactive or mentally retarded child, may be overwhelmed by a diversity of stimuli. Adolescents or adults may be overwhelmed by their own emotions and lack the structure and confidence to function in a stimulating but unstructured environment. Cognitive planning of the major steps leading to a desired goal, e.g., a long-term project of constructing a cardboard house with furnishings from a variety of materials by an adolescent group of girls (Summerville, 1983), provides the necessary structure with a creative freedom within it.

The therapist's attitude towards the client also can be either nondirective or structured. Creativity is enhanced for some clients through the therapist's unconditional acceptance of them as individuals as well as of their creations. For other clients the therapist's encouragement to ride out frustration and to work with a structure helps to promote creativity.

Spontaneity and expansiveness, as well as openness to inner stimuli and self-acceptance, are other characteristics of the creative personality. These aspects may be enhanced through application of Luthe's Creativity Mobilization Technique (1976). This technique consists of producing about 15 paint and brush exercises in about a 30-minute period. These exercises focus on a nonstriving activity and on bypassing goal-oriented, intellectually controlled involvement. Since the product is not the primary goal, inexpensive poster paints and newsprint are suggested as materials. This activity is repeated four times a week for 6 weeks. After the first week emotional or "brain-disturbing" material starts to emerge. This is manifested in the use of dark colors, especially purple, and emotional and physiological manifestations, such as crying, laughing, dizziness, anxiety. Manifestations associated with memories are allowed to follow their own natural process. Personal observations and reflections are recorded in a diary. These abreactions lead to expressions in lighter colors, often accompanied by joy expressed by singing and dancing. The creative expression is ultimately generalized to other areas of living.

A simpler variation of the creativity mobilization technique is doing multiple paintings to different types of music. This latter technique also allows bypassing of the left hemispheric analytical activity and mobilizes the right hemisphere. Many right-brain enhancing visual expressive activities are presented by Edwards (1979).

The different stages in the creative process can be enhanced through different media. The image of a bridge connecting two separate ideas, parts, or shores may be helpful in making internal connections. Transformation of an idea through expressing it in different media also enhances the incubation phase. Fluid media can be used in the conversion phase in exploring different possibilities without making closures. The expressive or verification phase again benefits by the client's exploring qualities of a particular medium; the final product is a creative dialogue between the individual and the medium used.

According to Kramer and Wilson (1979), "creative art expression is characterized by economy of means, inner consistency, and evocative power" (p. 50). The creative product achieves an existence independent of the creator and verbal explorations are contraindicated. The acknowledgment of the validity of the creative act, however, is important. In the therapy setting a periodic review of the client's portfolio containing all the work produced has a synthesizing and creative value.

The creative process may be distorted or aborted in any of the different phases of creativity. The individual may be overwhelmed by the stimuli in the input phase, or s/he may be too anxious in the incubation phase and form premature closures. The conversion phase is dangerous for some individuals, in that the openness to different possibilities in a primary process mode of thinking robs them of the free will to make closures. Some individuals lack the persistence and ego strength to actualize the creative insight. Working with selected art media may help to overcome the different difficulties.

The creative process involves all the levels of the ETC, and the creative expressions can be manifested on all of these levels.

In the therapy setting, an individual discovering a new level of expression or a new level of experience of him/herself may be seen as a creative act.

DIFFERENT LEVELS OF EXPRESSION IN ART THERAPY

The presence of different modes and levels of expression in art therapy has been pointed out by different authors. Naumburg (1950, 1966) states that in helping to reveal the symbolic significance of the picture, the therapist asks the client to describe the mood portrayed in the drawing, the order of the colors applied, and the meaning of the picture. According to the levels of ETC, this inquiry focuses on the affective level in describing the mood, on the perceptual level in reflecting upon the order of the colors, and on the cognitive/symbolic in stating the meaning.

Betensky (1973b) states that an involved art experience arouses at the same time physical, emotional, and rational levels. Physically, such an experience produces an awareness of increased inner sensation, such as increased heartbeat. Emotionally, the experience touches the individual deeply by bringing up strong feelings. Rationally, there is an increased rate of information processing which brings together previously disconnected pieces of information. The focus on the art product makes this unifying experience real and creative by integrating the different levels of expression into a coherent whole.

The art experience or task can be broken down into several steps on different levels of the ETC. Landgarten (1981) uses the following steps to increase concentration span for geriatrics: (1) portray feeling through line or color; (2) identify the situation; (3) add a person; and (4) fill in the background. Each of these steps can be expressed predominantly on one of the levels of the ETC. In identifying the level on which situation, person, and background are portrayed, the therapist can determine whether all the levels are congruent. The therapeutic goals can be set or modified according to the client's needs as reflected on the different levels present.

According to Robbins and Sibley (1976), in the beginning of therapy the media can be employed to gain control and distance, followed by a gradual increase in sensory stimulation and psychomotor release. The authors present an example of a progression from a cognitive level to a sensory level of media use. The progression proceeds from cutouts to tempera color to watercolor and finally to clay.

Lusebrink (1982) discusses the use of media in dealing with defenses, resistances, and coping mechanisms on the different levels of the ETC, as elaborated in Chapter 6. The expressions of these mechanisms can be transformed through the use of media on the different levels of the ETC, thus enhancing their transformation into coping devices.

The goals in therapy can be set predominantly on different levels, according to the client's needs. Levick (1967) states the following goals of using art therapy: (1) development of impulse control; (2) strengthening of ego; (3) uncovering of anger and reducing guilt; and (4) integrative and cathartic experiences. Robbins and Sibley (1976) differentiate goals in therapy in that some clients may need enhancement in their perceptual scope, some may benefit from a cathartic release of affect, and others may benefit from a cognitive approach to their feelings.

The transition between the different levels in these examples can be considered from the systems viewpoint as next discussed.

SYSTEMS APPROACH TO IMAGERY

The individual interacting with the media can be considered as a system. The systems approach assists in understanding the interactions taking place between the individual and the media.

The present application of the systems theory is a modification of Schwartz's (1984) proposed model of the general systems perspective to the psychophysiology of imagery and healing. Schwartz (1984) describes nine levels of physiological, psychological and social processes linking imagery and physiology: homeostatic-cybernetic self-regulation on a cellular level, classical conditioning, operant conditioning, motor skills learning, discrimination training, cognitive-emotional-behavioral-environment self-control, education or insight, motivation and belief, and social interaction. Schwartz (1984) proposes that these levels are organized hierarchically from micro to macro processing, namely from biological and physiological to psychological and finally to social levels. The imagery accordingly can be biological, psychological, and social, with the corresponding psycho-neuro-physiological processes involved with each of these levels of imagery. The combination of these processes associated with imagery proceed from micro processes to macro processes as the imagery evolves towards a higher level of the hierarchy. Self-generated imagery is seen as complex, multileveled, and multi-process.

A basic tenet of Schwartz's (1984) approach to imagery is based on the general systems principle that parts of the system interaction regulate each other and form emergent wholes. This approach differentiates between "negative" feedback and "positive" feedback. "Negative" feedback and decreased input contribute to the stabilization of the system. "Positive" feedback or added information leads to connection of different parts and to self-regulation. Disconnection of parts, in turn, leads to impaired self-regulation and can occur at any level of the system. Schwartz proposes that imagery can be used not only to foster self-regulation through positive and negative feedback loops, but also to foster disconnection. The action of imagery breaking or making connections can occur at any of the biological, psychological and social levels. Imagery also determines how the connections will be interpreted and whether the existing connections will be amplified or minimized.

Schwartz (1984) recommends the systems approach as an effective framework for understanding bio-psycho-social interactions. The systems approach posits that the higher or macro levels integrate information which on the different lower or micro levels appears to be disparate and competing. This approach is "friendly" to the micro level theories in that they are special cases of macro level theory. The systems approach also stimulates new discoveries and predictions not accessible at the micro level.

SYSTEMS APPROACH TO ART THERAPY

The therapeutic environment consists of therapist, client, and the media constituting a supra system. The therapist interacts with the client on the social and psychological levels which in turn affect the physiological level. The client interacts with the media expressing his/her psychological concerns and also responding to the media on the physiological level. Similarly, the therapist responds to the client's expressions and verbalizations. In art therapy, Nucho (1987) applies the general systems therapy from the psychocybernetics viewpoint. This model considers the flow of information in systems in a goal-directed manner whereby the feedback is provided through imagery and its concretization through media. Nucho considers the flow of information in the therapeutic process in a sequence of four phases: the unfreezing or warm-up phase, the doing phase, the dialoguing phase with the imagery product, and the ending and integrating phase. The systems approach also can be applied to information processing on the different levels of the ETC.

The client's internal processes, interaction with the media, and expression have the following characteristics of a system as defined by Bertalanffy (1968):

1. The expression and interaction with the media on the different levels of ETC function as whole, and changes occurring on separate levels are interrelated.
2. The characteristics of the expression and interaction on the different levels of the ETC are defined not only by the separate levels, but also by the levels being in relationship to each other.
3. Progress towards differentiation of the expression and interaction occurs by passing from the K/S level of the ETC to the hierarchically higher levels.
4. This progressive differentiation leads to enhanced cognitive and emotional functioning of the individual.
5. This progressive differentiation leads to the emergence of a hierarchical order in that expression on a particular level of the ETC has the characteristics of a system at a lower level. An example of this is an image denoting a symbol, which has kinesthetic, affective, structural, and cognitive components.

Schwartz's (1984) concepts of connection and disconnection can be applied to the imagery and interaction with media on the different levels of the ETC. Imagery and interaction with media can foster connection between the different levels, or they can lead to disconnection between the different levels. For example, in a creative expression, several or all the levels of the ETC are present or connected. On the other hand, the use of structured and resistive media can focus the expression on the cognitive level at the expense of the other levels of the ETC.

The therapeutic implications of the systems approach to imagery and visual expression in therapy are discussed in the following chapter.

SUMMARY

In summary, the use of imagery and visual expression in therapy can be conceptualized in the framework of the Expressive Therapies Continuum (ETC) and imagery systems.

The ETC consists of the following developmentally ordered levels: kinesthetic/sensory level, perceptual/affective level, cognitive/symbolic level, and creative level. Interaction with different media and expression of images take place on different levels of the ETC. This characteristic can be used in therapy in a goal-directed manner.

The interaction and transition between the different levels of the ETC can be described from the systems perspective. The interaction between the levels may lead to connection and emergence of a hierarchically higher level. The opposite takes place in disconnection between the levels when the expression and interaction are arrested on a particular level through a "negative" feedback leading to a reduced input.

Part II

Function and Processes of Imagery and Visual Expression in Therapy

CHAPTER 6

Connections and Disconnections between Levels of Representation and Expression

A young woman in a growth-oriented group setting shares the following dream:

> *I am high above the street in my hometown. The street is new and renovated, and the buildings are new. Then I am riding in a bus through the town. Across from me sits a woman with a large bowl of eyeglass lenses on her lap. They have sharp edges. I want to touch them but the woman slaps my hands. The backs of my hands are covered with many faint little scratches. Then I am holding a beautiful and rare red flower which is very precious. I look out the window and see the flowers planted everywhere in the gardens in front of very attractive little cottages.*

In another setting, a group dealing with psychosomatic illnesses, a middle-aged woman gives the following response to a guided daydream: "I cannot see anything. I can think that there is maybe a TV screen, but all I get is static." During sessions this woman usually describes her illness in minute details.

On an inpatient ward in a psychiatric hospital, a young man in his late teens, admitted for psychotic behavior, joins the art therapy group. He proceeds within a few minutes to create a scribbly looking picture with posterpaint (Fig. 6.1).

In which of these instances is it appropriate and advisable to use the verbal approach to imagery, and in which is it more appropriate to use the different aspects of visual expression? How does the use of media influence the different levels of imagery?

The previous chapters have discussed the levels and the expression

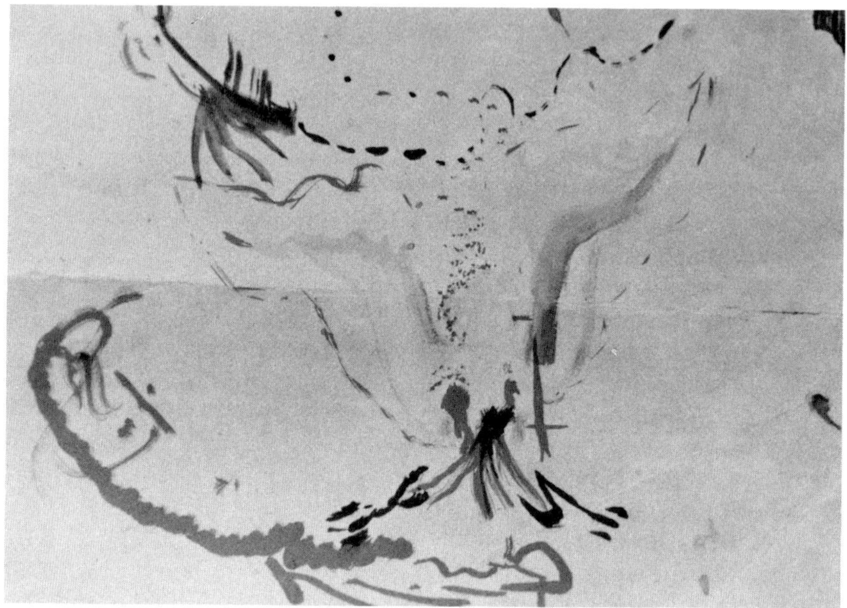

Figure 6.1. First painting by male schizophreniform patient.

of imagery and symbolism through visual means, the systems approach to imagery, and different levels of media applications in art therapy. This chapter attempts to combine the different variables into a general matrix, and to provide some rationale for the application of the different aspects and dimensions of imagery and art therapy. This chapter also explores the interaction between imagery, emotions, and resistances and their expression through different art media. The basis for the interaction between these different dimensions is the systems approach to imagery.

CONNECTION, EMERGENCE, AND DISCONNECTION OF INFORMATION PROCESSING

The systems approach to imagery and visual expression emphasizes the different levels of information processing and expression. This approach considers the therapy setting as a system consisting of therapist, client, and media. Each of these components constitute a subsystem functioning on different levels. These levels interact within a subsystem, and each subsystem interacts with the other two subsystems. The therapeutic focus of the interaction between these subsystems and between levels within each subsystem is on goal-directed functioning of the individual.

The levels of processes linking imagery and physiology can be organized from micro levels involving simple psychophysiological processes to macro levels involving complex interactions between internal processes and external environment. In a system, different levels regulate each other and form emergent new levels with qualities incorporating the previous levels (Schwartz, 1981, 1984).

According to Schwartz's (1984) systems approach to imagery and healing, the image fulfills three major functions. First, it can make or break the connection between the different subsystems and levels. Second, it determines how the connections are interpreted, either positively or negatively. Third, it determines whether the existing connections will be amplified or minimized.

Connections

Connections between two levels occur when the levels of information processing are in accord. The basic level involving imagery is psychophysiological, with emphasis on the motoric, sensory, and autonomous nervous systems. The subsequent levels are based on affective, perceptive, cognitive, and symbolic processes. These levels can be conceptually represented as the kinesthetic/sensory, perceptual/affective, and cognitive/symbolic levels of the Expressive Therapies Continuum (ETC) of Kagin and Lusebrink (1978).

When the levels are in accord, the information is transmitted and transformed from one level to another in a fluid manner and the organism functions in a goal-directed fashion. Table 6.1 describes each level's characteristics, healing dimensions, and emergent functions. The somatic and motoric components of the experience and expression on the kinesthetic/sensory level are transformed into an image through the formation of a schema or perceptual gestalt associated and/or modified by its affective component on the perceptual/affective level. Similarly, the transition from imagery as concrete representations on the perceptual level to the cognitive/ conceptual level of information processing occurs with increasing abstraction and complexity. In cases where the information is insufficient or the meaning of the information is yet unclear, meaning may appear in the form of a visual or verbal metaphor,

Table 6.1

Characteristics of Different Levels of Expressive Therapies Continuum (ETC) and Healing Dimensions and Emergent Functions on Each Level of Expression

Level	Healing dimensions	Emergent function
Kinesthetic Motor movements, gestures, acts of doing, exploration of materials	Energy release, rhythm	Form perception, affect
Sensory Tactile explorations, focus on inner sensations	Slow rhythm, awareness of internal sensations	Formation of internal images, affect
Perceptual Emphasis on form, formal elements concrete images	Organization of stimuli, formation of good gestalts	Interactions of schemata, verbal labeling and self-instructions
Affective Expression of feelings and moods, emphasis on color	Awareness of appropriate affect	Verbal labeling of feelings, internalization of affective and symbolic images
Cognitive Concept formulation, abstraction, verbal self-instructions	Generalization of concrete experiences, spatial relationships	Creative problem solving using verbal and imaginal interaction
Symbolic Intuitive and self-oriented concept formation and abstraction, synthetical thinking	Resolution of symbols through personal meaning; generalization of concrete personal experiences	Insight leading to discovery of new parts of self, integration of repressed or dissociated parts of self
Creative Creative expression leading to sense of closure and/or joy	Creative transaction with environment, creative self-actualization	

namely, as a symbol on the symbolic level. As was discussed in Chapter 3, symbols encompass the motoric, sensory, and imaginal components of meaning.

Further input on these levels may elaborate on the meaning and affective value of the symbolism, leading eventually to the emergence of the verbalization of the cognitive meaning and/or insight leading to the discovery of new parts of self. This sequence illustrates the emergent, creative qualities of information processing and imagery. The transition between the levels is often associated with interest, motivation, and joy because of matching with an established cognitive schema (Singer, 1974).

The client's interaction with media and his/her subsequent visual expression have an interactive effect on the client's different levels of internal representation and information processing. The visual expression may amplify internal images through their verbal and visual elaboration and modification. Art media themselves can act as amplifiers or reducers of the externalized images. Generally, fluid media will act as amplifiers and resistive media will act as reducers (Kagin & Lusebrink, 1978). The externally created image, be it visual or verbal, may lack the multidimensional richness and fluidity of the internal imagery. In most cases, however, the image will be truer to the individual's internal counterpart if expressed visually rather than verbally. With verbal expressions the therapist has to generate internal images in response to the client's verbal descriptions, thus influencing the perception of the imagery with the therapist's own idiosyncrasies.

The client's verbal reflection on the visual expression under the therapist's guidance leads to the alignment of the different levels of internal representation and information processing. This perceptual and verbal reflection may culminate in the "aha" experience, or in an insight. The transition from imagery to verbal expression depends on the client's developmental stage and level of mental functioning and on the complexity of information. The visual expression itself may be on the creative level of the ETC with the concurrent experience of the alignment of different levels and emergence of new qualities.

Disconnections

Disconnection between two subsystems or levels leads to less structured systems and deregulation. In the interaction between the individual and the media, the idiosyncratic qualities of both will determine whether the interaction will lead to connection or disconnection. Table 6.2 represents problems occurring in information processing and expres-

Table 6.2

Manifestation of Pathology in Expressions Reflecting Lack of Interaction between Levels

	Characteristics of Internal Experiences and Visual Expression and Counteractive Strategies	
Level	Characteristics	Strategies
Kinesthetic	Hyperactivity; affect expressed as destructive action; inability to pause between impulse and action; inability to take feedback of consequences of one's actions; perserveration in kinesthetic action	Effective limit setting; reduction of stimuli including isolation from environmental and/or affective stimuli; verbal or physical contact; therapist modeling and introducing forms
Sensory	Anxiety, overwhelming internal sensations without affective components; marked slowing down, may be manifested as fascination with ever increasing details of sensations or perceptions, or may be experienced as loss of will	Reflection of possible underlying affect; kinesthetic action
Perceptual	Rigid, concrete image formation and form perception; parts appear as isolated; inability to combine details into gestalts; geometrization of formal aspects of expression; lack of affect or controlled affect	Relaxation; representation through concrete handling of materials; expression of affect through visual means; exploration of sensations and/or symbolic meaning
Affective	Overwhelming affect; projection of affect on environment; affective images may appear as hallucinations; distorted form, or lack of form; muddy or intense colors, depending on diagnostic category and/or presenting problem	Emphasis on form, and cognitive operations to gain reflective distance; limit setting and use of structured and resistive media; defining of symbolic images
Cognitive	Presence of stereotypes; insistence on rigid structure and concrete images; inability to generalize; progressive analyses of details; loss of personal meaning; abstraction as means of emotional distancing	Exploration of concrete objects through touch; exploration of symbolic meaning; exploration of affective component; introduction of color
Symbolic	Identification with symbols; symbolic perception of reality coupled with physiognomic perception; stereotyped symbolism; abstract symbolism without personal or affective references	Exploration of affect associated with symbols; reality orientation in the present; concrete sensory and perceptual experiences; exploration of meaning and sequential manifestations of symbols

sion which reflect the lack of interaction or disconnection between the different levels. It also illustrates counteractive strategies enhancing the connection between the different levels. Disconnection may prove to be beneficial. As a result of disconnection, new connections may be created between the levels. In this case, the disconnection in psychoanalytical terms is defined as "regression in the service of ego" (Kris, 1952).

The case illustrations presented at the beginning of the chapter show applications of the concept of connection and disconnection between the levels of internal representation and external expression. The cases are considered from the viewpoint of the levels of information processing. As a rule of thumb, it is advisable to start working with the client on the level where the client is predominantly operating.

In the first example, the young woman had participated in art therapy group experiences before. The therapist suggested that she paint as many of the dream sequence frames as she felt necessary. The pictures of holding the lenses and the rose emerged as the most important images. Further exploration with the client of the perceptual and feeling components of the glass and the rose revealed that these contained the contrasting feelings of being sharp and possibly inflicting pain versus being soft and beautiful. This in turn led to the cognitive insight that she can be as sharp and cutting as glass, or as beautiful and soft as a rose. The visual resemblance of the roundness of the two objects, coupled with the different emotions associated with them, contributed to the emergence of this insight.

The second example of the middle-aged woman is a special case illustrating alexithymia or the inability to express and experience feelings. This would require not only attention on the exploration phase of media, but also cognitive stepwise instruction in image formation, use of recent memory, and the incorporation of nonthreatening perceptual elements. A more detailed description of this particular approach is presented later in the chapter.

In the third example, the young man was suffering from disturbances in both the cognitive and emotional aspects of information processing. As with many acute psychotics, he had the apparent need to express himself and organize his experiences through visual means. The drawing proceeded very fast and revealed a structure in its execution: a center and up/down direction, divided in left and right directions (Fig. 6.1). When asked to describe it he offered the following:

> In the middle is the angel of evil, puffing on his cigar, asking for mercy; right below him is a woman and a horse; they both are okay. There is also Jesus, and a sword. On the left is the devil; he has to be put in an isolation cell till he stops playing with his evil toys. On the right is a boy and a man climbing a mountain. They are both okay.

The fast scribbles represent a multileveled symbolism with universal meaning as indicated by the opposites of angel/devil and Jesus/sword. The implied imagery also has references to personal symbolism which could not be explored at that particular time due to the disturbed functioning of the individual. Nevertheless, the expression and the discussion of the picture were integrating and satisfying to him. On an intrapersonal level, this act integrated perceptual, emotional, and some contextual aspects for the client, which were reinforced on the interpersonal level through the dialogue with the therapist. The disclosure also gave structure and meaning to the motoric and sensory experiences that were predominant in his behavior.

Interaction between Imagery and Emotions in Therapy

Two aspects of imagery considerably influence the form and function of subjective imagery and therefore are important in therapy using imagery: (1) the interaction of imagery and affect; and (2) the interrelationship between imagery and resistances.

Subjective imagery and emotions have several commonalities and interrelationships. Like imagery, emotions have several levels on which they are processed, i.e., physiological, schematic, and cognitive counterpart levels. Both emotions and imagery are processed predominantly in the right hemisphere. The empirical evidence for these points has been presented in Chapter 2.

The reciprocal interaction between subjective imagery and emotions is particularly important in therapy. Imagery portrays emotions, and emotions can be aroused through imagery (Epstein, 1981; Horowitz, 1972). Images not only retain the emotions associated with them, but also retain the somatic correlates of these emotions (Ahsen, 1982, 1984). Images are instrumental in modifying emotional states and warding off threatening content and emotions (Horowitz, 1970). Control of imagery contributes to the control of affect as well as of behavior (Singer, 1974).

Negative emotions distort images by either transforming or arresting image flow. The physiological arousal concomitant to strong negative emotions tends to generate additional negative images, which are based on past experiences encoded at this level of arousal. Relaxation, on the other hand, can be incompatible with negatively charged emotions, and the images or the negative context of the images are changed.

Strongly charged emotions may be accessed through images by elaborating on the sensations associated with these images. Emotional discharge is beneficial because it helps reconnect the sensory, emotional, and imaginal levels. For the same reason, such an emotional discharge may be overwhelming because the information on all levels may be amplified due to the close relationship between imagery and emotion. From the systems perspective, the simultaneous connection of several levels may result in an information overload.

If the emotional and physiological components are disconnected from the image, the repression of the above components may manifest on the somatic level as illness. The inability to experience and express feelings, or alexithymia (Sifneos, 1973), is an extreme example of such a disconnection between the psychophysiological components, affect and imagery. Alexithymia (Sifneos, 1973) is characterized by marked constriction in experiencing emotions and difficulty in finding words for expressing feelings, along with an impoverished fantasy life and the subject's concrete and detailed description of circumstances surrounding an emotional experience. Actions are used to avoid conflict, as well as to express emotion (Sifneos, 1973; Sifneos, Apfel-Savitz, & Frankel, 1977). In speech, action words are used instead of adjectives (von Rad, Lalucat, & Lolas, 1977).

Alexithymia appears to influence the symbolic function. This is reflected in the alexithymic individual's difficulty in making the transition from concrete references to symbolic images (Demers-Desrosiers, 1982). The concept of alexithymia is further elaborated in Chapter 10.

In examining the case vignettes in terms of the emotions associated with the imagery, marked differences between the subjects can be noted. In the first example, the young woman first described her feelings as confusion and anxiety because she did not know where she was going. She felt excited at seeing the eyeglass lenses, but felt reprimanded when the woman slapped her "like a child who got her fingers slapped for putting them in the candy jar." She felt sad discovering the scratches on her hands, but became happy when holding the precious red flower. Her happiness increased seeing the houses with all the lights and flowers. In this case there is a rich range of emotions appropriate to the images.

In the second example, the only emotion the woman displayed was the anxiety in not being able to "see" anything.

The young man in the third example displayed high arousal; his images seemed to have affective values, evil or good, even though these emotions were not experienced while the client was painting or describing the meaning of the painting. The organization of images through painting and verbalizing about them seemed to have a calming effect on the client's state of arousal.

For the first individual, images and emotions were congruent, and the changing images seemed to resolve a negative emotional state. In the alexithymic individual there appeared to be a disconnection between cognition and the imaginal and emotional levels. With the psychotic client experiencing a high state of arousal, the emphasis on perceptual and cognitive aspects of imagery seemed to alleviate arousal, even though the emotional states themselves were not directly defined.

IMAGERY AND RESISTANCES

The disconnection between images and emotions and/or cognition are primarily related to resistances. Several image-related factors may indicate a lack of transition between the different subsystems of information processing: the absence of images, reiterated presence of images, and form and content of images.

The manifestations of resistance on different levels of information processing, and the disconnection between imagery, affect, and cognition have been described in the literature predominantly from the psychoanalytic viewpoint. According to the classical psychoanalytical approach, images are seen as cognitive manifestations of impulse-defense conflicts and symbolic representations of repressed content. "Screen images," such as blank images or realistic images with neutral content, may keep the cognitive and emotional aspects of conflicting ideas or memories from awareness (Horowitz, 1970, 1972, 1978; Kepecs, 1954).

The transition between imaginal and verbal modes represents the transition between states of consciousness and may manifest as blankness. *Blank images* can also be extreme examples of repression of conflicting ideas and memories. Resistance through foggy or blank screen images may be associated with a display of affect such as tears, anger, or frustration. Kepecs (1954) describes these phenomena as "the boundary of the borderland between consciousness and the unconscious" (p. 62); he also poses the question of whether resistance operates as a barrier or as a pathway between consciousness and the unconscious. Kepecs proposes that "blankness" contains visual memories that have lost their outlines and distinctiveness so that the memory becomes a homogenous field. These screens can be associated with an increase in muscular tension and loss of articulation of the visual field. The investment of energy in constructing or depicting the blankness of the screen rearticulates the field and allows the image or the memory to emerge.

The use of *realistic images* of neutral content as a defense or a resistance has been pointed out by Kern (1978) and Levick (1980). Kern (1978) refers to these as screen memories which ward off the traumatic event through displacement to a neutral scene, often an innocuous fragment of the early childhood scene. The dullness and banality of the scene attempts deflection of the individual's attention by "the roused defense apparatus of the ego" (p. 43). Thus a simple, pedestrian image may carry an attachment to strongly charged emotions.

Unbidden images, on the other hand, emerge into awareness without the individual having control over them; such images may seem alien or uncanny and often appear to have an external origin, e.g., hallucinations. Images generating fear, guilt, or hate also may be experienced as unbidden (Horowitz, 1970, 1972, 1983). The tension associated with the emergence of images in an analytical session can be due to the dynamic forces opposing the expression of a conflicting idea. The sudden manifestation of an image and the associated affect may be experienced as a surprise or even as shock; these feelings point to the "unbidden" content which has been previously repressed (Rubin, 1980).

Resistances to imagery, or the presence of "screen" images, can be considered in relation to the different levels of imagery and the different levels of information processing.

Resistances might be due to the avoidance of recalling stressful or traumatic images, emotions, and events on the different levels. A resistance can manifest itself through the increased use of motoric components to deal with the arousal or anxiety present. This may result from a predominantly motoric and somatic original encoding. Increased use of motor component may also be due to the disconnection of the perceptual or concrete representational level of the images from the affect associated with them.

Excessive motor activity and tendencies to act out on the kinesthetic level prevent image formation. Inattention to dim and fleeting images and prevention or excessive control of the primary process flow restrict image formation on the perceptual level (Horowitz, 1970). Clouded or foggy imagery may be present if feelings of joy or anger are resisted on the affective level (Shorr, 1978).

The repressed and emergent aspects of imagery may be present in the preverbal memories encoded in early childhood. The repressed content is more likely to appear in a symbolic image than in verbal form because images are closer to the original encoding.

The transition from the imaginal mode to the cognitive verbal mode of representation involves transition of information from the right to the left hemisphere. Here the transition may be repressed or disconnected because of the traumatic content or threatening negative emotional component of the images. Similarly, excessive imagery that inhibits interaction between the imaginal and verbal modes may be seen as resistance.

Either the failure to attach word labels to images or excessive verbalization, especially without words high in imagery content, indicates resistance to image formation, or a disconnection between the imaginal
and verbal modes of representation. Both rationalization and intellectualization are inhibiting to image formation. Analytical thinking in general prevents the presence of subjective imagery as well as the experience of emotion.

ENHANCEMENT OF CONNECTION AND EMERGENT FUNCTION THROUGH ART MEDIA

In using visual media in therapy, the therapist has to consider the
level of expression primarily used by the client as the starting point.
When evaluating the different levels of information processing and
expression, it is necessary to differentiate the levels of the imagery present. An expression may consist only of kinesthetic and sensory components as the precursors of image. An image may be a schema representing an object. Through line, form, and color the image may represent
emotion, or the image may be a symbol involving sensory and emotional
components. Images may have temporal and spatial qualities and relationships among them, or images may represent concepts and abstractions. Table 6.1 represents the characteristics of the different levels of
internal processes and expression involving imagery.

The first free picture produced in therapy may indicate the level of
information processing and expression preferentially used by the client.
In addition, like the first dream presented in therapy, it also may offer a
statement about the client's functioning in general and contain indications about the progress in therapy (Shoemaker, 1978).

In formulating a therapeutic plan, Tokuda (1973, 1980) evaluates the
client's first four or five drawings on the technical skill, pictorial nature,
level of thought, emotion, and volition portrayed. He considers the
following dimensions.

1. Theme, either of free drawing or set by the therapist
2. Motif encompassing one or more of the following: scribble, col-
   oration, design, deformation, inclusion of letters, abstract, and
   reality-oriented subject
3. Formal elements of the image: stroke, pressure, balance, perspective, color, detail
4. Space, differentiating realistic, inner, and imaginary space
5. Time, referring to past, present, and future

6. Image category, differentiating thought, sensory, hallucinatory, dream, and unconscious images

In addition to these aspects, Tokuda (1973, 1980) also considers the time required to create the visual expression, reaction level to inquiry, and the content of expression. Shoemaker's (1978) approach considers criteria similar to Tokuda's (1973, 1980), except that it elaborates the motif and formal aspects. Motif in the first picture reflects "synthessence" or a map of wholeness presented in the expression. The formal elements and their emotional impact reflect the amount of energy present.

The dimensions of motif and formal elements are helpful in differentiating the level of expression in terms of the ETC as represented in Table 6.1. The following examples from art therapy literature illustrate the choice of the starting level, the developmentally based emergent qualities, and connection between levels.

The client's *developmental* level or the level of regression as reflected in graphic expression is one of the first considerations for the therapist using visual expression in therapy. Small children benefit from sensory and motor experiences and manipulation of concrete materials on the kinesthetic/sensory level. Similarly, the mildly retarded young children and moderately retarded older children benefit from experiences involving sensory awareness and gross and fine motor skills (Uhlin & De Chiara, 1984). The use of emergent qualities based on developmental sequence are illustrated by the following examples.

Wilson (1977, 1985a, 1985b) points out that one of the first goals in therapy for the mentally retarded is expansion of their motor, sensory, and perceptual capacities, because the symbol formation is impaired. The transition to a level involving organized imagery can be enhanced by the therapist's modeling the drawing of circles and vertical lines (Wilson, 1977). The use of visual expression may assist the gradual shift from scribbling to drawing recognizable forms, eventually naming the forms, and attaching personal meaning to them. Similarly a gradual shift may be achieved from an object or visual expression standing for an inner experience to being representative of or symbolizing it (Wilson, 1985a). The developmental sequence illustrates the transition from the kinesthetic/sensory level to the perceptual, or even the cognitive/symbolic level. The new, higher level achieved represents the emerging function in that the individual functions on this level incorporating the previous levels in a new context.

For emotionally disturbed, mentally retarded children, the transition to the perceptual and eventually the cognitive level may be enhanced through reality-shaping using simplified, concrete, two-dimensional and three-dimensional models. The involvement with concrete objects leads to abstraction and systematic elaboration of concepts (Roth, 1978, 1987). The approach of reality-shaping reinforces the developmental sequence of exploration and manipulation of concrete objects on the kinesthetic/sensory and perceptual levels.

The expression of a child or individual who has not attained the symbolic stage of concept formation and representation can be seen as *presymbolic* in comparison to nonsymbolic expressions by individuals who are capable of symbolic expression but are not displaying this ability (Kunkle-Miller & Aach, 1983). In either case, clients may produce expressions on the kinesthetic/sensory level, but the regression to this level and the lack of progress to the perceptual level in an individual using nonsymbolic expression may be due to emotional impairment.

The *perceptual* level can provide a nonthreatening means to expression. Stember (1977, 1978) reports on using surface printing with abused children with delayed development. Printing of objects provides a structure and at the same time nondemanding exploration of colors or shapes. This exploration gives the children a sense of control and an opportunity to take small chances and to trust themselves. In addition, it provides an opportunity to find shapes and become sensitized to expression through forms.

Tracing emphasizes the visual/motor coordination necessary for the formation and preception of forms on the perceptual level. Hays (1982) found that children ages four to ten did not produce form responses to scribbles. Their responses to scribbles were more concrete than their responses to dot-to-dot drawings. Responses to the dot-to-dot drawings were of the associative type. In the case of dot-to-dot drawings, the child was asked to make dots on the paper and then connect them. Subsequently the child was encouraged to find shapes in the lines formed by the connected dots. Hays (1982) proposes that the emotional release was greater with making the dots than with scribbling because the dots released associative responses.

Another possible explanation for the larger amount of nonresponses to scribble drawings as compared to dot-to-dot drawings is again based on the greater amount of eye and hand coordination required in the dot-to-dot drawings, which leads to form perception.

The emphasis of the perceptual/affective level in the beginning of therapy is illustrated by Comfort's (1985) use of published pictures as a psychotherapeutic tool. The pictures are selected for their suitability to introduce clients to visual language, thus laying a foundation for future use of imagery as a means of communication in therapy. The pictures can be either content-oriented or "free" pictures. The therapist records the image selection, the client's verbalizations during this process, the associations produced to the images, and the reflections emerging in the subsequent discussion. Comfort (1985) states that the kinesthetic and emotional forces in the perceptual field contribute to new conceptualization of reality through abstraction. Abstraction is seen as a more effective defense mechanism than denial or repression. The labels and associations provided for the images build a bridge to the client's cognitive abilities.

The kinesthetic and perceptual aspects of expression leading to *affective* expression are emphasized by Rhinehart and Englehorn (1982) in their pre-image considerations of line, form, and color. The client is asked to supplement his/her verbalizations with free hand movement over the paper creating lines, forms, and color with brush and paint. The formal elements of expression are explored for their respective meanings, which contribute to the overall meaning of the image. The therapist may ask the client to repeat movements and exaggerate statements of line, form, and color. Rhinehart and Englehorn (1984) report that if the colors present are muddy, separation and clarification of colors gives the client an opportunity to clarify emotions.

In Rosenberg's (1982) approach, the perceptual and cognitive approaches are combined using modular drawings. The clients are encouraged to explore drawing within a drawing by expanding it into a sequence of drawings or by exploring one or more parts. Special emphasis is given to emotionally loaded parts, which are repeated several times. Choice and effective changes can be conceptualized through reordering and reorganizing the existing parts of a drawing. Rosenberg reports that the imposition of structure by the therapist serves a supportive role for clients who are vague and draw vague images, severely anxious clients producing erratic pictures, and dissociative and repressed clients showing a lack of order in their expressions. For clients with paranoid symptoms, the modular drawings provide an opportunity to view their projections with reduced anxiety.

Rhyne (1979b, 1983) and Carnes (1979a, 1979b) both use a *cognitive* approach based on Kelly's (1955) construct theory. Rhyne (1979b) provides an opportunity for the client to explore choices through drawing alternative solutions to a problem and verbalizing the constructs associated with the imagery. In a similar vein, Carnes (1979a) uses visual expression to depict a variety of possibilities for action. The client can experiment with new constructions and alternative solutions to the problem.

Considered from the systems theory viewpoint, such approaches illustrate the use of the emergent function and connections between levels of information processing in therapy. The development of cognitive/symbolic processes can be enhanced through a developmentally based progression of expression from the kinesthetic/sensory to the perceptual level as indicated by the work of Roth (1978) and Wilson (1979, 1985a, 1985b). This transition between the different levels of the ETC is schematically presented in Figure 6.2.

Rosenberg (1982) illustrates how elaborations and rearrangements on the perceptual level clarify conceptualization of a problem on the cognitive/symbolic level. Similarly, Rhyne's (1979b) and Carnes' (1979a) work indicates that problem solving on the cognitive level may be improved by concrete representations of the different aspects of the problem on the perceptual level. The elaborations on and connection with the perceptual level lead to concept clarification and rearrangement on the cognitive/symbolic level as schematically illustrated in Figure 6.3.

VISUAL EXPRESSION OF RESISTANCES AND DEFENSES

A hindrance of the information flow between levels and disconnection thereof in visual expressions is associated with different manifesta-

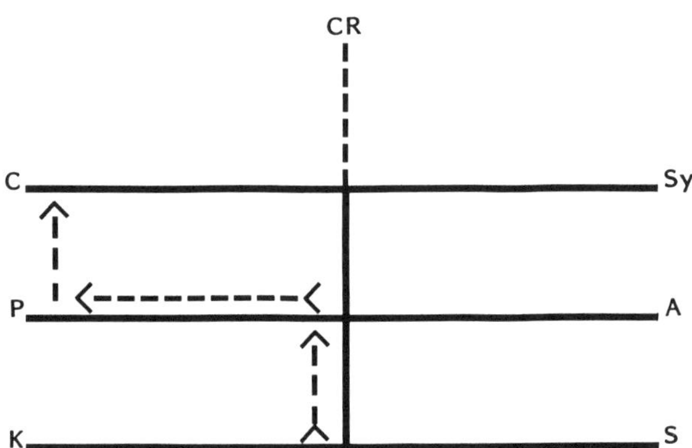

Figure 6.2. Developmental sequence of visual expression and media use with emphasis on perceptual and cognitive levels.

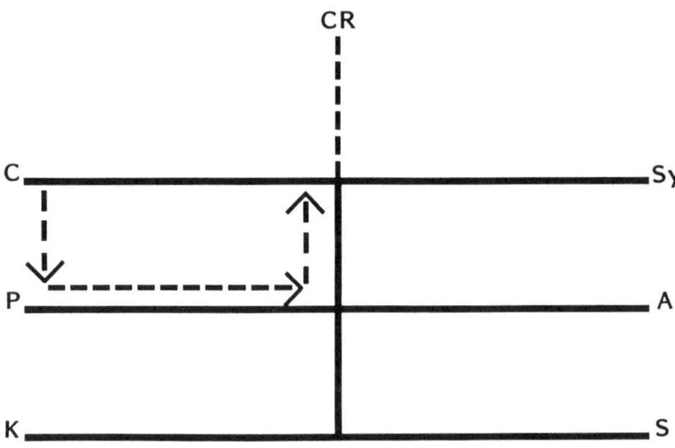

Figure 6.3. Problem solving with elaboration on perceptual level.

tions of resistances and defenses. The most common of the resistances with visual expressions are the following:

1. Claiming lack of artistic skills, which can be seen as overt and explicit resistance to visual expression
2. Visual expression used as resistance, characterized by noncomittal stereotypical images (Nucho, 1982)

Other types of resistances encountered in art therapy are resistance to completing the work, destruction of the visual expression, and copying. The latter can be seen as resistance to using creative abilities. Resistance to emotional stimulation or the presence of physical and emotional exhaustion may be also manifested through the use of pastel shades of colors, or innocuous and stereotypical, everyday subjects, such as a vase of flowers. Repetitious emphasis on an image without its undergoing a change or transformation similarly indicates resistance (Leuner, 1978). Images of resistances or defenses may be represented through the drawings of walls, fences, trenches, closed doors, barred windows. These repetitive and perseverative images indicate that the threatening content is sealed off from the conscious ego. Through the individual's drawing or constructing the structure of resistance, the defense may become less anxiety-provoking and may be gradually transformed to more mature coping mechanisms (Lusebrink, 1982).

Buchalter-Katz (1989) reports that directions to draw obstacles or barriers to recovery are helpful in dealing with resistances of depressed individuals.

The following characteristics indicate the presence of obsessional defenses in visual expressions: frequent use of stereotypes and patterned design; meticulous and perfectionistic techniques; repeated erasure and overpainting; excessive concern with detail; and indecisiveness, denial, and isolation of affect. All these characteristics relate to inhibition and defense mechanisms based on inhibition (Shaw, 1978).

The anxiety and fear associated with emergence of the repressed threatening material may be manifested in both the form and the content of an image. Form and content may also have a latent meaning indicating the nature of repressed emotions and drives.

In discussing the developmental aspects and the graphic manifestations of defense mechanisms, Levick (1983) differentiates between defenses based on inhibition and those based on motor discharge. Inhibition is seen as the motor counterpart for the following defense mechanisms: denial, reaction formation, isolation, repression, and intellectualization. Motor discharge, on the other hand, is associated with displacement, acting out, and identification with the aggressor.

The graphic manifestation of denial is seen in the absence of body parts or parts of objects in the visual expression of individuals capable of appropriate representations. Reaction formation is characterized by positive qualities portrayed about a situation or object that is known to be the source of painful feelings. Objects drawn singly on a page, or images drawn unconnected to other forms on the page represent ideas split from feelings in the defense mechanism of isolation. Repression manifests itself in visual expression by the omission of unacceptable thoughts or feelings. Displacement is represented by the images of thoughts and feelings displaced from the original object (Levick, 1983). Resistances and defenses, such as isolation, also may be portrayed through reinforced boundaries or encapsulation of the image represented.

Acting out as a defense mechanism manifests itself behaviorally in the therapeutic setting through the acting out with the media, or objects created with the media (Schnake, 1980). Identification with the aggressor may be manifested through images combining qualities of the individual and those of the aggressor (Kramer, 1971). In either of these two instances the expression of the defense mechanisms through media may emphasize the emergent qualities of the expression and creative transformation of the defenses.

In considering the defenses *related to inhibition* in the context of connection and disconnection between the different levels of expression, it appears that the expression is predominantly on the perceptual and cognitive/symbolic levels of the ETC. The affective level is disconnected and the kinesthetic/sensory level is minimally involved. The emotions associated with breaking through these are characterized by surprise, shock, anxiety, or even paranoia. Correspondingly, the images themselves may represent anxiety and dissociation. Connection between levels and emergence of a new level is associated with joy.

Dealing with Resistances in Art Therapy

The overt resistance to visual expression in claiming lack of artistic skills is counteracted by the therapist's assurances that artistic performance is not expected. Exploration of media gives opportunities to overcome resistance to visual expression. Nucho (1987) in her psycho-cybernetic model of art therapy designates this activity as the first or unfreezing stage of art therapy.

Whether the resistances are supported or confronted depends on the individual's ego strength and length of therapy. If supportive therapy is indicated, exploration on the perceptual level of the formal aspects of the visual expression gives form and structure to the resistance and strengthens the ego. Verbalization about the product likewise focuses on the formal aspects (Albert-Puleo, 1980; Lusebrink, 1982; McNiff, 1981; Hesse, 1981). An effective example of this approach is Riley's (1979) art experience, suggested with resistive adolescents, who are asked to portray their "secret" through visual means and discuss it then in formal terms, such as its size, color, etc., without revealing the personal meaning.

A client's persistent use of global or poorly defined images can be approached in a supportive manner through emphasis on detail, either verbally or through perceptual exploration of the visual expression. Visual rendering of objects explored through the different senses enhances detailed perception and differentiation.

The images of resistance may undergo transformation if expressed through different media, especially through media that lend themselves to transformation, such as clay or construction paper (Lusebrink, 1982).

Where uncovering therapy is indicated, a change of levels in the imagery and information processing can be achieved through the use of media with emphasis on the kinesthetic level or affective level, as was discussed in Chapter 5.

The use of media can increase the emergent qualities of information processing on different levels. The use of media can also contribute to the disconnection between different levels, either by choice of the client or the therapist. The client's insistence on the use of media on a particular level may reinforce the disconnection between the levels and the corresponding subsystems; for example, the insistence on the use of pencil or any other resistive media in a controlled manner by the obsessive-compulsive reinforces the cognitive controls and repression of emotion. Changing to other resistive media that can be controlled but have also a motoric or sensory component, such as stone or wood carving, may facilitate connection between different levels, especially involving emotions.

The therapist has to consider when free choice of art media for the client is beneficial, and when it is likely to reinforce disconnection between subsystems and the levels of information processing.

The illustrations and case vignettes at the beginning of this chapter may be used to illustrate the presence of a particular level of information processing; the transition between the levels, either emergent or resistive; and the use of media.

In the first vignette, the young woman experienced the images in a dream; they were involved and emotionally colored, so we therefore presume that they are symbolic and have a meaning beyond the obvious concrete object references.

The requirement to select a few important frames from a complex dream sequence is akin to selecting important pictures from a multitude of magazine cutouts; in both cases the individual relies on the emotional and intuitive aspect of information processing to select and form a meaningful gestalt or configuration. The use of a felt-tip pen in a semistructured way enhanced the emotional and symbolic aspects of the dream expression in the first vignette.

In the second example, the middle-aged woman was not able to generate images in response to the guided daydream (presentation of a story by the therapist using words with high imagery content). It appears that here is a disconnection or blockage between the verbal and imaginal modes of representation. On further consideration there also appears to be an inability to form images, and the only image formed seems to portray the anxiety present—the image of a TV screen with static on it. This image, the general lack of ability to express feelings, and the presence of psychosomatic symptoms pointed to alexithymia, as was earlier discussed. The disconnection not only seemed to be between verbal and imaginal modes, but also is a more innate inability to experience and express affect.

Because she was unable to form images from the information, the presentation of a guided daydream was inappropriate for this woman. A gradual introduction to visual expression and imagery, using recent memory and tactile exploration of concrete objects, may increase her ability to form images. A playful exploration of media on the kinesthetic/sensory level would improve her expressive means. If she were offered a free choice of media, it would increase her anxiety, and a good guess is that she would choose a pencil, namely a medium familiar to her, emphasizing the cognitive aspect of information processing.

In the third example, the young man used fast strokes to create a complex structured image. This image indicated the fluid transition present between the kinesthetic, perceptual, and cognitive levels. The reinforcement of the cognitive level through verbalization revealed that the image held a complex symbolic meaning. Although the symbols seemed to portray feelings, as did the verbalization, the true meaning and the appropriate connection of feelings and life experiences were missing.

The client's free choice of poster paint was intuitively correct. Poster paint provided enough fluidity for his fast expression and the color enhanced the symbolism present with its emotional undertones, thus contributing to the structural organization, and the emergent qualities of the expression. Subsequent verbalization and reflection introduced the cognitive component. The whole sequence had an emergent quality and flow of information leading to insight.

Indications and Contraindications in Using Verbal vs. Visual Expressions of Imagery

The use of imagery and its expression through visual media in therapy is primarily determined by the client's and the therapist's preferences for modes of representation and expression, either verbal or visual or both. The therapist's training, familiarity, and comfort with visual and creative expression are the determining factors in whether visual media are used to express images. The therapist's own resistances to the use of media may determine the preferred use of verbalization in therapy, regardless of the therapist's training as an art therapist.

In assuming that the therapist is prepared to facilitate the client's expression through visual means, the client's preferred modality for representation, resistances, and the therapeutic goals set by the therapist and client determine the modality used.

The following discussion considers the use of verbal and visual expression in therapy on different levels of information processing. From the information-processing viewpoint, internal experiences are expressed visually (emphasizing the right-hemispheric processing innate to imagery) and then discussed verbally with the therapist (using predominantly left-hemispheric functions). The decision whether to use art media or to rely on verbal expression in the therapeutic setting can be made along the client's preferred modes for representation and expression. Individuals who are predominantly verbal or verbalizers will benefit from verbal approaches to therapy, at least initially. Similarly, individuals who have difficulties in verbalizing their experiences, but who have rich visual imagery—i.e., visualizers—may feel more comfortable and will share more by using the visual expression.

Developmentally, this division is important in therapy with children because small children, at least up to age five, may have a limited ability to express their inner experiences and emotions verbally and may require an external concrete means of processing information. Art therapy with an emphasis on the creative and the therapeutic application of media is recommended for small children (Rubin, 1978; Uhlin & De Chiara, 1984).

One of the contraindications in using either verbalization or visual expression is the presence of resistances impeding the progress in therapy. *Excessive verbalization* can be seen as resistance, and it may imply the repression of threatening material, possibly in the form of images. When such resistances occur, transition to the right-hemispheric functioning is desirable. The failure to make this transition might be associated not only with resistances, but also with lack of adequate expressive and imaginal means. Gradual introduction to imaging and to art media may be advisable. Enhancement of imagery was discussed in Chapter 2. Warm-up experiences, using media on different levels of the ETC was discussed in Chapter 5. In instances where excessive verbalization is indicative of such defense mechanisms as intellectualization and rationalization, art experiences with emphasis on the sensory components (e.g., finger paints or clay) are especially effective in reestablishing a connection with the emotional component.

Lack of verbalization can be another form of resistance. The use of collages of cutout figures or objects with "balloons" of written statements for each (Landgarten, 1981) combines visual media with the concurrent retention of the verbal cognitive component. The client's selection of "published" images and one-word association in the form of a written label similarly integrate right- and left-hemispheric functions

(Comfort, 1985). If a client's imagery-forming capacity is adequate, the therapist may introduce guided daydreams and ask the client to portray visually three most important instances of the daydream. The guided daydream provides a general structure which the client can elaborate with subjective images and verbal associations.

Lack of verbalization may also be associated with overdetermined global images. The lack of verbalization may indicate that a new part of the individual's personality is emerging, for which s/he still does not have verbal labels. Elaborations of the images and feelings with visual media allow the new parts to be explored gradually in their emergent and, to some extent, ambiguous state. The freedom provided through the use of fluid media, such as watercolors or soft water clay, provide means for trials and reshaping of the emergent structures. Awareness of the physiological states present, i.e., heart pounding, increased breathing rate, or any motoric action such as clenched fists or a swinging leg, provide entry points to image formation and expression of emotion.

An *excessive motor component* may be a basis for not using visual means of expression. In general, visual expression may be counterindicated where there is an excess of imagery flow, emotion, or motoric action present. In some instances art media can be used to control the excess flow of information by using highly resistive media such as stone, wood, and plaster casts. Nevertheless, the therapist is wise to consider the integrative abilities of the client, since working with resistive media may lead to disintegration of the original form of the material without achieving any therapeutic benefit. In less extreme cases, the presence of an excessive emotional or motoric component can be contained by limiting the choice of media and giving a structure to the session and allowing some freedom of choice within this structure.

Table 6.2 presents some counteractive strategies for persistent difficulties and/or perseveration at the different levels of expression. Outcome studies comparing differences in the effectiveness of using verbal and visual expression of imagery in therapy do not exist, however.

In art therapy the focus can be on the therapeutic effects of the expression through media (art as therapy) or on the psychodynamic functioning of the client as manifested in the visual and verbal expression (art psychotherapy).

Rosal (1985), in comparing the effects of art as therapy and art psychotherapy, found that both types of therapy improved significantly the behavior and locus of control of children with classroom behavior disorders in relation to a control group. Rosal suggests that the process of creativity in visual expressions and art may go beyond the act of sublimating. The child's movements and inner experiences are reflected and reinforced visually through the marks produced on paper. This produces a direct link between behavior and outcome.

SUMMARY

Schwartz's (1984) systems approach to imagery in healing provides a prototype for applying the systems approach to imagery and visual expression in therapy. The interactions between therapist, client, and media can be conceptualized as a system where different parts influence and regulate each other. The therapist, the client, and the media can be considered as subsystems.

Imagery has different components and can be expressed on different levels of information processing. The media provide a means to concretize the image as well as contribute to its connective, emergent, or disconnective qualities. A particular medium may enhance or inhibit the expression on a specific level, or the medium may help to form a connection or disconnection between two or more levels. Several examples from the literature illustrate the developmentally based use of media to increase perceptual and conceptual functioning.

Affect is an important component of subjective imagery. Motor activity, emotions, and imagery influence each other in that motor activity may help or prevent the expression of emotions and imagery. The same is true for effect of emotions or imagery on the other two components.

Images may represent resistances and defense mechanisms. Lack of images and excessive verbalization can be seen as resistance. The use of verbal or visual expression of images depends on the personal preferences and style of the therapist and client as well as their own resistance to visual expression.

The case vignettes discussed in this chapter provide views from different perspectives on the interaction between the client, media, and therapist: emergent, connective or disconnective, emotional, and defensive or resistive viewpoints. The discussion of the media used illustrates the effect of amplification or minimization of the connection between different levels of information processing.

Thus the multidimensional matrix discussed in this chapter provides an approach to the client's needs on an individual basis, dealing with emergent as well as resistive qualities in a goal-directed manner.

CHAPTER 7

Active Imagination, Guided Daydreams, and Dreams

A male art therapy student illustrates the following dreams with two drawings: "My friend and I are diving into deep water to retrieve treasure from a sunken ship. There are sharks in the water threatening us, but we proceed with the diving. The scene changes and my friend and I are in a small boat being pursued by several boats with policemen" (Figs. 7.1 and 7.2).

A female therapist organizes the most important images of a rich and complex dream in the following five frames arranged on three levels:

I am by a work table on which there is an active baby who seems to have features of my boyfriend. I attend to his needs. The scene changes and my boyfriend and I are entering a plaza. A festive crowd is approaching the plaza from the opposite direction. It is led by a jolly man in a jester's costume. The last scene which stands out is a cellar where somebody pushes in a gurney with a mummy on it. There seems to be a life in it, though, since the mummy is slightly moving. Someplace there also seems to be a baby mummy (Fig. 7.3).

A woman comes home from work frustrated about the unresolved problems of a meeting she was leading. She airs her frustration with a few strokes of a marker on a piece of paper. She proceeds to elaborate by filling out areas while she is thinking about the meeting and the problems there (Fig. 7.4). During the night she has the following dream:

I am waiting by a railroad track on a sandy hill for a train. A voice says, "The train does not stop here anymore." I am going down the hill to a highway by the ocean. A French driver offers me a ride in a taxi. I climb in and I want to go to the left, but the driver says that it is not the right direction and we have to go to the right. I am apprehensive about the possibility of an explosion there.

Upon awakening she realizes that the dream landscape is based on her doodle of the previous night—to the right, along the line dividing the sandy and the blue color areas, is indeed an encapsulated form which looks like a contained explosion. The woman realizes that in the meeting on the previous day she was avoiding confronting people, and it apparently was the way to solve the problem.

Figure 7.1. Dream drawing I: "Diving for Treasure."

Figure 7.2. Dream drawing II: "Pursuit by Police Boats."

INTRODUCTION

This chapter deals with the flow of imagery present in active imagination, guided daydreams, and dreams. These three forms of imagery have several characteristics in common: (1) the images are related mainly to self; (2) they involve external input only minimally or not at all; and (3) they seem to have a direction independent of the conscious will of the individual. In addition, they display spontaneous changes in the flow of the imagery and, as self-directed thought, they are influenced greatly by affect. All three forms of imagery flow have a large visual component, and in therapy situations drawing or painting is often used to portray the images (Jung, 1960, 1969; Leuner, 1977, 1978, 1984). The individual's attitude in all three forms is passive in that s/he submits to the flow of imagery with a minimally judgmental attitude; at the same time, the individual is an active participant in the setting provided by the flow of imagery.

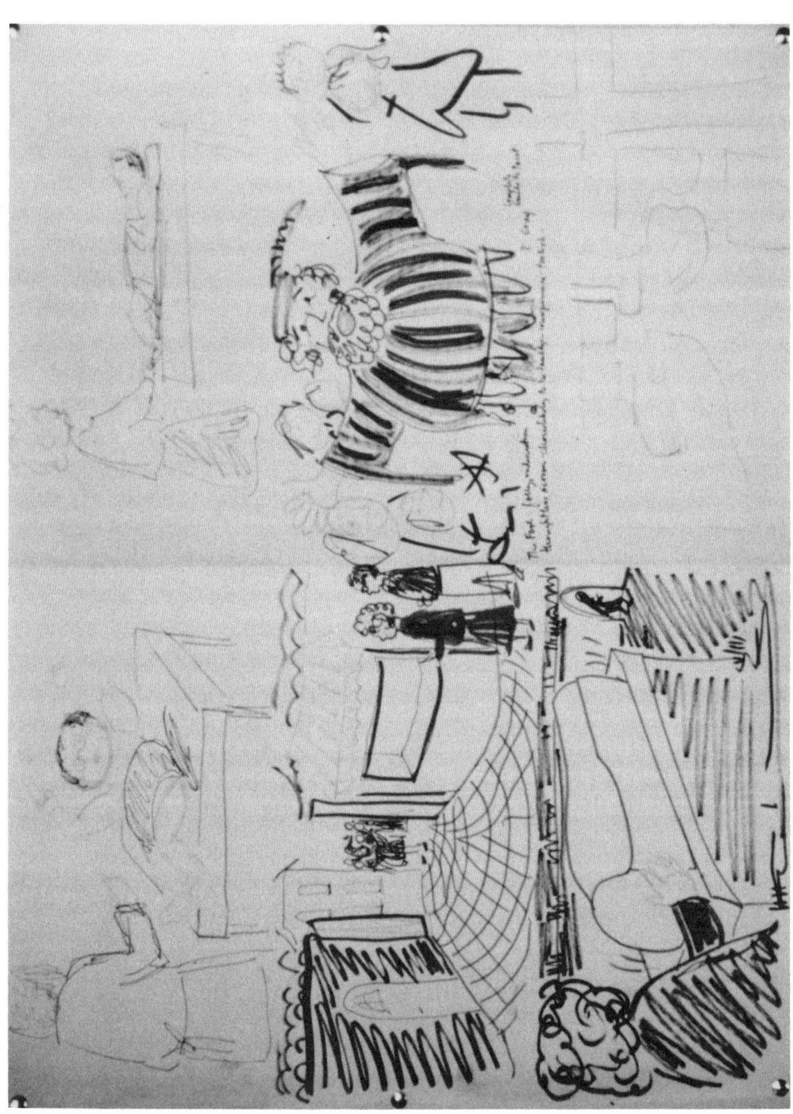

Figure 7.3. Serial dream drawing: "Work, Play, and Problem."

Figure 7.4. Doodle drawing as basis for dream scenery.

The Flow of Imagery and Fantasy

The flow of imagery in fantasy and daydreams and its function have been investigated by Singer (1976) and Klinger (1978).

Singer's (1976) approach to the characteristics and function of fantasy and daydreaming is discussed in the next chapter in relation to depression in adolescence. The present chapter focuses on the structural flow of imagery and levels of consciousness, with emphasis on their manifestation in dreams and dreamlike imagery methods in therapy.

Klinger (1978) defines the flow of consciousness as all the changes that take place in the consciousness over a period of time. These changes include imagery as a form of thought in all the sense modalities and also the changes in affect. Moment-to-moment thoughts have a coherent quality determined by motivational factors and emotional cues. The sequence of the flow of consciousness follows the induction principle:

> At any given moment the next thematic content of thought is induced by the combination of a current concern and a cue related to that concern. The "cue" is construed as either a cognitively meaningful stimulus in the external environment or a symbolic event in the stream of the individual's own consciousness. (Klinger, 1978, p. 250)

This induction principle also holds true for the imaginal stream in fantasy. The changing imagery carries with it affective responses that act as cues for changing the thematic content.

Shifts in the fantasy sequence occur every 5 to 6 seconds in silent thought. The length of a fantasy segment while thinking aloud is about 30 seconds (Klinger, 1978). In addition to current concerns, these shifts often occur in response to fantasy segments with a strong affect that disrupts the segment. Based on the affect present, either the segment is redirected or a new segment is initiated. Fantasy serves an adaptive function in that a person recombines and reorganizes information, often emphasizing aspects that s/he may have overlooked in a reality context. The affect present serves as an evaluative component of the person's current concerns and incentives and efforts in dealing with them (Klinger, 1978).

Dreams and fantasies form a continuous ideational stream (Klinger, 1971; Starker, 1974) and display an interchangeability in function (Faber, Saayman, & Papadopolous, 1983). The particular characteristics of waking fantasy and dreams, however, are influenced by the physiological state in which they are experienced, i.e., relaxed wakefulness or the different stages of sleep. The sequential segments in fantasy appear more organized as compared to play and dreams, where the sequence of events seems to be more erratic. Nevertheless, dreams mainly reflect the dreamer's current concerns, especially emotionally charged concerns (M. Kramer, 1982). Similar to fantasy, the segments of dreams may change in response to the emotional arousal associated with these concerns (Klinger, 1971).

CONSCIOUSNESS AND THE UNCONSCIOUS

The imagery present in active imagination, guided daydreams, and dreams may be reality-oriented and reflect life situations and current concerns; or the images can be internally oriented in that they metaphorically and symbolically represent and deal with aspects of self and problems of which the individual is not consciously aware. Whether the focus of the experience and its interpretation has a reality context and is mainly oriented to the immediate past, or refers to the individual's distant past and childhood or to more mythological themes depends upon the individual's experience and the therapist's approach. In the first dream example (Figs. 7.1 and 7.2), the diving may be seen in reality context as an adventure, or in the Jungian context of individuation as reaching the inner treasure of self (von Franz, 1968).

Images possess different temporal references and reflect differences in the psychic depth represented in them. The range of the images reflecting the psyche covers a continuum from representations of the psyche's conscious contents and operations to the contents inaccessible to conscious awareness or the unconscious.

The cognitive-behavioral approach proposes that the enduring characteristics of an individual's cognitive organization are based on cognitive structures or schema (Meichenbaum & Gilmore, 1984). These cognitive structures are interdependent with affect, in that affect plays a modulating role in cognition. The information processing based on cognitive structures is limited in that at any given time a person can process only a small amount of given internal and external information. The range of information processing is delimited by the attention paid to a particular input at any given time.

From the cognitive viewpoint, the unconscious is a dynamic process of thought, not a static depository of memories. The unconscious is organized on three levels involving developmentally sequential modes of mental operations, namely, sensory motor actions, mental representations, and abstract thought. The memory processes change with age, and at each successive developmental level, the same event is constructed and reconstructed differently (Fischer & Pipp, 1984).

The most commonly known depth-psychology viewpoints of the unconscious are those as defined by Freud and Jung. In Freud's structural model the unconscious is defined as the Id, consisting of drives which are the major source of psychic energy barred from consciousness through ego defenses. The Id also comprises repressed memories, fantasies, and emotions that were conscious before repression took place

(Brenner, 1955). Thus the repressed material constitutes a personal unconscious related to the experiences of the individual.

Jung differentiates between the personal unconscious and the collective unconscious. Consciousness is seen as a fluid state containing both conscious and unconscious elements. Jung (1969) defines the personal unconscious or the "fringe of consciousness" as:

> everything of which I know, but of which I am not at the moment thinking; everything of which I was once conscious but have now forgotten; everything perceived by my senses, but not noted by my conscious mind; everything which, involuntary and without paying attention to it, I feel, think, remember, want, and do; all the future things that are taking shape in me and will sometime come to consciousness: all this is the content of the unconscious. (p. 95)

The collective unconscious is universal and detached from anything personal, and its contents can be found everywhere in the human race (Jung, 1956). The collective unconscious forms the archetypal psyche, or the depository of a priori patterns for instinctual activities. These patterns emerge in consciousness in the form of archetypal images, which contain the meaning of the instinct (Jacobi, 1959). The archetype also contains the potential for the spiritual goal towards which the instincts and images evolve.

ACTIVE IMAGINATION

A conscious connection can be established with the unconscious, particularly with the archetypal images, through the method of active imagination involving a flow of fantasy. Jung's (1960, 1969) approach to a flow of imagery presupposes certain conditions: a passive acceptance of the flow of imagery with an active participation in the imagery.

In Jung's view (1960, 1969) active imagination provides an indirect view to approach the archetypal images and the individual's feelings and meaning associated with them. The emergence of the images contributes to the understanding of the meaning of the underlying archetypal pattern. Thus, for example, the manifestation of the image representing a wise old man or woman may carry with it the archetypal configuration of an inner guide with a particular meaning for the individual experiencing it.

In active imagination, images seem to have a life of their own, and their symbolic flow develops according to its own logic. The starting point for the flow of active imagination is marked by concentrating on an image, which then becomes enriched with details. The unconscious produces a complete story through the movement of the images. Jung (1969) cautions against interrupting the flow of events with conscious thoughts. Nevertheless, the material is produced in a conscious state of mind and differs from dreams in that it is closer to everyday thought patterns and has more direct feeling values than dreams. In active imagination, though, the themes present have a literal semblance to everyday reality only as an expression of the underlying unconscious processes.

Jung (1969) points out that these images do not necessarily need to be interpreted. Their meaning, if further elaborated upon, should not be reduced to the conscious content as the common denominator, but should be investigated through amplification in a process similar to that for dreams. In amplification the therapist may add examples from historical and mythological contexts and symbolism, thus elaborating on the possible meaning of the images. The impersonal images present in active fantasy can be expressed and explored through painting or drawing. In this manner the patient can process the archetypal material without being overwhelmed by it. The patient is advised to keep the pictures so that their unconscious archetypal content can be incorporated in consciousness. This process brings about a change in personality (Jung, 1960, 1969).

"Paintings from the unconscious" (Jacobi, 1955) or the "picture method" (Henderson, 1973) of visually expressing the emerging images is used in Jungian analysis and also in the Jungian approach to therapy without the intervening step of active imagination. The pictures give a "body" to the images that express inner experiences, which are urgently felt but are incomprehensible and cannot be expressed in words (Jacobi, 1955). This method consists of several steps: first, the picture is created; next, the individual experiences the picture as it makes an impression on the creator's psyche; in the last step the impression is compared to the therapist's interpretation of it. The visual expression puts in motion the psychic energy associated with the image and provides it with a structure. The assimilation of the picture through conscious reflection is a prerequisite for a lasting transformation of the unconscious contents. Depending on the patient, at times the visual expression is regarded as sufficient by the therapist, or interpretation may also be carried out for the details of the picture, not only the main images (Jacobi, 1955). The visual expression is considered to provide a broader view than the verbal description alone, but it has to be given a permanent form through a thorough analysis (Henderson, 1973).

Lyddiatt (1971) developed a method of spontaneous painting and modeling based on Jung's principle of active imagination. In this method the individual paints from the unconscious by deliberately responding to a mood in letting the hand move without conscious guidance. Lyddiatt does not use interpretations in her work with patients. The purpose of the painting is to link the unconscious with consciousness. The intellectual, emotional, and moral understanding necessary for complete assimilation is achieved in this case through painting. Lyddiatt (1971) considers the following three stages as necessary for the spontaneous painting method: giving form to the imaginative material, experiencing the forms created, and feeling more alive as a result of it. At times the created productions need to be lived with or experienced on a prolonged basis. This method is not seen as a substitute for psychotherapy; nevertheless, it is effective with patients who may not have the ability to understand their pictures in intellectual terms.

Spontaneous production of imagery can be seen on a continuum with directed or guided imagery. In the direct visualization methods the general theme of symbols to be imagined is presented by the therapist. In directed daydreams an important role is assigned to the directional suggestions of symbolic ascent or descent (Dessoille, 1966). This approach is incorporated in psychosynthesis (Assagioli, 1965; Gerard, 1964), whereby the downward movement leads to contact with symbolic representations of internal or interpersonal conflicts. The symbolic upward movement is used for resolution of conflicts, sublimation, and symbolic linking of spirit and matter (Gerard, 1964).

GUIDED AFFECTIVE IMAGERY

Leuner's Guided Affective Imagery (GAI) (1977, 1978, 1984; Leuner, Horn, & Klessman, 1983) method is the best known of European oneiro or daydream therapies. It is based on psychoanalytic principles and uses imagery predominantly in a structured manner; its focus is on stimulating self-regulating tendencies of the ego and the self-healing powers of the psyche. This approach, introduced in 1948, represents one of the earliest extensive uses of imagery in therapy, and it is one of the most documented in regard to its effectiveness. Its effectiveness is also backed up by controlled studies (Leuner, 1978; Wachter & Pudel, 1980). The aspects of GAI emphasized here relate primarily to the function, changes, and visual expression of imagery in therapy.

In GAI imagery the therapist introduces one of the standard themes: e.g., on the basic level, meadow, brook, mountain, house, and edge of the woods. The client, in a relaxed state and using creative fantasy, elaborates on the presented theme and tells the therapist about the emerging imagery contents. In addition, the client is encouraged to draw psychic maps of the inner landscape or sketch the emerging images on paper. The client is also advised to keep a written journal of mental imagery and paint his/her choice of the contents at home. This journal and the paintings are then brought to the therapy session where the therapist reads the journal aloud to the client and discusses with the client the possible meaning of the written images as well as those of the painted ones. In this manner the GAI method is similar to the active imagination method, whereby the unconscious content is presented in images, which then are concretized, reflected back to the client, and explored for meaning.

Leuner bases his approach on the observations that under emotional stress people can have very vivid imaginative experiences and on the presence of hypnogogic imagery formed in relaxed conditions. Imagery and the hypnoidal state influence each other in a circular fashion: relaxation leads to a slight hypnoidal state inducive to image formation and the progressive presence of imagery produces a more pronounced hypnoidal state. The guided imagery is only slightly under the voluntary control of the individual, and the imagery possesses a remarkable state of autonomy.

The image usually used to start therapy is apt to be a meadow because of its pleasant characteristics. The client develops his/her own imagery associated with the meadow; the therapist may expand it with additional images. The imagery is explored for obstacles, threatening areas, or goals. The imagery motifs undergo change through "symbolic transformation" (Leuner, 1978, p. 130) in the course of 20 to 30 sessions, indicating that the different imagery motifs are dynamically related.

No interpretations are made on the basic level of the GAI. The themes are worked and resolved in terms of perception in two directions: first, cognitively, by focusing on the perceptual structures, and second, emotionally, by animating these structures with feelings and moods. Moods may be portrayed through landscapes and weather, e.g., a frozen landscape would indicate constriction and lack of feelings. Generally, feelings are slower to emerge than the cognitive aspects of imagery, therefore adequate space and time must be allowed for the feelings to develop in the presentation of the themes. The imaginal contents can change continuously, and these changes are often precipitated by the slightest change in emotions (Leuner, 1984).

Leuner (1977, 1984) differentiates between fixed images and shifting images. Fixed imagery repeats itself without undergoing any change and indicates a presence of conflict areas. In this case the same imagery is explored several times until the imagery begins to shift as the core conflict is activated. The fixed images point to an element of emotional rigidity characteristic of neurotically and psychosomatically disturbed clients. Shifting images change from time to time and are not particularly charged with affect.

The symbolic content of strongly emotionally charged images may contain a significant meaning for the client. The transition from the symbolic to the verbal expression of the conflict is seen as relatively difficult, and it takes time for the therapeutic process to cross the threshold between these two modes of representation.

Perceptually contradictory images, which are at odds with the natural world, indicate conflicts, similar to fixed images. The therapeutic strategy is to allow the client to find his/her way out of obstructed or conflictual situations, thus fostering the client's initiative and active motivation. Magic means of escaping difficult situations are seen as regressive and are not condoned. The therapist leads the client back over and over again to the conflictual areas with the presentation of the standard themes of the GAI. Defensive structures are closely examined perceptually for their construction and the details of mechanisms involved.

Through the perceptual analysis the client learns to penetrate each imagined scene cognitively and bring it into the total context. At the same time the client also becomes aware of the emotional tone of the imagery. The symbolic figures present in the imagery can be seen from the subjective and objective viewpoints. From the *subjective* viewpoint these figures are assumed to represent unconscious behavioral tendencies of the client, similar to Jung's concept of the "shadow." These are to be integrated in the conscious personality. For example, the animals present in imagery are approached and stroked, thus making them friends of the client. From the *objective* viewpoint, the imagery figures are seen as the client's referential figures, and in the GAI they are fed and satiated, thus eventually leading to reconciliation. Their characteristics and the client's feelings about them are explored in the course of the discussion of the images. Different themes of the imagery are dynamically associated with each other as is seen in the phenomenon of "synchronous transformation." In the course of therapy changes even occur in imagery themes which are not directly associated with the therapeutic interventions, such as aspects of landscapes (Leuner, 1978).

Leuner (1984) reports that conflict-free scenes also have been observed to lead to a client's somatic improvements. These mainly are encounters with persons emanating positive feelings and peaceful scenes and aesthetic nature experiences that create happy moods and feelings of well-being. Leuner sees the effectiveness of these images in the gratification of the client's archaic needs for security and emotional warmth. Gratification of these needs is also achieved with images and themes of water: drinking it, bathing in it, and swimming in it. Leuner calls the therapeutic use of the conflict-free scenes "the second dimension of the GAI," the first dimension being centered around conflicts.

Instead of being structured with a thematically defined motif, GAI can also be used to bring an acute conflict into focus spontaneously. With psychosomatic problems a journey through one's own body can be used to inspect the different bodily organs.

The GAI procedure can be used starting with children 7 years old. It is not recommended for adults with an IQ below 85, nor for adults with organic brain syndromes or psychosis (Leuner, 1978). It appears that the imagery procedures require the presence of anticipatory mental images and the ability to separate reality from inner images.

In regard to the advantages of using oneiro or daydream therapies, Frétigny and Virel (1968) point out the advantages of using imagery: it can be used with people with a low level of sophistication who are incapable of systematic reflection, with people who rely on rational thinking, and with those who have a tendency to rumination. The main advantage of using imagery is its orientation towards the individual's affective experience.

The therapeutic effectiveness of GAI is manifested in relaxation of defenses, symbolic representation of conflicts, release of suppressed impulses, trying out alternative and new solutions, and creativity, including representation of future possibilities through imagery (Leuner et al., 1983). The changes observed in the GAI flow of imagery are similar to those described by Klinger (1971, 1978, 1980) in the flow of consciousness and fantasy.

Faber et al. (1983) found that waking dreams influenced nocturnal dreams because there was a shift in symbolic and affective themes in nocturnal dreams after waking dream experiences. The dreams showed a significant increase in the frequency of archetypal content, thus demonstrating "a very strong relationship between endogenous, self-generated, dynamically relevant stimuli upon the reported content of nocturnal dreams" (p. 158).

Therapeutic Use of Visual Expressions of Guided Imagery

The GAI (Leuner, 1977, 1978, 1984; Leuner et al, 1983) method uses visual expressions of the imagery that appears especially important to the client. It also uses sketches and diagrams as supplements to the verbal descriptions of the imagery present.

In art therapy the imagery experience can be separated from its visual expression and the subsequent verbal discussion. First, the client, who must be in a relaxed state, experiences the imagery on a theme presented verbally by the therapist. Since the client does not share the imagery from moment to moment, in this approach the therapist has to observe the client for signs of affect or anxiety and distress and intervene directly if necessary. At the end of this presentation either the therapist asks the client to select three or more important scenes from the guided daydream, or suggests three particular scenes which the client contemplates before opening his/her eyes. Usually the scenes selected by the therapist are the initial scene in the daydream, such as the meadow, followed by the obstacle encountered on the journey, and then the goal, such as the top of the mountain or the source. The client is encouraged to represent visually any other important or anxiety-provoking scene. This approach emphasizes the transformation of the imagery by dividing it into the main segments.

Usually poster paints or watercolors are recommended for the visual depiction, emphasizing the affective component of the experience. The exploration of the pictorial and descriptive details and the integration of the images take place through the act of painting. Usually the individual becomes involved in the creative aspect of painting the images, which in itself has an integrative value. The exploration of affective or other aspects can follow the completion of the painting. The visual examination of the expression brings to the client's awareness the changes and transformations that have taken place during the imagery journey.

The obstacles can be explored visually for their emotional impact, meaning, and context in regard to the other images present. Often the obstacles become incorporated in a transformed context in the final picture. For example, for a young man, a fallen tree that blocked his way to the mountaintop became incorporated as a part of a solid octagonal log building on the top of the mountain. The unusual or contradictory forms or scenery indicative of conflict stand out in the visual expression and can be elaborated for their affective values and meaning. Similarly, the size of the images portrayed and their closeness to or distance from the viewer can be explored for affective meaning.

The visual reinforcement of the images experienced in the guided daydream helps to reinternalize the images, which then emerge again in a changed context or even in dreams.

STRUCTURE AND FUNCTION OF DREAMS

Dreams are considered to be a mental activity on a continuum with waking fantasy and hypnogogic and hypnopompic images, whereby the character of each of these mental activities is determined by the state of the physiological arousal in which the activity is experienced (Klinger, 1971).

In cognitive psychology dreams are seen as a cognitive activity, albeit an involuntary one (Foulkes, 1985). Dreams are formally organized because they appear understandable from moment to moment and they have a narrative with sequences of events in which the characters and the settings show continuity. The formation of dreams has to involve the same structures and processes as in waking experiences for them to be coherent thematically. Dreams occur in the absence of external sensory stimulation, and their content is based on the dreamer's memories, knowledge, beliefs, feelings, and sensations. These form the basis for the stimuli during dreaming and the dream consciousness that interprets them (Foulkes, 1985).

During sleep imaginal dreams occur in the REM stage of sleep. Rapid eye movement sleep (REM), in addition to eye movements, displays signs of general physiological arousal, whereas tonus in the head and neck area is markedly decreased. The gross body movements are more frequent immediately preceding and following REM periods than within the REM periods (Schwartz, Weinstein, & Arkin, 1978). The eye movements do not seem to relate to individual dream images, but appear to occur in accordance with the head movements that the individual would make if the dream activities took place in waking reality (Herman, 1984).

The content of REM dreams in the first part of night refers to the previous day's residues, but it becomes more detailed, complex, and unusual as the night proceeds and more remote memories are incorporated into the dreams. Dreams at the night's end are again present-oriented. The dreams from non-REM sleep are reported as brief, either thoughtlike or as isolated images, based on recent memory. Thus the expression in dreams changes from conceptual to perceptual, depending on the stage of sleep (Webb & Cartwright, 1978).

The dreams reported upon falling asleep or from the hypnogogic stage of sleep are similar in their imaginal character to REM dreams but about three times shorter. They have a regressive or defective imaginal character based on momentary memory fragments (Foulkes, 1985). Lucid dreaming (LaBerge, 1980; Ogilvie, Hunt, Tyson, Lucescu, & Jeakins, 1982) is experienced towards the morning hours, and is characterized by its real lifelike quality and the dreamer's awareness in dreams that s/he has some control over the dream. Lucid dreaming seems to be linked to the enhancement of analytic-reflective and waking spatial abilities (Ogilvie et al., 1982).

According to M. Kramer (1982), dreams serve a mood-regulating function. They process and interpret information in relation to the self which appears in about 95% of adult REM dreams. Dreams are based on the activation of memory, emotions, and sensations. They interpret and integrate motoric and perceptual knowledge and other mental activities which do not reach awareness during the waking state. The dream experience simulates waking experience, including spatial organization and temporal directions (Foulkes, 1985). The experimental data seem to support "a broad generalization that there is a division of labor between waking and dreaming mentation with the former being primarily concerned with intellectual information and instrumental responses, and the latter being specialized for affective information and responses" (Webb & Cartwright, 1978, pp. 244–245).

COGNITIVE DEVELOPMENT OF DREAMS

Dreaming is a symbolic activity, which takes place in the absence of the referent objects in reality and requires a sufficient symbolic maturation to permit symbolic processing. The content and frequency of children's dreams depend on their age and are related to stages of symbol development (Foulkes, 1985). Dreaming also requires an ability to recall the nocturnal mental content and to express it either verbally or through visual means.

The developmental aspects of dreams have been investigated by Foulkes (1977, 1982, 1985). Similar to drawing, children's dreams reflect what they know instead of what they see or do. Foulkes' classification of the development of children's dreams reflects Piaget's (1962) sequence of the development of symbolic representation, as discussed in Chapter 3. In this context, symbols are defined as the mental representation in the absence of objects or events they represent in reality.

In the preoperational period (3–5 years), children seldom report dreams upon being awakened from REM sleep. Their dream reports are very short, and the themes present involve body states, such as hunger or sleep, and animal characters. Absent from small children's dreams are movement of physical activity, self-representation or known human characters, and narrative planning. The dreams are static, reflecting the static mental imagery present during this period.

During the period of transition to concrete operations (5–7 years) the dreams are significantly longer, even though the frequency of dreams has increased only minimally. The content of dreams during this period shows important changes from the preoperational period: increase in physical movement, shifts from animal characters to known and invented humans, shifts from body states to social interaction, and the appearance of a primitive narrative or theme linking the events into a linear sequence.

In the period of early concrete operations (7–9 years), both the length and the frequency of dream reports increase significantly over those of the previous developmental periods. Self-character participation, both in movement in the dream scene and in social interactions, also has increased significantly. The dreams are unified by a plot, and the dream characters may have thoughts and feelings, reflecting the emerging awareness of inner mental life.

During the period of later concrete operations (9–13 years) the length and the frequency of the dreams are similar to those of adults. The dream content reaches a high point in physical activity and social interaction and self-participation is further increased, as is the presence of strangers. Feelings are diversified, although most of the dreams are reported without feelings being present in dreams. The dream content reflects the preadolescents' waking interests and behavior.

The dreams in the period of early formal operations (13–15 years) have fewer instances of physical activity and of active self-representation. There is an increase in novel characters and dream settings reflecting the increased ability to abstract from reality and to create new situations.

Childhood dreams during REM and non-REM periods do not differ in the early stages of development. Reports of the presence of non-REM dreams increase in the period of early concrete operations. It appears that the emergence of formal operational reasoning contributes to the appearance of the more fragmentary images and thoughts characteristic of non-REM dreams.

Considering that the developmental stages of dreaming and dream content depend on cognitive development, dreaming appears to be a form of consciousness with a developmentally dependent interpretative system. Dream processes mature along with the expansion of mental representation and symbol formation. Dream content is represented in multisensory imagery, with the visual imagery predominant. Nevertheless, dream imagery apparently represents what the child or the individual knows rather than representing exclusively perceptual memories or "pictures." Thus dream imagery is constructed and represents a broad base of experiences, knowledge, sensations, and feelings (Foulkes, 1985).

Two additional aspects of the dream developmental sequence of imagery are important in therapy: (1) self-portrayal and its active participation in dreams; and (2) the amount of kinesthetic or physical activity present in dreams. Self-portrayal is present in dreams starting with the stage of early concrete operations (7–9 years). The presence of self-portrayal is preceded by dreaming of activities by others in the stage of transition to concrete operations (5–7 years). Foulkes (1985) points out that self-portrayal in dreams requires the ability to separate the self who watches from the self who acts. The presence of physical activity in dreams starts to increase in the period 5–7 years and reaches its high point in the stage of later concrete operations (9–13 years). Dream imagery and activities seem to reinforce the necessity for the kinesthetic and sensory basis of acquiring novel knowledge during the period of concrete operations. This is in contrast to the following stage, that of formal operations, when dreams, similarly to the waking stage, reflect the increased ability to abstract from reality.

PSYCHOANALYTIC AND COGNITIVE APPROACHES TO DREAMS

Freud (1967) conceptualized dreams as a mental activity present during sleep which protects the sleeper from the unconscious mental activity threatening to interfere with the sleep. Freud distinguished between the manifest dream content, latent dream content, and dream work. The manifest dream content is the conscious mental activity during sleep which the individual later recalls as a dream. The latent dream content consists of three categories: nocturnal sensory impressions, current concerns, and repressed wishes and primitive desires originating in early childhood. The dream work is "the unconscious mental operations by which the latent dream content is transformed into the manifest dream" (Brenner, 1955, p. 167). For Freud the essential dream part was the repressed latent content. The manifest dream represents a gratification of the repressed wish; this representation of the gratification can be distorted or disguised so that the manifest dream may appear even frightening instead of being pleasurable. In the dream work, the latent content is translated into visual images through the use of primary process representation.

The changes in the psychoanalytic method which have taken place in the approach to dreams are based on the more recent view that the primary process undergoes maturation (Holt, 1967; Noy, 1979). Fosshage (1983) proposes that primary process serves an integrative and synthetic function, using primarily visual and other sensory images with strong affective values. Similarly, dreams serve an integrative function, and the manifest dream content directly incorporates emotionally laden and meaningful experiences. An intrapsychic conflict may result in a discrepancy between manifest and latent dream contents similar to that in waking thought. The mastery of it depends on the dreamer's acceptance of the conflict along with the defenses used. The main function of dreams, though, is seen as "the development, maintenance (regulation), and, when necessary, restoration of psychic processes, structure, and organization" (Fosshage, 1983, p. 657). Dreams display psychological development and new levels of psychic organization. Dream vagueness may not necessarily be indicative of defensive processes, but may imply the presence of yet unformed and unclear intrapsychic processes (Fosshage, 1983).

The cognitive approach to dream analysis is concerned with the instigation and the structure of dreams (Foulkes, 1978, 1985; Klinger, 1971). Dreams are seen as synthesized through the active processing of information from memory storage, except that dreaming uses parallel processing to a greater extent than waking thought (Neisser, 1967). The cognitive viewpoint accepts Freud's view that dreams are verbal thought processes represented in pictorial form but rejects Freud's interpretation of wishful fulfillment as the main purpose of dreams. One of the reasons for this rejection is that all waking thoughts are not interpreted in regard to the underlying wishes, and this possibility should be considered also for dreams (Foulkes, 1978). In this aspect the more recent psychoanalytic approach is closer to the cognitive approach than Freud's views of dreams.

From the cognitive viewpoint, dreams consist of diverse sequences which can be activated through current concerns (interrupted or unfinished goal-directed activity) and the affect related to them. If the motive for a particular dream sequence is a current concern, then the affect associated with this concern can either interrupt the ongoing dream sequence or initiate a new sequence with its ideational flow related to the affect. The affect can elicit additional responses from the memory that are in some way related to the current concern. Thus sequential organization of dream segments seems to be based on the antecedents instead of consequences of the thought (Klinger, 1971).

Affect is present mainly in REM dreams. These dreams initially reflect current concerns, especially those high in emotional intensity (M. Kramer, 1982). These affective responses may interrupt the ongoing segment of a dream or determine the ideational flow of the next segment. The imaginal character of dream symbols may be formed to fit several of the activated ideational schemata (Klinger, 1971).

An example of this is present in the first example (Figs. 7.1 and 7.2). Apprehension bordering on fear is the emotional component of the first dream segment. This emotion elicits the second sequence being chased by policemen. The second segment provides another view, literally a "surface" view of the dream setting, as compared to the first or "in-depth" view. The images of the sharks, sunken ship, and the policemen are symbolic in that they can be seen in several different contexts.

Drives can be part of the motivation for a particular dream sequence, but not the only motives. Similarly, wish fulfillment may be part of current concerns but does not encompass all of an individual's current concerns. The symbolic images in dreams are plurisignificant, elicited by the activation of several instigators which are represented by the symbol fitting all of them. The symbolism in dreams can display a morphological fusion, whereby the construction of images is different from the present in the waking state. The symbolism can also incorporate sequential fusion, where different or disjointed sequences are combined (Klinger, 1971).

Klinger (1971) defines the symbols present in dreams as plurisignificant and multidetermined in that a symbolic sequence incorporates several ideational schemata, reflecting several of the dreamer's concerns, affects, and associative chains.

The difficulty of remembering dreams is at least partially caused by the fact that dreams are processed differently than waking thought and their encoding is not as effective. Images and inner speech are two codes of representation in dreams. These codes are formed by the structures and operations supporting them. Foulkes (1978) suggests that the structures supporting the narrative dream formation are propositional and linguistically based. Especially in REM dreams, the verbally coded propositions are assigned visual representations, which can be more literal in the perceptual than in the verbal mode of representation.

Dreaming is absent with right hemispheric damage, after hemispheric disconnection, and with organic impairment of verbal functions, indicating that both hemispheres are involved in the formation of dreams. Foulkes proposes that REM dreaming contributes to the interhemispheric interaction and visual/verbal integration (Foulkes 1978, 1985).

JUNG'S APPROACH TO DREAMS

In addition to the personal and cognitive references discussed here, the Jungian approach also acknowledges the presence of a deeper, archetypal level in some dreams.

Several aspects of the cognitive view of dreams are present in Jung's approach: dreams are a part of a natural self-regulating system (Jung,

1968); dreams do not conceal, but teach; dreams are selected by the conscious situations of the moment; and dream associations relate to events that are linked by strong emotions as part of a complex (Jung, 1974). In these aspects the recent psychoanalytic approach to dreams (Fosshage, 1983) does not differ much from Jung's views. Jung points out, however, that the causal or reductive approach, based on the components of personal memory, breaks down when the contents cannot be reduced to personal experiences. This happens when the images representing the collective or archetypal layer of the psyche emerge in dreams (Jung, 1956). Such dreams are designated by Jung (1974) as big dreams versus little dreams or dreams dealing with everyday affairs. Big dreams are easily remembered and make a lasting impression on the individual.

Direct associations elicited by the personal contents of dreams circumambulate or center around emotionally important nodal points of the image flow in dreams. This approach is different from the free-association method, which is based on a causal chain of associations. Dream amplifications can take place through the individual's references on the object level. For archetypal images that amplification can be achieved by introducing mythological images and themes.

The dream associations are interpreted either subjectively or objectively. The subjective level refers every part of the dream and all the dream characters to the dreamer himself. On the objective level dream images are assumed to refer to real-life objects or to persons of special importance to the individual.

Since the individual's arbitrary will is inactive in dreaming, Jung (1956) sees dreams as objective manifestations of the psychic processes. The dreams are linked associatively to the existing conscious situation, and can either be complementary or compensatory to it.

Instead of placing importance on individual dreams, Jung (1974) considers dream themes based on dream series. The keeping of records of dreams and their interpretation is considered very important. Drawing of the dream images is encouraged.

Similar to active imagination, the themes that emerge from adult dreams over a period of time lead to self-development and individuation.

EXPRESSION OF DREAMS IN ART THERAPY

Dreams have a temporal and a spatial structure. The temporal structure of the dream is manifested in the dream narrative which has a beginning, middle, and end. Subsequent dreams during the same night may elaborate on different aspects of the dream theme. Dreams also have a spatial structure in that they present a three-dimensional space within which the action takes place with definite directions, such as up/down, right/left. At times the structure of forms is fused, combining two or more references. There can also be a temporal fusion present in dreams in that references from different times of the dreamer's life are fused or represented simultaneously. Temporal fusion can be manifested also in the different ages experienced by the dreamer in the dream. The morphological and sequential fusions seem to be initiated and influenced by the affect and state of arousal present during dreaming.

Affect seems to play a major role in dreams in that it can exert the following influence on dreams: (1) change the dream image, (2) change the dream sequence, (3) change the dream theme, and/or (4) wake up the dreamer if the dream images fail to provide an outlet or defenses for the affect.

A visual representation of dreams expresses the content and structure of images and the affect present in dreams. The meaning of the visually represented dream images can be explored either through verbal and visual associations. The associations also can be sensory or bodily kinesthetic experiences, the meaning of which can be arrived at through exaggerating them (Perls, 1969).

The visual expression of dreams can take place with particular emphasis on one of the different levels of the Expressive Therapies Continuum (ETC) (Kagin & Lusebrink, 1978). The choice of the medium and the structure imposed by the therapist influences the expression in that the emphasis can be either on the formal aspects on the perceptual level, on the emotions on the affective level, or on conceptual organization on the cognitive/symbolic level of the ETC. The component parts of symbols can be explored at the perceptual or affective level.

The perceptual level of the ETC emphasizes the formal and structural aspects of dreams. The drawing of a dream scene or an aerial map clarifies its formal and structural aspects. A subsequent dream may reincorporate the structure of a drawing as is seen in the third example (Fig. 7.4), where the forms and color areas become the structure of the dream landscape. In addition, the color and the expressive qualities of form in the doodle carry the affective component of the dream symbolism: The sandy hill metaphorically represents the lack of affect, and the encapsulated red and blue dynamic lines on the right denote contained but potentially explosive feelings.

Similar to guided affective imagery, moods in dreams may be conveyed through weather and through the moods of the dream landscapes. Distorted forms in dreams, similar to other visual expressions, are indicative of the interaction of affect on form. The affective component can be amplified through elaborating on the sensory aspects of the dream images, either experientially or through art media which emphasize the sensory level.

The cognitive and affective aspects of dreams and their mutual interaction is explored through sequential dream drawings (Lusebrink, 1987). The client is asked to represent the most important aspects of a dream in three to nine sequential frames. This approach structures and brings into focus the shifts in dream themes, which for the most part are influenced by the affective response to the previous dream segment.

The first dream example (Figs. 7.1 and 7.2) gives a dream portrayal using poster paints, with emphasis on the affective aspects. The images of sharks and policemen appear to represent two aspects of the same feeling: apprehension or fear. The associations to these images can be obtained on either an objective or a subjective level. The Gestalt approach (Perls, 1969; Rhyne, 1973) which could be used to establish a dialogue between the persecutor and persecuted aspects of self, is based on the assumption that all parts in the dream represent the different aspects of the dreamer himself. The dream sequences and the visual representation provide three levels of "depth" on which the dream can be explored: surface, middle area, and in-depth. The images on the surface or present level can be explored by the Gestalt approach. On the middle level, in this case "in the water," the persecutory figures appear as sharks represented in phallic shapes. The Freudian approach with references to the past seems to be appropriate here. The "depth" level of the sunken ship may benefit from the Jungian approach with the sunken treasure possibly referring to the self or inner core of the individual.

The second example (Fig. 7.3) illustrates the cognitive approach to a long and complex dream. The five frames selected are organized on three levels representing three different affective states, which presumably initiated the changes in the dream imagery. The first two frames represent feelings of "work," including a work table, which becomes an important image in subsequent dreams. This level may be described as reality-oriented, but it has some symbolic implications in the image of the baby. The middle level represents joy and a festive mood, but the setting does not have direct memory references. The structural form of the setting is circular or mandala-like, indicating possibly the archetypal structure of a center. Again this structure is repeated in later dreams. The jester, like the baby, has symbolic implications. The last frame is on the bottom level of the paper representing basement. The mood of this drawing is apprehension and also awe, and the mummy forms appear to be alive and have a symbolic meaning. The structure imposed by the frames and also by the use of colored markers (resistive medium) emphasizes the conceptual and cognitive approach to the dream without getting too drawn into its emotional or associative aspects.

In applying Leuner's (1984) consideration of unusual forms of imagery as an expression of conflict, the mummy forms represent the most conflictual images in this sequence. In using dream sequences the individual has the choice on which level and on which frame they prefer to work. In the therapy setting the therapist inquires which image seems to be the most important or attracts the client's attention the most. All these images can be explored for their objective and subjective meaning. The last frame in this example represents a cognitive aerial view approach to the dream. Apparently it was not the appropriate level on which to pursue the dream investigation, since it did not hold interest for the dreamer.

The dream sequences at times provide a distance from the dream content and affect associated with it by presenting a stage, movie, or painting within the dream. These sequences benefit from the serial drawings of dreams which show the antecedents of the dream for which the reflective distance was needed.

SUMMARY

Active imagination, guided daydreams, and dreams represent the flow of thought, especially imaginal thought, which is self-directed and expresses and reflects the influence of affect on thought.

The partially structured approach of Leuner's Guided Affective Imagery expands on the dynamics of this flow, the changes and fixations present, and the synchronic transformations of the images. Leuner emphasizes the importance of the perceptual reflection and integration of the imaginal thought with affect. The therapeutic strategies employed by Leuner (1984) on the basic level of the GAI follow the initial strategies used in art therapy (Betensky, 1973b; McNiff, 1981) with the emphasis on the perceptual and cognitive elements.

The approaches to dreams discussed cover the developmental aspects and the cognitive view of dreams, as well as the psychoanalytic, and Jung's synthetic methods. These approaches reflect and deal with different levels of the psyche. The cognitive method regards dreams as being based on current concerns. The psychoanalytic approach investigates personal memories and experiences represented in dreams and the primitive drives that elicited them. Jungian analytical psychology adds another dimension to dreams with the concept of the archetypal psyche.

The content of dreams can accordingly be approached on different levels. On the level of current concerns the dream is examined for its elaborations and affect, which then can be reinforced or corrected in the light of reality-oriented conscious decisions. The dream content can be analyzed for repressed content through free associations and thus incorporated into the consciousness. Finally, the structure present on the archetypal level seems to be the synthesizing and healing agent of the psyche.

Dreams and daydreams and their symbolism can be explored through visual expression at the different levels of the ETC. The visual expression depicts and integrates the structural and affective aspects of the dream imagery and highlights its important segments and the changes precipitated by affect. The application of daydreams and the dream images present in depression are discussed in the following chapter.

Chapter 8

Daydreaming and Adolescent Depression

Jim, a 16-year-old adolescent, was brought to therapy sessions by his mother. Jim had become increasingly withdrawn and was spending more and more time by himself in his room. He also had been truant from school and, with some other youths, had gotten in some trouble with the authorities.

Jim's mother and father were recently divorced. He was the youngest of four boys. Jim's evaluative drawings in the initial session showed depression. In the Kinetic Family Drawing (Burns & Kaufman, 1970), he did not include himself, indicating his isolation from the family. For several weeks in the therapy sessions Jim was resistant and unwilling to express himself or venture to explore the art media. When asked to do specific assignments, such as portray a number of feelings, he complied, even though he only used the color black. His expressions were realistic with emphasis on the cognitive aspects. The feelings portrayed with the most personal reference were sadness and bravery. He was preoccupied with trying to get a car, but he did not share much other information about himself.

After trying different approaches, the therapist presented a guided daydream of going up the mountain (Leuner, 1978). This session was successful in that Jim became involved in the act of drawing, even though he did not elaborate on his drawings verbally. The basic theme of this daydream is departure from a meadow and going up a mountain. On the way up there is an obstacle on the path (Fig. 8.1). After overcoming the obstacle, the participant is asked to imagine taking a brief rest in a mountain meadow before proceeding to the top of the mountain. On the mountaintop there is a temple with something mysterious in its inner room. In Jim's case the path changed and became steeper after the stop to rest, and the scenery also changed (Fig. 8.2). The tree in the first drawing changed from a dead tree to living one, and a blackened, undefined area changed to a gravesite in the second drawing. The temple itself seemed to have symbolic meaning as did the figures inside guarding the treasure chest (Figs. 8.3 and 8.4). Both of the last two drawings had a compulsive, protective quality as portrayed in the stone slabs. Jim related to the treasure itself as concrete treasure and money—instead of as a metaphor for inner treasure. This interpretation characterized Jim's present state of limited resources of fantasy and his preoccupation with money. In the following session the therapist presented Jim with another guided daydream. This one was of entering a cave and finding someone there seated by a fire. The participant is asked to imagine being engaged in a dialogue with this person, who then offers him a parting gift. For Jim the person in the cave was a cloaked old man who offered him a high-school diploma (Fig. 8.5). A transformation from the previous daydream was seen in the form of the old man, when compared to the stiff and forbidding guardian shapes in the first drawing. Also, the image of the concrete treasure was transformed into the abstract treasure of a diploma. The therapist interpreted the transformation as a positive sign in the flow of imagery instead of insistence on fixed images (Leuner, 1978).

The therapy included series of guided imagery, which seemed to free Jim's own flow of inner imagery and daydreaming. The images Jim shared were at first negative and persecutory. Eventually he was able to obtain a physically active temporary job which increased his self-esteem and self-respect. Jim's depression had lifted considerably. The last painting Jim made before terminating portrayed a cloaked guide leading a sheep up the mountain. Jim used color in this painting. Noteworthy is the elaboration on the scenery (Fig. 8.6), and the incorporation of the cloaked figure from earlier daydreams.

Figure 8.1. Guided daydream: "Going up the Mountain." 1. The obstacle.

Figure 8.2. Guided daydream: "Going up the Mountain." 2. The path after the obstacle.

Figure 8.3. Guided daydream: "Going up the Mountain." 3. The entrance into the temple.

Figure 8.4. Guided daydream: "Going up the Mountain." 4. Inside the temple and the treasure.

Figure 8.5. Guided daydream: "Going into Cave." 5. Encounter with a cloaked old man.

Figure 8.6. Termination: Free painting.

Introduction

This case example illustrates the use of daydreams in therapy with a depressed adolescent. The present chapter explores the development and role of daydreams as part of the internalization of images and flow of thought, and their importance in adolescence in particular. The application of daydreams in therapy covers depressive daydreams, depression in adolescence, and the role of daydreams in therapy.

The presence of imagery and its flow is influenced by the state of consciousness, and can be perceived on a continuum from cognitions and problem solving to daydreams to dreams during sleep. In daydreams the reality-directed, problem-solving oriented imagery is under the direction of conscious awareness. Dreams define the other polarity whereby the individual has a minimal conscious influence on the flow of imagery. The intermediate range between these two is characterized by varying degrees of conscious influence, as seen in daydreams, guided daydreams, and active imagination. Unbidden images and hallucinations represent instances of inner images intruding into consciousness. Hallucinations are an extreme case wherein the images are perceived as reality-based occurrences. The underlying mechanisms for daydreams, hallucinations, and dreams are similar in their development and capacity and can be transformed from one into the other (Starker, 1982). There is a continuity of content (Beck, 1970) and affect (Starker, 1982) across the waking and sleeping fantasy.

FUNCTION OF DAYDREAMING

Daydreaming is seen as a form of information processing, especially processing information relating to self and current concerns, including problem solving. Daydreams help to integrate new information with the existing structures and to empathize with and integrate experiences one has not actively experienced. In adolescence, daydreams are used to consolidate a sense of self and to prepare for future action. Daydreams foster divergent thinking and thus provide a possibility for rehearsing alternate reactions and seeing alternate views (Singer, 1973, 1976, 1979). In their convergent capacity, daydreams integrate input from different sensory and internal channels, including affect (Starker, 1978). As is the case with imagery in general, daydreams reflect the underlying structures; at the same time daydreams are constructed in the process of daydreaming, instead of being stored as ready-made entities.

Conditions fostering daydreaming are similar to those fostering image formation in general. A degree of privacy, reduced physical activity, reduced external stimulation, and relaxation all contribute to increased daydreaming. Similarly, sensory deprivation and a monotonous external environment lacking variety are conditions that lead to attention being directed inward and to subsequent daydreaming.

Reminiscences have the least interruptions in daydreaming. A shift towards daydreaming also seems to occur in dealing with complex and abstract material not related to self. In relaxed states there is a tendency for visual imagery to replace abstract thought (Singer, 1976). Generally, gross physical activity and attention to the external environment inhibit daydreaming and directing attention to internal processes (Singer, 1966).

The *themes* of daydreaming are predominantly future-oriented, especially dealing with important interpersonal relationships (Singer, 1976). Another prominent theme present in daydreams is that of current unfinished concerns (Klinger, 1971).

Affect is a significant structural component in daydreaming, and daydreams provide a vehicle for processing and integrating emotions. Klinger (1971, 1987) proposes that emotions have a major influence on the flow of thought. Starker (1982) found that "affective disposition" is continuous across waking thought, daydreams, and nocturnal dreams. Mood and daydreams influence each other in that a certain mood may provoke mood-congruent daydreams, and daydreams may create a certain mood. Anxiety and bizarreness of thought also seem to maintain continuity across the different levels of consciousness. Similarly to interrupting dreams and waking up the dreamer, anxiety may disrupt daydreams (Starker, 1978, 1982, 1984–1985).

Bizarreness of thought displays unusual, strange images, which often seem at odds with occurrences in nature. Starker (1978) points out that bizarreness could possibly be accounted for by some individuals blocking select incoming stimuli, which, in turn, is manifested as a lack of structuring of stimuli. In dreams the opposite effect seems to be true, in that dreams are more bizarre towards the morning as they deal with more complex information (Webb & Cartwright, 1978). While processing diverse internal stimuli, these dreams seem to integrate more distant memories and match them with the current information. The affect present in the previous day's concerns seems to be the determining factor which activitates long-term memories with a similar affective component. The difficulty of matching and structurally integrating images from different time periods evoked by a similar affect appears to contribute to the increased bizarreness of the early morning dreams.

Patterns and Styles of Daydreaming

Affect and content in daydreams differentiate the different daydreaming styles. Singer (1976, 1978), using the Imaginal Process Inventory scales (IPI), found that daydreaming seems to fall between three of four major clusters, or factors: positive-vivid daydreaming, guilty and negatively emotionally toned daydreaming, and anxious distractibility in daydreaming. Another factor that differed from the positive-vivid daydreaming in some behavioral manifestations was controlled thoughtfulness.

The factor of *positive-vivid daydreaming* is composed of high scores on scales dealing with future oriented daydreams, positive reactions to and acceptance of daydreams and visual imagery. High scoring on these and other scales suggest an active mental life, freedom and flexibility of fantasy, acceptance of inner life, and the use of daydreams in problem solving. Singer (1975b) reports that high-scoring subjects were more apt to use metaphorical thought. The factor of *controlled thoughtfulness and objectivity* in fantasy at times overlaps the positive-vivid daydreaming pattern. The controlled thoughtfulness style emphasizes curiosity about physical and natural events, as compared to the positive-vivid daydreaming style with its predominant emphasis on people.

The *guilty-negatively toned* daydreaming patterns consist of scores high on guilty and hostile-aggressive daydreams, fear of failure, as well as achievement-oriented and heroic daydreams. Individuals manifesting this daydream pattern may experience self-doubt, guilt, and periods of depression.

The *anxious-distractible* daydreaming patterns are characterized by daydreams consisting of many rather fleeting and loosely connecting fantasies emphasizing anxiety and worries. The scales contributing to this factor reflect frightened reaction to daydreaming, past-oriented daydreaming, mind-wandering, and distractibility. Individuals rating high on this factor do not enjoy daydreaming and do not use daydreams as resources.

Starker (1982) elaborates the different daydreaming patterns into daydreaming styles by further differentiating them and including characteristics of dreams associated with particular daydreaming styles. The positive-vivid daydreaming pattern is the basis for the *positive fantasy style*. It is characterized by positive, visual daydreams, positive mood, minimal negative emotions in "worst possible" daydreams, with self-exclusion from such daydreams. The negative daydreams are short in this style of daydreaming. The *conflictual fantasy style* is based on the guilty-dysphoric daydreaming pattern. This style is characterized by minimal positive emotions in "best possible daydreams," self-exclusion from such daydreams, nightmares, insomnia, and childhood sleep disturbances. The *anxious fantasy style* is an elaboration of the anxious-distractible daydreaming pattern. It also includes characteristics of the guilty-dysphoric daydreaming pattern, such as low positive mood, negative emotions in dream recall, and insomnia. Nightmares, though, are more strongly related to the conflictual daydreaming style than the anxious daydreaming style.

Daydreaming Styles and Dreams

The structure and affect associated with the different daydreaming styles are consistent in daydreams and dreams. The positive fantasy style daydreamers have frequent vivid dreams with positive affect. Similarly, the conflictual fantasy style is characterized by more negative affect and more bizarre dreams than those of positive fantasy style. The anxious daydreaming style has most emotional, bizarre, and negative dreams, which display the greatest variation in their content. The negative dreams of the conflictual daydreaming style could be explained as that the processing of current concerns occurs not only during waking thought but also is continued during dreams. The negative daytime thoughts characteristic of this style are carried over in the nocturnal dreams and nightmares.

Recall of dreams is also related to daydreaming styles. The positive daydreamers have a high recall of their dreams, whereas the conflictual and anxious daydreaming styles are negatively related to dream recall (Starker, 1974, 1977; Starker & Hasenfeld, 1976). Starker (1984–85) points out that "daydream patterns are one manifestation of broader, more pervasive fantasy styles which are expressed whether waking or sleeping" (p. 246).

Play as Antecedent of Daydreaming

Developmentally, daydreams can be seen as internalization of make-believe play (Singer, 1973). Play uses gestures, images, and words in helping the small child to assimilate new information and to form new structures to accommodate this information. Play combines and transforms the behavioral, affective, imaginal, and cognitive aspects (Singer, 1979). Through play the child assimilates external reality in his/her frame of reference, and at the same time accommodates the reality as represented by external objects (Piaget, 1962). In the psychoanalytic view, play represents the child's attempts partially to satisfy his/her drives, and work through and master the conflicts that the child is unable to deal with in reality (A. Freud, 1965). Creative, exploratory play, on the other hand, is present when the biological drives are satisfied (Klinger, 1971; Singer 1973). Both play and fantasy can be present without a previous conflict, and can enhance and enrich life (Singer, 1973). Singer (1973) views creative play "as a normal outgrowth of the fundamental processing activity of the child. Such cognitive activity involves not only the external environment, but also requires the child to attend to the brain's processing of long-term memory" (p. 199).

According to Piaget (1962), the most elementary form of play or ludic symbolism is the use of a symbolic schema as reproduction of sensory motor schema outside its direct context. Piaget describes symbolic play as evolving through three major stages: symbolic play, socialized play, and play oriented to reality adaptation. During the stage I (2–4 years) assimilation predominates accommodation; in stage II (4–7 years) and stage III (7–11 years) accommodation becomes increasingly predominant.

Stage I, symbolic play, coincides with the preconceptual stage of intellectual development. At this stage the child has arrived at object permanency. Play at the preconceptual stage involves symbolic combinations as compared to play during the last stage of the precedent sensory-motor stage of development involving imitation using objects and body. The symbolic play during stage I involves complex combinations, as well as compensatory and liquidating play. The liquidating combinations involve unpleasant or difficult situations which are dissociated from their unpleasantness through the symbolic play, thus assimilating reality to the ego. The internal images during this stage have a "magic" quality, namely, they are not differentiated to reality-based input. The verbalization is idiosyncratic, fused with images, and does not have an independent, socially shared meaning. The images assimilated at stage I of play become schemata in the next period (Piaget, 1962).

During the preconceptual stage of development, play is the most effective way of representing and using inner imagery, since the imagery at this stage has a static quality. Dreams are static, primarily representing bodily needs, and animal figures are present (Foulkes, 1977, 1982). Furthermore, during this stage the child is in the sensory-motor stage of graphic development, and expresses him/herself graphically through scribbling and making simple forms, such as circles.

Stage II of play, or socialized play, coincides with the preoperational stage of development. During this stage, play becomes increasingly more imitative of reality and displays collective symbolism (Piaget, 1962). Dreams become more dynamic and animals are replaced by members of family. In boys' dreams, images of untamed animals may express conflicting feelings (Foulkes, 1977, 1982). In graphic development this stage is defined as preschematic, whereby the child represents objects in a spatial relationship to himself and his body space, instead of objective space. Color is used in an idiosyncratic manner (Lowenfeld & Brittain, 1970).

The representational imagery still has a static quality at this stage, and therefore the concrete objects and concrete graphic expressions are necessary for handling dynamic images. The overt verbalization during this stage serves a similar role, in that it allow the child to describe and formulate his actions.

Stage III of play, or reality-oriented play, coincides with the developmental stage of concrete operations (7–11 years). Here the child uses play in a reality-oriented, cognitive, and constructive manner. This stage of play involves socialization through games with rules. The symbol becomes an image for adaptation to reality instead of assimilation to the ego, as it was the case in the earlier stages. The imagery during this stage is dynamic, and uses anticipatory images; the speech becomes internalized (Piaget, 1962). Dreams display motor activity and aggression, especially in boys' dreams (Foulkes, 1977, 1982).

The stage of concrete operation encompasses in graphic development the schematic stage (7–9 years) and the stage of dawning realism (9–12 years). The schemata used in the schematic stage represents the child's active knowledge of the object, which is depicted in a definite order in space relationships, including a baseline. The schemata are highly individualized; schema deviations represent either autoplastic experiences or have emotional significance to the child. The color represents a relationship to the object. The drawings during the stage of dawning realism reflect the child's greater visual awareness and representation of details. Schema deviations are no longer used to express emotions (Lowenfeld & Brittain, 1970).

During this period the play becomes increasingly internalized as daydreams. Solitary play is less predominant and less verbal, but drawing may be used to depict the daydreams and to provide feedback in clarifying them (Singer, 1976).

Daydreaming in Adolescence

Intellectual development in adolescence is marked by the stage of formal operations, whereby the adolescent is able to "think about thought" (Piaget, 1962). Daydreaming in adolescence can be seen as a developmental step in the process of internalizing concrete operations. The young child uses play to assimilate reality input and to externalize different parts of himself, including role play. The gradual transition from play to daydreaming provides an internal mechanism for role modeling, problem solving, and dealing with assorted current concerns.

Adolescence is seen by Blos (1962) as a second individuation, as compared to Mahler's (1963, 1965) first individuation, when the child establishes object constancy. The main tasks of the second individuation process are the separation from parental dependencies and familial love objects which are replaced by reliance on a peer group. The previous mental organization has to be loosened in adolescence (Blos, 1962). The increase in daydreaming seems to be the vehicle within which this restructuring can at least partially take place.

From the psychoanalytic viewpoint, adolescence can be divided into preadolescence, early adolescence, middle adolescence or adolescence proper, late adolescence, and postadolescence (Blos, 1962). These different phases are discussed briefly with an emphasis on the role of daydreaming or fantasy and the contribution to self-identity in each phase. Blos designates latency as a preparatory phase for adolescence. During this period the child consolidates his/her ego, and the sense of self which in turn replaces the reliance on parents. The child's ability to differentiate between reality and fantasy increases. In Blos' view, daydreams during preadolescence increase as part of reaction to and containment of the libidinal and sexual drives.

In early adolescence, identification with parents is replaced by identification with peer groups. The increased fantasies help to redirect and contain the earlier acting out. The content of daydreams during the ages 10 to 13 is action- and adventure-oriented (Singer, 1979). In dreams, same-sex characters predominate. The interaction with family decreases, while that with peers increases (Foulkes, 1977). In gifted adolescents, guilt and fear daydreams decrease from age 10 to 15 years (Henderson, Gold, & Clarke, 1984; Taylor & Fulcomer, 1979; Taylor, Fulcomer, & Taylor, 1978). Lack of daydreaming skills, on the other hand, may result in boredom (Taylor & Fulcomer, 1979).

Middle adolescence is characterized by more mature behavior, but the new sense of independence also increases the individual's sense of loneliness (Muuss, 1980). Fantasy life peaks during ages 14–17 years. There is a divergence in daydreaming between gifted adolescents and average. Daydreaming peaks in the average adolescents at around 14 years of age, whereas in the gifted it increases linearly until up to age 17. The gifted use their daydreaming skills as an excellent medium to deal with problems (Gold & Henderson, 1984; Henderson et al., 1984).

Daydreaming provides the adolescent with a means of adapting to change (Gold & Henderson, 1984). In addition to problem solving, romance, sex, and achievement are the predominant subjects of daydreams during this time. Daydreaming also provides a sense of freedom from parents, which consequently then can be expressed in action (Singer, 1976). In dreams there is a decrease in overt expression of activity (Foulkes, 1977). Diaries kept during this time heighten an awareness of inner life for adolescents. Much of this transition depends on a flexible ego and positive self-image, as well as stable emotional environment and supportive parents. All these factors facilitate and contain the inner rearrangement without undue stress. If a stable outer environment is not present, the adolescent may cling to the old and familiar forms, which at the same time he has already outgrown. In this case the inner environment is perceived as stable, even though it remains immature. During this time the self-image undergoes a transformation, and often there is an insistence on a negative self-image (Muuss, 1980).

Depression in Adolescence

Depression exaggerates the inner experience of the loss of childhood, as well as the negative self-image of the adolescent. From the system's viewpoint, at a time when it is important for the adolescent to have an open inner system, in depression there is an insistence on a closed system. This conflict is experienced especially acutely if the depression is present in early adolescence. During this time the drives are prominent, which increases the tension between the depressive, containing elements, and the outward pressure of the drives. The fantasy element itself may be denied and repressed because of its negative content (Muuss, 1980).

The object-loss theory of adolescence proposes that in order in to pursue autonomy and independence, adolescence disrupts earlier object attachments. Major disruptions present in adolescence are the dramatic changes in the body and its functions. Other disruptions and losses may come through parents' death or divorce, or even through imagined loss (Blos, 1962).

The *cognitive model* of depression (Beck, 1976) is based on the assumption that the individual's conceptions about his somatic sensations determine his feelings. Visual images as well as fantasy may affect the sensations in the body and feelings, which in turn may be cognitively misinterpreted. Objective observation of thoughts and images provides a distancing effect.

According to Beck (1976) cognitions precede depression, and negative cognitive appraisal of stimuli and situations assist in maintaining the depressive symptoms. Maladaptive thoughts can also occur in a pictorial form. The cognitive schemata are seen as relatively stable and invariant (Kovacs & Beck, 1979). The modification of the distorted cognitions can take place through the separation of the depressive symptoms in their emotional, motivational, cognitive, behavioral, and physiological components. Concentrating on a symptom cluster or a problem area may lead to improvement in other areas. Beck sees the depressive cognitive organization as a closed system incapable of accommodating contradictory information. The discovery of an opening of this system and introduction of new information and different points of view leads to improvement.

Levels of Depression in Adolescents

Cytryn and McKnew (1972, 1974, 1979) categorize depression in children and adolescents on three levels:

1. Masked depressive reaction, which may be associated with a variety of emotional disorders, such as hyperactivity, aggressive behavior, delinquency, psychosomatic illnesses, and hypochondriasis.
2. Acute depression, whereby the precipitating cause is associated with a real object loss.
3. Chronic depression, which results from the accumulation of many separations and losses from childhood on.

Lesse (1974) elaborates on several acting-out behaviors which can be interpreted as masked depression: acts of vandalism, sexual promiscuity, drug abuse, destructiveness, in addition to temper outbursts, sadistic or masochistic behavior, and compulsive eating or working (Lesse, 1974). Hypochondriasis and psychosomatic illnesses also can serve as masks for depression with increasing frequency from early to late adolescence (Lesse, 1981).

In addition to these masked symptoms, the depressive process in children and adolescents (Cytryn & McKnew, 1974, 1979) can be manifested and expressed on three levels:

1. Fantasy, as expressed through dreams, spontaneous play, free drawings, and associations to stories and TV shows. The themes of fantasy are either depressive, or aggressive and violent, including inadequate or damaged self-image. The fantasy entails themes of mistreatment, thwarting, blame or criticism, loss and abandonment, personal injury, death, suicide.

2. Verbal expression of hopelessness, helplessness, guilt, unattractiveness, worthlessness, and suicidal ideation.
3. Mood and behavior displaying psychomotor retardation and sadness, including crying.

The opponents of the concept of masked depression point out that though at times such behavior can mask depression, not all delinquent behavior is to be thus interpreted. The criteria differentiating masked depression from other disorders of childhood are unclear (Carlson & Garber, 1986; Chiles, Miller, & Cox, 1980). The cognitive features of depression include low self-esteem and poor self-image, negative expectations of future, and self-blame or criticism (Beck, 1967). Adolescents may show their loss of motivation in poor school performance, or try to escape depression through social withdrawal and the use of mood-altering drugs (Chartier & Ranieri, 1984).

The depressed themes in fantasy are present in most depressed children; the verbal manifestation of depression is less frequent, and the depressive mood and behavior the least. The above manifestations of depressive themes in fantasy and verbalization can be considered a pattern of defenses against depression. These levels of defensive systems are progressively less effective in protecting children against depression.

Fantasy acts as a defense in masked depression, along with acting-out behavior, denial, projection, introjection, avoidance, and splitting. The verbal manifestations of depression are encountered most with receding chronic depression, along with dissociation of affect and reaction formation. In chronic depression the defenses fail (Cytryn & McKnew, 1974).

Depressive Fantasy Themes

Exploration of fantasy themes is important in early detection of depression. The fantasy element may be the best indicator of the depressive element in masked depression, since the behavior component may reflect at this stage only acting out or psychosomatic symptoms. Depressive mood and behavioral manifestations were found to be the least stable factors in identifying depression in adolescents. The negative and violent fantasy themes remain present throughout the depression (Cytryn & McKnew, 1979).

In surveying 254 children and adolescents, Silver (1988) found that in response to a Draw-A-Story task, strongly negatively themes were higher in the depressed subjects than in normal subjects. The Draw-

A-Story consists of 14 stimulus drawings, selected because of previous predominantly negative associations produced in response to them by children. The stimulus drawings include the following categories: four human representations (boy, cowboy, bride, and man smoking pipe), five animal representations (chick, mouse, angry cat, snake, and dragon), four scenes (old and young tree, parachute jumper approaching ground, volcano, and castle), and an object (knife). The individual is asked to select two of the images, then imagine and draw something happening between them. The visual and verbal responses were evaluated on a 7-point scale ranging from strongly negative themes (1 point) to strongly positive themes (7 points). The intermediate scores of 2 and 3 represent moderately and mildly negative scenes, and 5 and 6 mildly and moderately positive themes, respectively. The median score of 4 is given to ambivalent, unclear, or unemotional content. The illustrations judged as representing strongly negative themes portrayed the principal subjects as dead, dying, helpless, trapped, thwarted, sad, isolated, or cruel; the corresponding environments included knives, smoking guns, prisons, or tombstones.

The formal elements in visual expression, such as free drawings or paintings, can be used as indicators of depression. In an adult depressed psychiatric population, Wadeson (1980) found that the pictorial characteristics or formal elements present in patients' drawings were different when they were more depressed as compared to drawings made when they felt less depressed. The depressed drawings were characterized by less color, more empty space, constriction, disorganization, and less completeness and meaningfulness than the drawings from non-depressed individuals. The themes portrayed in drawings by hospitalized adult suicidal patients were self-hate, harming others, hopelessness, isolation, and anger. The image of a spiral also was often present in their drawings, especially the inward or the downward spiral. The associations to the image were whirlpool, turmoil, anxiety, narrowing possibilities.

Depressive Dream Themes

The negative imagery present in depressed fantasy and visual expression is also present in the dreams of depressed individuals. Themes of rejection, abandonment, punishment, and experiencing oneself as ugly and undesirable were reported significantly more by depressed individuals than by normal controls. Depressed individuals also experienced a distorted time perspective in dreams in that their dreams dealt with the past and were not future-oriented (Beck & Hurvich, 1959). Dreams of depressed divorced women increased in masochism (Trenholme, Cartwright, & Greenberg, 1984) and had more negative content than those of divorced women who were not depressed (Cartwright, Lloyd, Knight, & Trenholme, 1984). Dreams reported by adult psychotic depressed patients were barren and bland. Actually, as depression lifted, the dream content increased in anxiety and hostility (M. Kramer, Baldridge, Whitman, Ornstein, & Smith, 1968; Kramer, Whitman, Baldridge, & Lansky, 1966). Several dream themes, such as masochism and dependency, remained present even after depression lifted. The dreams of remitted depressed individuals, as compared to normal controls, had a higher proportion of negative themes and were rated higher on masochism and externalized scale. These dreams involved crying, feeling sad, rejected, deserted, thwarted, deprived, blamed, injured, etc. The hostility was displayed through hostile acts in the environment, including actions by inanimate objects, such as bullets flying, storms blowing, knives flying (Hauri, 1976). These themes are similar to the strongly and moderately rated negative themes of the Draw-A-Story tasks (Silver, 1988).

The negative contents of fantasy and dreams are helpful in the early detection of depression. Drawings, spontaneous play, selective projective techniques, and dreams, as discussed, elicit and portray the negative fantasy material.

Depression and Daydreaming

The depressed adolescent seems to be caught in a cycle of guilty-dysphoric daydreaming pattern through a repetitive negative flow of thought and interpretations of current concerns. Depression scores correlate positively with daydreams involving guilt, fear of failure, and hostility. Depressed individuals' mental activity reflects mind-wandering, distractibility, and boredom, as well as uncontrolled thought patterns through increased daydreams; the latter can create a frightened reaction in the individual (Giambra & Traynor, 1978).

In regard to the causes of events, depressed adolescents believe that negative events or failures are internally caused, stable, and global. In comparison, nondepressive individuals perceive such events as externally caused and specific to the instance, and therefore changeable (Krantz & Rude, 1984; Siegel & Griffin, 1984). In a seeming paradox to attributing an internal cause to negative events, adolescents who scored high on depression measures displayed an *external locus* of control by perceiving outcomes of events beyond their control.

In masked depression, the adolescents attempt to cope with the negative thought patterns and depressive feelings through acting out, delinquent behavior, or psychosomatic illnesses. The adolescents need to develop inner resources through fantasy and symbolic avenues to deal with the depression instead of being bound and reacting to specific occurrences that are interpreted negatively. Since the inner depressive structures are experienced as stable, the adolescent has difficulties achieving this goal of making a transition from a concrete approach to a more symbolic one.

The transition to the symbolic mode of thought is especially important for depressed adolescents. The flow of imagery in symbolic thought echoes the adolescent's own active daydreaming process, and therefore can be accepted by the adolescents without too much resistance. The advantage of dealing with symbolic images is that they are ambivalent and can have either positive or negative values. The symbolic level of information processing provides the ambiguity needed in the imagery of the depressed adolescent.

Daydreaming and Aggression

In masked depression, aggression is an important component of the individual's behavior as it is in the fantasy images. Aggression can be seen as an adaptive measure against affective pain, and as such it may precede the overt manifestations of depression whereby the aggression is directed against the source of the pain (O'Connor, 1986). The affective pain of the individual can be converted into aggressive action either against the environment, as for example in delinquency, or against self, as in psychosomatic illnesses, drug abuse, and suicide.

Imagination, play, and daydreaming skills can be employed in the reduction of aggression. Aggressive daydreams and play have been investigated in regard to their role in the reduction of aggression (Singer, 1973). High-fantasy children were able to reduce their aggression through imaginative play, but this was not true for low-fantasy children. In daydreams only individuals high on daydreaming skills were able to work towards the solutions of the anger-provoking situations, whereas low daydreamers reverted to action. General themes, which included aggression among other themes, were less likely to result in overt aggression than direct focus on aggressive themes. Imaginative children in play also were able to take roles other than self, and to develop empathy (Singer, 1978).

Singer (1973) found a significant correlation between high-fantasy level and concurrent inhibition of motor activity, resulting in lower levels of overt activity. Singer points out that this refutes the cathartic drive model of aggression reduction through aggressive play or daydreams.

Imagery Approaches to Depression

In depressed individuals structure and content as well as the mode of processing daydreams have different effects on the negative thought processes and depression. There appears to be a difference in the visual and verbal processing of depressive stimuli. The depressed stimuli were rated as more vivid when processed visually (Baker & Jessup, 1980).

Schultz (1978) investigated the effect of different imagery approaches on depressed adults. He compared the effects of angry or aggressive imagery, socially gratifying imagery, positive focused imagery, and nondirected imagery on depression. Engagement in directed imagery produced significantly lowered levels of depression than free imagery. There was a differential effect of imagery on different depressive themes. In subjects whose depression was characterized by themes of dependency, or who were self-critical, the levels of depression were lower after aggressive and socially gratifying imagery. With the free imagery approach, the depressed subjects were able to generate positive imagery, but were not able to block the negative thought intrusions. Subjects high on positive-vivid daydreaming pattern experienced a greater decrease in depression after socially gratifying and positive imagery than after aggressive and free imagery. Subjects displaying guilty-dysphoric daydreaming patterns, on the other hand, showed increased depression after positive daydreams. The appropriateness of the imagery to the individual's concerns have to be considered in the therapeutic approach. If the socially gratifying imagery is of current concern, it may generate greater affective arousal in the individual than other types of imagery.

Schultz (1978) hypothesizes that the interruption of the depressive cycle involves the generation of strong affects and their maintenance through directed-imagery procedure. Affect influences thoughts in a circular fashion in that a strong negative affect produces negative thoughts which in turn influences the affect. This is particularly true in unstructured daydreaming. Starker and Singer (1975) suggest that the negative organization of fantasy and orientation towards future play important roles in maintaining depression.

Guided imagery approaches, such as Leuner's Guided Affective Imagery (Leuner, 1978, 1984; Leuner, Horn, & Klessmann, 1983), provide structure and basic symbolic images which contain both positive and negative aspects. The depressed adolescent can endow these images with his own feeling and meaning, which in the early stages of therapy may be negative. The negative images undergo transformation in the subsequent daydreams, and the positive aspect of the symbolic images begins to emerge. In the example at the beginning of the chapter, this transition was seen in the figure of the guardian of the treasure, who emerges as a positive guide at the termination of the therapy.

Beck (1970) found that guided or structured fantasies were useful in facilitating adaptive behavior and realistic appraisal of problems. The negative affect could be reduced through successive repetition of the fantasy, whereby the content of the fantasies became more realistic. The repetitions in some case reduced the affect, even though the content of the fantasies did not change. In Beck's view the repetition of a fantasy and its rehearsal produce cognitive restructuring.

ART THERAPY APPROACHES TO DEPRESSION

Young children need objects and concrete images to act out and portray their fantasies, feelings, and concerns. With latency-age children, the expression of aggression can take place through concrete visual configurations, such as making clay figures or drawing images. The expression of aggression through clay images may also lead to positive, protective maneuvers in the child's interaction with the therapist's clay figures. Thus such interaction, after several destructions of the clay figures symbolically representing either the self or the therapist, the client may start protecting these figures, thus reversing the negative imagery and negative feelings associated with it (Popkin, 1980; Schnake, 1980; Weiss, 1981).

In reporting on a single case study, O'Connor (1986) found that expression of hostility through play therapy was followed by depression in a latency-age depressed child. O'Connor interpreted this sequence as the child at first experiencing pain, which is then directed as aggression towards the source of the pain. If the child fears that the aggression will drive the loved person away, then depression follows the aggressive act. Depressed children in general identify with the victim and misfortunes, displaying perseveration of negative themes and rigidity in play behavior (Portner, 1982).

For adolescents, cartoon strips of a character performing aggressive acts may substitute for the clay play. Similarly, guided daydreams provide the structure and the distance needed for the depressed adolescents to deal with their negative and destructive imagery. The kinesthetic component of the aggression itself can be explored through throwing or wedging clay followed by a reintegrative experience of forming an image out of the wedged clay. A structured approach leading to a product is recommended for delinquent adolescents who display masked depression. Thus the wedging of clay can eventually lead to a finished clay product; similarly working on leather with metal tools can absorb the aggression through the repeated pounding of the tool on the surface of the leather to produce a design.

The visual representations of daydreams can be expressed and processed with an emphasis on either their content, structure, or affect. The visual expression is particularly important in dealing with the daydreams of adolescents with guilty-dysphoric and anxious-distractible daydreaming patterns. The negative thought patterns of the guilty-dysphoric dreaming style can be objectified through the visual expression and then dealt with on a cognitive level with emphasis on reality feedback. On a symbolic level, the negative thought pattern can be complemented and counteracted by its opposite, i. e., positive thought pattern. The visual expressions also may reflect how the negative affect influences the content of the daydreams.

The adolescents with the anxious-distractible daydreaming pattern benefit from the visual expressions of daydreams in two major ways. First, the anxiety can be expressed directly through the visual media, and thus given an image, which in turn can be processed for its content. Second, the visual expression provides structural means to integrate the disrupted or short daydream unit into larger cohesive statements.

As the daydreams are a developmental sequence to play, the visual expression of daydreams provides a developmentally based structural and affective support.

SELF-ESTEEM, DAYDREAMING, AND DEPRESSION

Self-esteem is affected by daydreaming as well as depression. Self-esteem, as the individual's perception of his own worth (Battle, 1980), and as a reflection of one's body and self-image (Chartier & Ranieri, 1984) is significantly negatively correlated to depression. This correlation was found to apply to all aspects of self-esteem, except the social (Yanish & Battle, 1985). Negative self-esteem and depression are also influenced by attributional styles. Individuals with internal, stable, and global attributions have more depressive symptoms than those who attribute difficulties to external, unstable, and specific causes (Seligman et al., 1984; Yanish & Battle, 1985). The external attributional style and projection on external causes could be seen as a coping mechanism, albeit not very effective, and it is used in masked depression which may be associated with delinquent behavior. Loss of self-esteem in depression can lead to acting out against the environment (Howard, 1981), and the acting-out juvenile delinquents and the aggressive, oppositional children may act "bad" instead of "sad" (Lesse, 1974; Petti, 1981).

Dealing with self-image and self-esteem also can become entry points on dealing with adolescent depression. Lewis and Michalson (1983) conceptualize self as having both subjective and objective aspects. The subjective self refers to the existential, most universal aspects of an individual as being different from others. The objective self is seen as the categorical self, having distinct characteristics such as gender, age, and abilities. Either of these aspects of self can be explored through visual expressions.

Nucho (1983) sees the self-system as pivotal for change, and the strengthening and modification of the self-system in depression as a central task for therapeutic intervention. Nucho bases her art therapy interventions on Gates' (1978) differentiation of the self in four factors: body self, interpersonal self, achieving self, and identification self. The *body self* consists of one's physical, mental, and emotional endowments, and abilities. The *interpersonal* self consists of relationships, both intimate and more casual interactions. The *achieving* self refers to the individual's work roles, performance, and accomplishments. The *identification* self refers to values, ideals, and ethical and transpersonal attitudes. Examples of art therapy experiences strengthening the body self are: representational and abstract self-portraits, favorite animal, place, season, and collage about the ideal self. The interpersonal self can be strengthened by the following art experiences: representational and abstract family portraits, best friend, self in grade and high school, important people in one's life, and visual portrayal of problematic relationships. Techniques of strengthening the achieving self are exemplified by the portrayal of one's workplace and ideal workplace, proudest achievements, greatest disappointments, and difficulties conquered. The identification self can be strengthened by exploring favorite team, actor or actress, ideal friend, or person one envies the most. Collage lends itself to many of these art experiences.

Any of these experiences can be elaborated in further fantasy explorations. The visual images provide concrete starting and returning points for exploring the different characteristics of the self-image.

Imagery combined with cognitive approach to modify self-image was the basis for Reardon and Tosi's (1977) Rational Stage Directed

Therapy (RSDT) in modifying self-concept and emotional states in delinquent girls. The imagery was used to encounter directly those internal and external events that activated irrational cognitions, which were then substituted with a more rational self-talk. The RSDT improved the overall self-concept, as well as the specific dimensions of identity, behavior, physical self, and moral self of the Tennessee Self-Concept Scale, along with decreased levels of self-reported depression and anxiety.

Visual expression of the self-image provides a basic starting point in dealing with depression, especially in adolescents. Clarification and consolidation of the adolescent self-image helps to built the adolescents' self-esteem, which in turn facilitates dealing with the losses and depression in adolescence.

SUMMARY

Daydreaming is a form of information processing especially active in adolescence. Developmentally, it can be seen as the internalization of the use of play in problem solving and adaptation to reality. Daydreaming is enhanced by a decreased motor activity, relaxation, and inward-directed attention. These conditions exist in adolescence when there is a shift in information processing from direct motor action, and a concurrent shift from reliance on the use of concrete objects to symbolic and formal thought patterns.

The themes of daydreaming are predominantly problem solving, either future-directed or dealing with current concerns. Affect is an important component of daydreaming in that it influences thought. Affect and anxiety are continuous across states of consciousness, including dreams. Daydreaming can be divided into three main patterns: positive-vivid, guilty-dysphoric, and anxious-distractible. The daydreaming patterns also show continuity with nocturnal dreams.

Daydreaming provides adolescents with the means to deal with the stresses experienced in the transition between childhood and adulthood. In depressed adolescents this avenue for dealing with important age-appropriate developmental aspects appears to be at least partially shut off. As a consequence the adolescents either are not able to make the transition to the internalized process of daydreaming, or regress to earlier patterns of dealing with tension, anxiety, and depression by acting out, or somaticizing them into psychosomatic illnesses.

The thought content and fantasy are negative and self-damaging in depression. The depressive daydream themes and dream themes are similar in their content, portraying rejection, abandonment, punishment, blame, sadness. The daydreams and dreams also display aggression and hostile acts in the environments, including actions through inanimate objects. The use of structured daydreams helps to interrupt the perseverative quality of thought patterns in depression. The imagery approaches are useful in dealing with depressed adolescents in that these approaches parallel the daydreaming processes present in adolescence. Structured imagery approaches are more effective in dealing with depression than unstructured approaches. Daydreaming ability itself is an important factor dealing with aggression and depression. Individuals high on daydreaming skills can use these skills to solve problems and lower their aggression, whereas individuals with low daydreaming skills experience boredom and/or revert to overt action. Self-esteem and self-image are other important aspects which are impaired in depression. Visual expression of daydreams can improve self-image and self-esteem, thus creating a supportive base for dealing with depression.

The visual expression through art media supports the necessity of having concrete objects to deal with images during the different stages of play. Even in latency, with the advent of concrete operations and anticipatory images, visual expression gives form and structure to the images. The visual images also reflect the affect associated with them. The visual expression gives the adolescent a reflective distance on daydreaming, which then can be processed, evaluated, and changed in regard to its negative content.

CHAPTER 9

Images of Disintegration and Integration in Psychosis and Schizophrenia

Visual expressions in schizophrenia reflect disturbances both in form and cognitive processes. They also represent regression to earlier and more primitive modes of expression. The cognitive secondary elaborations give way to direct expressiveness of the elementary forms of perception and the process of imagery formation. The disconnection between the different levels of information processing and representation is distinct and often irreversible in schizophrenia, whereas the transition between levels is rapid in the acute phase of the schizophreniform disorder. The spontaneous visual expressions in schizophreniform disorder and schizophrenia become a rich source for observing the structure and functions of imagery. A study of the verbal reports of imagery indicated that the imagery distortion is significantly higher in subjects with schizophrenic characteristics as compared to psychopathological nonschizophrenics and normal control subjects. Imagery distortions were defined as the occurrence of an unexpected spontaneous addition or change in the image, surprising the individual (Lanyon & May, 1979).

The degree of disintegration and integration present in the visual expressions of schizophreniform patients and schizophrenics over a period of time differ considerably. The approaches using art media in therapy with these two groups differ correspondingly.

191

THE SCHIZOPHRENIC EXPERIENCE OF PERCEPTUAL
AND COGNITIVE DISTURBANCES

Schizophrenia is characterized by disturbances in perception, affect, cognition, sense of self, psychomotor behavior, volition, and relation to the external world. The emotional turmoil and confusion is more acute in schizophreniform disorder (lasting less than six months) as compared to schizophrenic disorders, even though the symptomology presented may not be distinguishable from schizophrenic disorder. Schizophrenic disorders by definition are of longer duration than six months (DSM III-R) (American Psychiatric Association, 1987). Most of the references here use the older classifications of reactive and process schizophrenia (Fine & Zimet, 1959). In the present work the terms schizophreniform and schizophrenic disorders are used referring to reactive and process schizophrenia respectively, unless specified otherwise.

In schizophreniform disorder, the illness has a different premorbid history and is assumed to have a different etiology from schizophrenic disorder. Schizophreniform patients have a premorbid history of adequate social, economic, and sexual adjustment, and the onset of the psychosis may be traced to an external precipitating factor. In schizophrenia there is an insidious and gradual development of the illness starting early in life. Specific precipitating factors are absent.

Extensive descriptions of the subjective schizophrenic experiences of perceptual and cognitive disturbances have been surveyed by Friedman (1974). Friedman points out that these self-reports, as they primarily are, may not represent the whole range of the schizophrenic experience, but only the schizo-affective end of this range. In the acute schizophrenic break, perceptual experiences are described as more acute, direct, and vivid than in normal perception. The individual is sensitive to the background stimuli and, as a result, has difficulties in perceiving distinction between figure and ground. Eventually the rush of incoming stimuli leaves the individual anxious and exhausted. Some schizophrenics report being closed off from sensory stimulation and their perception as being wavy and blurred. People and objects may appear terrifyingly large or shrink to a very small size (Fig. 9.1). Objects may look flat and far away. Space may appear vast, limitless, and bathed in a stark, bright light. Synesthesia may be present in that the senses of sight and sound are linked to other senses. Cognitive experiences may be characterized by a feeling of intense aliveness, and brilliant flashes of insight or thought may be experienced as fragmented, racing, and being out of active control (Fig. 9.2). Pressured thoughts may have an image-like quality. The individual may experience being flooded by mental images. Thinking may be nonverbal and symbolic, especially when the individu-

Figure 9.1. Changes in objects and environment in visual field as represented in drawing by schizophreniform patient

al is anxious. Thinking occurs in images instead of words, and there is confusion between figurative and literal meaning. An enormous range of associated thoughts may be present. Individuals may experience a loss of the sense of time, and with it, the ability to sequence time and the sense of logical order. The individual experiences mental exhaustion,

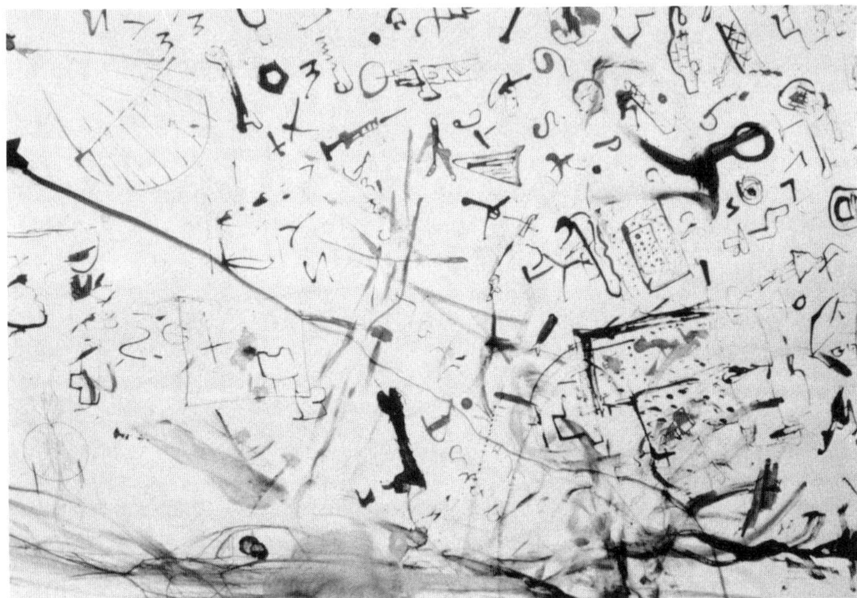

Figure 9.2. Drawing representing external and internal stimuli impinging on schizophreniform patient's consciousness.

similar to sensory exhaustion, after a period of racing thoughts. Some individuals report a marked slowing down of thoughts, thought blocking, and confusion. Over a period of time the schizophrenic experience results in a progressive loss of the sense of self and depersonalization (Fig. 9.3). The chronic schizophrenic may represent dissociation as projection of the astral body (Fig. 9.3), whereas schizophreniform individuals may experience a symbolic death and being in heaven (Fig. 9.4).

The dynamics of the schizophrenic visual expressions have been covered by Arieti's (1967, 1973, 1974, 1976) extensive writings on schizophrenia. In referring to the visual expressions of schizophrenics, Arieti (1974) states that "painting is an effort to adjust to new vision of reality, to crystallize it, to arrest it, or to delay further changes" (p. 354). He differentiates four phases of schizophrenics' experience as reflected in their visual expressions (Arieti 1973, 1974).

1. Acute eruption of conflict. The visual expression produced during this phase may be difficult to distinguish from the visual expressions of nonschizophrenics.

Figure 9.3. Mirror image of body as portrayed by male schizophrenic patient.

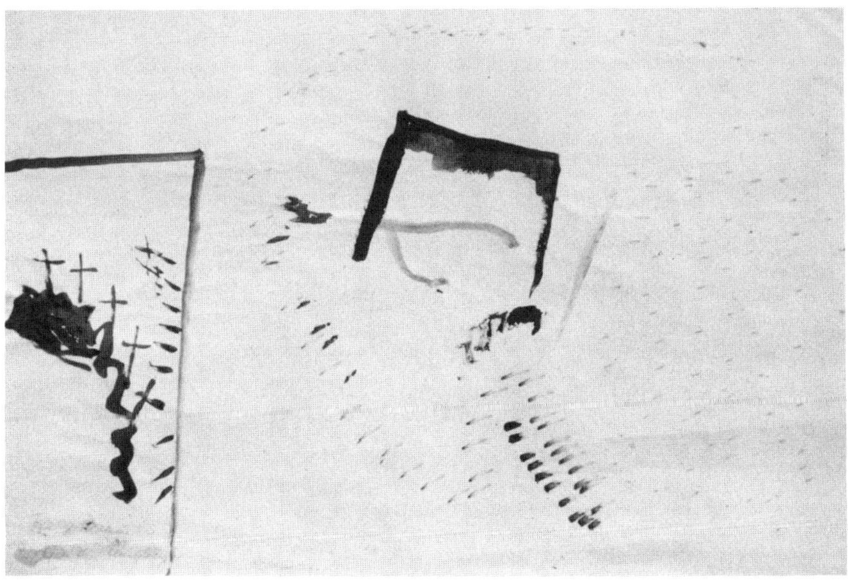

Figure 9.4. Schizophreniform patient's drawing representing dying and being in heaven.

2. Gradual disintegration of secondary processes. The visual expressions are characterized by the emergence of primary processes such as predicate thinking and active concretization.
3. Crystallization of the primary process in more rigid and stereotyped forms.
4. Disintegration of the primary process.

Arieti (1973, 1974) states that the schizophrenic experience of patients who recover is contained within the first two phases. Chronic schizophrenics who continue to disintegrate nevertheless resist the disintegration with defenses that characterize the typical schizophrenic visual expressions: simplification, stylization, stereotypy, ornamentation, mannerism, spatial alterations, and overfilling.

Arieti (1973, 1974) sees the schizophrenic's use of stereotypy as an attempt to arrest the rapid changes perceived externally and experienced internally. Stereotypy provides a continuous reinstatement of the same experience of reality. Mannerism (the excessive emphasis on a particular style), ornamentation, and overfilling present in the schizophrenic's visual expressions seem to serve the purpose of "filling an empty life with formalisms and decorations" (p. 364). The spatial alterations are the result of the perceptual flux experienced by the schizophrenic, and the consequent concrete perception of each isolated object or part of it.

Arieti (1973, 1974, 1976) emphasizes the presence of two primary-process characteristics in schizophrenic thinking: concretization of concepts and the acceptance of objects being identical based on their similarities or predicates. In concretizations, abstract ideas are transformed into concrete representations. The schizophrenic psyche seems to be still capable of abstractions, but they are not sustained, especially in anxiety-provoking situations.

In the identity between objects based on similarities, some general likeness based on form, detail, or visual appearance determines the identity between two or more objects. In an acute episode the schizophrenic may also experience an inability to perceive wholes and may exert a conscious effort to reconstruct the wholes. These efforts at reintegration then follow the principles of the primary process instead of the secondary process, and the parts replacing the missing ones may be based on similarities instead of identities. Condensations of forms present in the visual expression of schizophrenics may be seen as the result of such reintegration based on primary-process principles. Arieti (1974) points out that perception is a constructive process, where the wholes are constructed from parts, according to the secondary-process rules.

According to Arieti (1974), a large part of the functioning of the brain can be divided into four levels which organize the stimuli in progressively higher constructs. The first level registers crude sensations, the second level processes perceptions and recognitions, and the third level deals with the voluntary recall of past sensations and experiences. The third level is more complex in that the individual must have the ability to produce a mental image of external stimulus. The symbols on this level are denotative, instead of connotative. The fourth level deals with the processes of highest abstraction. Arieti (1973, 1974) believes that in the schizophrenic syndromes the symbols first lose their connotative power, retaining only their denotating ability. In further regression the elements of thought become completely perceptualized.

Visual Expressions of Schizophreniform Patients

The inner upheaval and the experience of self and environment in both the schizophreniform disorder and schizophrenia are such that the individuals resort to nonverbal and earlier forms of representation and communication. Volmat (1956) reports that 30% of psychiatric populations produce spontaneous drawings. Lusebrink (1977) found that 62 patients, or 55% of a group of 112 young males, ages 18–35, diagnosed as reactive schizophrenics, produced visual expressions in art therapy sessions. In addition to the two functions of arresting fleeting experiences and filling in a void of experience as described by Arieti (1973, 1974), the visual expressions of schizophrenics also serve the following purposes: (1) depicting multileveled internal imagery containing affect; (2) recreating an internal symbolic experience, which at times is more real and insistent than the perceptions of the external reality; and (3) communicating these experiences to others and in this process, discovering their meaning.

The following studies of schizophreniform visual expressions use the older nomenclature, "reactive schizophrenics," instead of referring to patients suffering from the schizophreniform disorder. The specific duration of the disorder present is not described in these studies, but it is assumed that the characteristics of visual expression described here are applicable to the visual expressions of schizophreniform patients. In describing the specific studies, though, the diagnostic terms reported in the respective literature will be retained. The majority of the work of the schizophreniform patients discussed here was produced in therapy, in either individual or group sessions.

Friedman (1974) points out that the different subtypes of schizophrenia may experience different clusters of cognitive and perceptual disturbances, and that differences in subjective experiences might respond differently to treatment. The same point has been made regarding the visual expressions by schizophrenics (Miljkovitch & Irwine, 1982). For reactive schizophrenics, the distinction between paranoid and nonparanoid patients appears to be important.

Perry (1953, 1962, 1973) reports a symbolic imagery sequence in the reconstitutive process in schizophrenia. These observations are based on his work with acutely disturbed undifferentiated or catatonic schizophrenic inpatients, mostly in their twenties and early thirties. The visual expressions of the symbolic images were an integral part of the process and therapy. Perry (1953, 1962) sees this process as centering around the reorganization of self and leading to a more integrated personality.

Perry (1953, 1962) discusses the imagery sequence from the Jungian point of view. The patient initially presents a negative self-image, which is compensated by an overblown self-image, often of mythological proportions. As the patient decompensates, he establishes a location at the world center, or cosmic axis. At this point the patient may have a feeling of participating in some form of drama or ritual. Themes of dismemberment, or delusions of having died and arrived at an afterlife are present. As the regression proceeds, the patient may experience being taken back to the beginning of time. A conflict arises between two opposite forces: good versus evil, chaos versus order. This strife may be interpreted in terms of warring current political parties or world powers. The patient may experience a threat from the opposite sex or may fear being turned into the opposite sex. This conflict eventually is resolved and the patient experiences an apotheosis as royalty or divinity, and enters a sacred marriage. A new birth of a superhuman child may take place. The later stages of the reconstitutive process are characterized by the patient's actively planning the formation of a new society. Plans and representations of a fourfold structure of the world or cosmos are presented in the visual expressions in the form of a mandala.

Perry (1973) points out that understanding and accepting this primordal imagery becomes a major task in therapy. The imagery itself is not seen as pathological. The pathology is present in the relation of the ego to the images and to the self in that the ego identifies with or becomes overwhelmed by these images. The symbolic imagery itself is often beyond words. The visual expression is used to depict externally the phases of the spontaneously occurring reorganization of the psyche. The mandala in its fourfold structure becomes the organizing element of the psyche. The verbal interpretation of the images helps to convert the "raw, archaic modes of image and emotion into more differentiated concepts and values" (p. 64). The imagery has a strong affective component presenting an "affect image": "the image renders the meaning of the emotion, while the emotion lends dynamism to the lost affect" (p. 64). The creative visual expression parallels and reflects the essence of the reconstitutive process: organization, disorganization, and reorganization, or integration, disintegration, and reintegration. According to Perry, this therapeutic work should not be directed but, rather, "the psyche has to be allowed to proceed with its own intentions" (p. 64).

Lusebrink (1977, 1980) bases her observations on work with acute reactive schizophrenics, ages 18–35. The most outstanding characteristic of this sample of visual expressions seems to be the difference between the expressions of the patients with paranoid and nonparanoid ideation.

As a group, the paranoid-type patients were less likely to participate in art therapy sessions, especially group sessions. Those who participated used mainly an abstract expressive style, either geometrical or conceptual. At times, letters and writing were included on the expressions. In the paranoid patients' work, the themes present progress from the abstract or designlike to the concretely personal (although they do not deal with the basic conflict). At times, the visual rendering of hallucinations seems to relieve some of the paranoia associated with the hallucinations. In later stages of the reconstitutive process, symbolic forms and references are introduced in the visual expressions. At first the symbolic forms are variations on the mandala form. The reality-oriented drawings may have symbolic or metaphorical overtones, e.g., a trapdoor that cannot be opened, a door that leads only to another door, an opaque or jammed TV screen, or a stopped-up sink. A transition takes place from a linear, geometric, and controlled expressive style to a more flowing and curvilinear one. The area initially covered is small, mainly in the upper part of the page, and it expands with the progress in recovery. Similarly, color-use changes from predominantly black-and-white, and the use of pencil to a larger color range, using paints.

For the nonparanoid patient, visual expression is most important in the acute stage. The expressions are fluid, executed in a fast, sketchy style, and cover most of the page. Upon closer inspection, each stroke assumes a symbolic meaning for the patient; thus paintings that at first appear to be only a surface covered with quick random strokes may reveal an underlying plan or meaning. This significance may not be shared verbally with the therapist in the acute phase, but the patient distinctly remembers and shares it with the therapist upon review of the work later in the reconstitutive process. Themes of fear and destruction alternate with cosmic and/or astrological themes. The positive experience of "being in heaven" may be portrayed through rhythmical brushstrokes (Fig. 9.4) or mandala-like structures. The visual expression in the acute phase is highly symbolic, even colors and numbers may assume symbolic meaning. The colors used may be vivid but not in jarring combinations. Pale colors used by reactive schizophrenics may indicate extreme sensitivity to sensory stimuli.

A large kinesthetic component is present in the early expressions of the acute phase. Expression in visual images and activation of the symbolic component subdues the kinesthetic component. The symbolic images reveal a theme that unfolds over a period of time. Several of the nonparanoid patients in Lusebrink's (1974, 1980) sample followed, with some variations, the sequence described by Perry (1953, 1962). The fear of destruction, symbolic death, and integration of opposites are expressed symbolically in well-defined forms. The clinical behavior at this time often becomes more regressive, in contrast to the organized visual expression. This organization predicts the reintegration of the behavior by one to three weeks. As the symbolic stage subsides and the behavior improves, the visual expression assumes a more cognitive and linear style. Similar to Perry's (1953, 1962) descriptions, the social awareness emerging at this time is reflected in visual plans and charts concerning time dimension; retracing the past; categorizations, such as charting the staff members along their different roots of origin; and planning for the ideal community. Like the first picture in therapy, the last picture is often predictive of the ensuing course of recovery. This expression again has symbolic undertones, expressing either the confidence of recovery or apprehension of future acute episodes.

The forms in the visual expression of reactive schizophrenic patients do not display the conglomerations and the neomorphisms encountered in the work of chronic schizophrenics. The forms may show some affective distortion or some dissociation, but the organizing aspect of the psyche in regard to form and structure prevails and the forms retain their original reference, rather than becoming bizarre and idiosyncratic. The threatening affect in the acute phase may be handled by establishing emotional distance, as expressed symbolically through images of constellations of planets with references to family, eclipse of sun and moon, or abstractions based on physics symbols. The integration of opposites and the emergence of an integrated self is portrayed symbolically as, for example, the Virgin Mary, Old Wise Man, Princess, Prince, or scion of noble birth.

The transition to the symbolic level of representation and expression appears to be one of the determining factors separating the individuals who recover from the acute episode from those who either proceed to decompensate or arrest the process through defensive but largely ineffective maneuvers.

Wadeson (1980) observed in the visual expressions from 56 reactive schizophrenic patients that depiction of psychiatric illness contained the following categories.

1. Feeling states such as confusion, depression, anger, and also positive feeling states including elation, happiness, and energy
2. Depiction of brains, whereby the disordered expressions reflected the disorganization present
3. Representation of physical illness
4. Locus of illness

The drawings of hallucinations and delusions mainly depicted paranoia, confrontation with and conquest of evil, as well as religious subjects, such as an encounter with Christ, being a Savior or the Virgin Mary, or of being singled out or visited by God. Other topics included recent historical events such as persecution by the Nazis, the assassination of President Kennedy, or the Middle East conflict. These themes are similar to those of conflict and resolution reported by Perry (1953, 1962) and Lusebrink (1974, 1980).

Celentano (1977) reports a consistent pattern of growth observed in the visual expressions of schizophrenics in a short-term hospital. The initial agitated, completely disorganized character of the visual expressions gradually changed to more organized expressions in the following manner. At first the display of visual configurations was nonrepresentational and cryptic in symbolic meaning. Eventually the expressions moved towards recognizable objects, and finally to realism. During this process the spatial organization changed from two-dimensional design to three-dimensionality. This sequence of changes in the visual expressions is similar to that reported by Lusebrink (1974, 1980).

It appears that the visual expressions of acute schizophreniform patients are first on the kinesthetic level and reflect the presence of motor activity and disorganization of cognitive functions. The inherent sense of form (Arnheim, 1977), however, is not impaired in this stage, and it reemerges as the patient assigns symbolic meaning to the kinesthetic traces. The schizophrenic, on the other hand, may try to counteract the disintegrative tendencies with an overemphasis on form without the symbolic meaning. The excessive dominance of form stifles the life of the visual representations and leads to stereotypical repetitions either on perceptual or cognitive levels.

Representations of Body Image, Space, Movement, and Time by Schizophreniform Patients

The concepts of body image, space, movement, and time are closely related. Space is first experienced in relation to the body and moving through space. Space is also experienced by the body moving through space. The traversing of a distance in space creates its relationship to time by the length of time it takes to move through this space. Fast and slow movements, in turn, influence differently either the distance covered or the time it takes to cover a given distance. The concrete representations of changes in these experiences are represented in the visual expressions.

The *body image* of the schizophreniform patient undergoes rapid changes in size, represented as micropsy or macropsy (Fig. 9.1). The diffusion of ego boundaries and the increased sensory awareness of either body functions or external minute details seem to contribute to this confusion and change. The body may be experienced as distorted; faces especially represent the negative self-image. The acute paranoid schizophrenic is more likely to represent the body or its parts visually than the schizophreniform patient. The schizophreniform patient's main focus is on the symbolic aspect of the experience at the cost of bodily awareness. Representations of the brain are common (Lusebrink, 1980; Wadeson, 1980), and reflect either the disorganization or the mazelike aspect of the brain.

Movement is experienced through activation of the body and the psyche. In visual expressions movement is portrayed through the expressive movement of a line and through the portrayal of moving forms. Psychic movement is indicated by the dynamic arrangement of forms and the emergence and changes of themes over a period of time. The dimension of movement, too, is impaired in schizophrenia.

The schizophreniform patient expresses himself in the acute phase with fast and fluid strokes. These strokes are, for the most part, rhythmical and have symbolic meaning. The forms depict fast-moving objects such as cars and planes, and the objects may possibly be going out of control (Fig. 9.2). Many forms may cover one page. The *relationship* between these forms, however, reflects a sensory overload and the fluidity of the changing experience in contrast to the condensation of forms and conglomeration of unrelated forms of *Bildsalad* encountered in the chronic schizophrenic expressions. Changes in the psychic movement are reflected in the unfolding and changing of themes over a period of time as seen, for example, in Perry's (1953, 1962) sequence of the reconstitutive process.

The experience of *space* undergoes rapid changes for the acute schizophreniform patient. Extremes of space are represented conceptually and symbolically as expansion of space with loss of body references. Visually, this is represented as cosmic constellations or heaven. The closing in and disappearance of space is present in regression. Visually this may be presented as large, looming forms, or in extreme regression, as fog or ascending waters. Changes in the experience of space may alternate by space expanding and contracting. The depiction of changes may be present in the same drawing or can be reflected in changes in the expressive styles. For example, traditional style with a conventional expression of space may alternate with a regressed or archaic style within the same day (Simon, 1970, 1974). The space portrayed may assume a symbolic meaning, such as being in hell, heaven, on other planets, or in another land (Fig. 9.4). Organization of space seems to be important. The patient's spontaneous drawings of maps of places and events important to him can be seen as spatial organization of information. In later stages of recovery, space again is presented in reality context but may still have symbolic undertones.

Acute schizophreniform patients express preoccupation with *time*, either conceptually or structurally, such as a symbolic representation of the face of a clock. One patient in the recovery stage tried to arrange the clock on a 10-hour basis instead of 12. Other authors (Billig & Burton-Bradley, 1978; Perry, 1962; Plokker, 1965) have included in their work reproductions of drawings by schizophrenics with the faces of a clock but have not elaborated on their meaning.

Art Therapy with Schizophreniform Patients

Schizophreniform patients display a tendency towards spontaneous visual expressions during the acute phase of their illness. This need for visual expression subsides with the improvement of the individual's functioning. The spontaneous expressions through different media, including poster paint, seem to be effective in the therapy of these patients (Celentano, 1977; Lusebrink, 1974, 1980). The expressions allow the patient to arrest the overwhelming and changing inner psychic processes in the time and space frame of the concrete work. At the same time, visual expressions facilitate the emergence of inherent organizing tendencies to form gestalts. Gantt (1979) points out that nonverbal group experiences reinforce the reversal of ego boundary diffusion because these group experiences have definite tasks with a beginning, middle, and end. Gantt recommends that the art media used with acute patients should be restricted to pastels, manila paper, and clay, and that the use of fluid media be reserved for more integrated patients. The patient also benefits from reverse interpretation, with a focus on the direct reinforcement of reality.

The schizophreniform patient with an excessive symbolic stance benefits from art experiences different from those of the paranoid patient. The patients with symbolic ideation benefit from media that promote organization and reality grounding with a concurrent exploration of the unfolding symbolic changes. The reality grounding is promoted with structured tasks, possibly with a sensory component. The amount of structure required depends on the individual ego strength and stage of regression. Group work is difficult in the initial stages of acute regression, but is recommended along with individual work during middle and later stages of the recovery.

The patient with paranoid ideation benefits from relaxation and work involving movement and the use of color. The goal for this type of patient is to move from the concrete or abstract expression to more fluid expressions involving symbolic meaning. The evolution of positive changes in forms and themes can be enhanced through the introduction of color, first with resistive media. For example, a highly paranoid and anxious patient in an acute stage was drawing a progression of geometrical figures with a black pencil. With the introduction of colored pencils, the patient colored the geometrical figures green, and by adding a brown line to each, converted them into trees with concurrent emotional relief. Assuming that color represents the affective component, the use of color indicated the first step towards the connection of form and affect, or the representation on the perceptual level with the affective component of this level.

Jones and Rush (1979) report on a study of patients preoccupied with delusions of control by unseen destructive forces described as demons or devils. In a supportive group setting, art therapy provided the possibility of exploring these "devils" in graphic form. The process involved two steps.

1. Drawing on a small piece of paper. This allowed the expression of fantasy and at the same time required visuo-motor and cognitive involvement. The small piece of paper discouraged expansive big muscle movement leading to loose and destructive behavior.

2. Projection of the small drawings on a wall into life-size images. Each individual elaborated on his work verbally by identifying with it. In this process the unconscious material was elicited by projections into images, which were then dealt with as a percept. This procedure facili-

tated the integration of the split-off, destructive forces into the personality.

The schizophreniform expression is characterized by the changes in imagery and the levels of expression, reflecting the internal psychic movement. The visual expressions on the perceptual level enhance the structural aspects of the flow of internal imagery. The visual feedback from the expression reinforces the structural aspects of the internal imagery and strengthens the cognitive functioning of the patient.

EXPRESSIVE QUALITIES AND PSYCHOPATHOLOGY OF FORM IN SCHIZOPHRENIC ARTWORK

The spontaneous visual expressions of schizophrenics have been extensively described and reviewed by several authors (Anastasi & Foley, 1940, 1941a, 1941b, 1941c; Billig & Burton-Bradley, 1978; Plokker, 1965; Prinzhorn, 1972; Volmat, 1956). Most of the work of schizophrenics discussed here refers to spontaneous expressions, produced outside the therapeutic sessions. These expressions warrant the terms "art expressions" or "schizophrenic art."

Prinzhorn's *Artistry From the Mentally Ill* (1972), first published in 1922, was one of the first studies devoted to the work of schizophrenics incorporating the expressive aspects of art. Prinzhorn based his observations and insights about the expressive qualities of spontaneous schizophrenic artwork on a collection of 5000 samples from psychiatric institutions in Germany, Switzerland, Austria, Italy, and Holland dating from 1890 to 1920. In his approach Prinzhorn presumed that any motor discharge can be a carrier of the expressive process. The integration of the expressive movement is guided by the artist either consciously or unconsciously. The observer adds forms from his own preconceptions to the perceptions of the work.

Prinzhorn divided the schizophrenic expression into six categories.

1. Objective, unordered scribbles.
2. Work displaying ordering tendencies, which use linear arrangement, regular pattern, and symmetry.
3. Playful drawings which include reproductions of individual objects without any intention to order, and ornamentation of the surface according to formal rules.
4. Playful drawings with a predilection to copy scenes from sur-

roundings; at times these scenes are presented in a bird's-eye view.

5. Visual fantasy, which includes commonly understandable configurations, as well as distortions of the environment.
6. Symbolism with increased personal significance.

The formal elements of spontaneous visual expressions of schizophrenics are extensively reviewed in Volmat's *Art Psychopathologigue* (1956). Volmat's approach is partially influenced by earlier French authors dealing with this subject, and their interest in structural psychopathology with an emphasis on the understanding of form and the dynamic aspect of its development and change.

Volmat (1956) proposes that schizophrenic art has the following basic psychopathological characteristics.

1. Geometrization, especially present in paranoid art, characterized by emphasis on the pure forms, such as squares, lozenges, and arched diagonals.
2. Stereotypies, the most characteristic structural elements of the schizophrenic style, distinguished by the repetition of a drawing or design as a whole over and over again. Stereotypies represent invariable fixation and lack of flexibility, with tendencies to deformation, simplification, and mechanization.
3. Iterations, similar to stereotypies, formed by immediate repetition. Iterations or perseverations differ from stereotypies in that the repetition encountered in iterations is based on a motor act. These productions "lack air" or display "horror vacui."
4. Dissociation, characterized by a succession of superimposed or juxtaposed views, often present in contrasting colors. In dissociation the separation of the plan and object becomes apparent with a concurrent rise in the disequilibrium in composition.
5. Tendency towards stylization, representing a compromise between the external image and the internal affective experience. Stylization results in simplification and repetition of forms. It is characterized by the use of simple geometrical forms such as triangles and circles in repetitious combinations.

Navratil (1969, 1976) summarizes the changes of schizophrenic forms by the presence of the following tendencies.

1. Physiognomation. The expressive qualities are affectively exaggerated or present in an unusual manner.
2. Formalism. All the expressive qualities may be either repressed or excluded, resulting in overemphasis on the formal aspects.

3. Symbolism. A new vehicle may be created for the expression of meaning through the use of symbolism, which gives the expression a special secret or mysterious meaning.

Navratil (1976) proposes that all the characteristics of the schizophrenic expression can be traced back to these three tendencies. Formalism encompasses stereotypy with its ordering and calming effects, geometrization, emphasis on symmetry, reinforcement of outlines, and reduction and/or abstraction, as well as amplification of forms. Physiognomation and symbolism are manifested in the deformations, especially of the human figure. The tendency to symbolization also is present in unusual combinations and fusion of forms.

The disintegration present in the schizophrenic artwork manifests itself in the division of expression into two or more opposite or unrelated areas, and in the fragmentary character of the forms present. The forms may be twisted, deformed, elongated or, at times, condensed and piled up on each other. Disintegration is counteracted by the encapsulation of forms. Volmat (1956) points out that as the forms disperse, the themes present may become richer and correspond to personal conflicts. With increasing regression, the individual expresses himself more and more in symbolic language, representing both personal and universal symbolism. In deeper regression the personal symbolism disappears and is replaced by the emergence of archetypal forms. At a regressed level there is no distinction between perception and representation, and no separation exists between the individual's ego and the outside world. The evolution of the schizophrenic visual expression during the course of illness parallels the evolution of the illness, and often precedes it.

At times the schizophrenic will use an external model, such as a vase of flowers, for the art expression. This serves to release the anxiety experienced in face of the dissolution of personality and the encroaching loss of reality. The academic and conventional character of the art expressions reflects the striving to maintain a reality contact.

Schizophrenic art expressions reflect the perturbed figure/ground relationship; a left/right or up/down split in the relationships of forms and/or colors may be present. Color use by schizophrenics can be either vivid or harsh, or the colors used can be pale and lightly tinted, indicating emotional emptiness.

Table 9.1 represents a compilation of the characteristics of pictorial expression of schizophrenics based on Volmat's (1956), Plokker's (1965) and Navratil's (1969) work. It reflects the pathology of forms, lack or distortion of spatial organization, over- or underemphasis on the expressive qualities, and the presence of perseveration in the expressions.

Table 9.1
Characteristics of Pictorial Expression in Schizophrenia

I. Changes in spatial structure
   A. Depersonalization and isolation
      1. Emphasis on distance
      2. Desertlike empty space
      3. Floating figures
   B. Regression to earlier modes of graphic expression
      1. Shift in baseline
      2. Mixture of plane and elevation
      3. Transparencies
      4. Disproportionate size relationships
   C. Visual defenses against threatening ego-disintegration
      1. Strict symmetry
      2. Encapsulation
      3. Decorative sheets
   D. Altered modes of organization
      1. Lack of organization, *Bildsalad*
      2. Figure/ground alternations
      3. Splitting in two sides or opposites
II. Changes in form
   A. Inarticulate forms
      1. Loss of details
      2. Partial representation
      3. Stereotypic forms
   B. Distortion of form:
      1. Geometrization
      2. Deformation
      3. Physiognomation
      4. Elongation
   C. Inappropriate forms
      1. Mixed body positions
      2. Transparences
      3. Interpenetration and agglutination of forms
      4. Condensations and neomorphisms
III. Changes in expressive and graphological qualities
   A. Line quality
      1. Faint lines
      2. Controlled
      3. Disorganized scribbles
   B. Use of shading
      1. Lack of shading
      2. Overemphasis of shading
   C. Use of color
      1. Faint colors
      2. Strong color contrasts

Table 9.1
(Continued)

D. Altered modes of expression
  1. Perserveration
  2. Combination of visual and written expressions
IV. Content
  A. Purely psychomotor expression
  B. Decorative sheets
  C. Depiction of loose associations
  D. Nonthreatening everyday objects and scenes
  E. Portraits, faces
  F. Symbolic:
    1. Personal
    2. Cultural
    3. Archetypal
  G. Religious

The Comparative Approach to Schizophrenic Visual Expressions

The visual expressions of schizophrenics have been compared to children's drawings, works of primitives, and art from different times and different cultures, including contemporary and modern art. Psychopathological art expressions enter the realms of imaginary categories, which are also present in the great productions of myths, religions, and art in general (Volmat, 1967).

In a series of comparative studies Billig (1966, 1968, 1970, 1971, 1973) investigated the regression and integration of spatial representation and movement in the schizophrenic artwork. Billig (Billig 1968; Billig & Bradley-Burton, 1978) compares the visual depiction of space by schizophrenics during the different stages of regression as being similar to the development of spatial integration in the art of early civilizations. Billig and Bradley-Burton (1978) found in crosscultural studies of schizophrenic art expressions that latent universal spatial structures are repressed by cultural developments and that "personality disorganization reactivates these early structures and they appear in a preestablished pattern, corresponding to the levels of disintegration" (p. 230).

The regression and restitution of the schizophrenic spatial representation seem to follow the stages of human ontogenic and phylogenic development. The similarities between schizophrenic visual expression and children's drawings were already pointed out by Prinzhorn (1972). The regression in the structure of the visual expression of schizophrenics can be seen as the reverse of the graphic development as classified by Lowenfeld (Lowenfeld & Brittain, 1970), i.e., scribble stage, preschematic stage, schematic drawings, and dawning realism.

Billig and Bradley-Burton (1978) point out that "the simultaneous presence of regressive and restitutive mechanisms contribute to unstable images and to a partial breakdown of the structure of the visual world" (p. 231). The visual expression of the schizophrenics, though, is not unique in some of its expressive aspects. Plokker (1965) compares the styles of schizophrenic expressions to those present in modern art: expressionism, cubism, and abstract art. The modern artist's work has an underlying structure and it shows a freedom of choice in the expression. The schizophrenic's work often lacks a structure. The schizophrenic does not have much choice in his expression because his work expresses emotions and experiences which he cannot adequately express in words, often because of the strange or novel quality of his experience. The modern artist's work presents social consciousness to varying degrees. This element is lacking in the schizophrenic's work, which appears bizarre, gruesome, repulsive, or incomprehensible. Plokker (1965) points out that real art is alloplastic, representing sublimated experiences that can reach audiences larger than the artist himself. The schizophrenic work is autoplastic, expressing individual tensions, problems, and experiences.

Rennert and Mode (1969) compare the representations of "mixed beings" or fantastic animals encountered in art, especially in primitive and mythological art with those present in schizophrenic expressions. The sphinx is an example of a fantastic being that the authors compare with similar mixed beings encountered in paranoid schizophrenics. Rennert and Mode propose that the mixed creatures in art and in schizophrenia express an attempt to deal with inner threat and fear through concretization. In art these monsters have cultural roots and religious implications. They are asexual and sobering in their character, representing a sterilized image with functional anatomy. In schizophrenic visual expressions the creatures represent isolated individual experiences and they display strong erotic and sadomasochistic traits. They present an image that is grotesque, ornamental, and repulsive, with excessive anatomical disproportion.

In general, however, the comparative method indicates that there are basic structural and formal commonalities in cultural art and in visual expressions of schizophrenics that follow the same rules in universal development of consciousness, graphic expression, and the human need and creative striving to form gestalts (Bader, 1972; Navratil, 1969; Plokker, 1965; Prinzhorn, 1972; Volmat, 1956). The similarities and differences in the dynamics of creativity between creative individuals and schizophrenics have been discussed by several authors (Arieti, 1976; Arnold, 1953; Ehrenzweig, 1971; Perry, 1973; Plokker, 1965; Storr, 1972).

Representations of Body Image, Space, Movement, and Time by Schizophrenic Patients

The body image of the schizophrenic is less differentiated and more regressed than that of the schizophreniform patient (Fig. 9.3). The representation of the body may be embryolike, or it may illustrate the disappearing ego boundaries by transparencies, elongations, and sketchy outlines. The body image may be distorted or contain condensations and neomorphisms. The schizophrenic portrait becomes masklike (Plokker, 1965). The internally experienced split may be portrayed as a concrete "split" in the head, as two contrasting halves of the face, or as a missing half or quarter of the face. The eyes are empty, without pupils. Paranoid ideation is indicated by the emphasis on the eyes. A severe regression is indicated by a rendering of a nude body containing a double image of a body and a face, whereby the breasts become eyes and the navel a nose. Halbreich and Assael (1979) point out that the abbreviation and condensation of head and body results in the formation of "cephalopodes" with limbs of "podiae" protruding from the fused form of head and body. The authors compare the characteristics of cephalopodes with masks and identification with the magic power of masks. Graphically, though, encephalopodes are early representations of humans by children around age four (Kagin, 1978). Thus the presence of cephalopodes in the drawings of regressed schizophrenics also may indicate a severe regression in body image and in its graphic expression.

In the cases where expressive *movement* is present in schizophrenic work, the kinesthetic expression is either disorganized or fragmented, or forms a repetitive pattern of iterations. However, most of the chronic schizophrenic work lacks kinesthetic movement. The forms are static, either encapsulated or presented in a very tentative way. The forms do not relate to each other, or they have idiosyncratic meaning. The repetition of the same themes and stereotypy characterize the lack of psychic movement over a period of time.

The regressive aspects in the representations of *space* by schizophrenics were discussed earlier (Billig, 1968, 1970; Billig & Burton-Bradley, 1978). The space in chronic schizophrenic expressions is characterized primarily by its strangeness and otherworldliness. Unlimited space is represented visually as an empty desert, sea, or ocean. The emptiness and the static quality of the space represented indicate that movement has come to a standstill (Plokker, 1965; Volmat, 1956). Plokker (1965) states that distortion of space also may be presented through altered proportions between foreground and background, lack of depth, transparency of objects, and their overlapping. The horizon line ascends on the page and disappears in regression, then reappears at the bottom of the page with an improvement in the mental state (Rennert & Mode, 1969). Depiction of movement and the organization of space increase with the improvement of the individual and thus become prognostic indicators (Volmat, 1956). In evaluating spatial representation in schizophrenic drawings, the patient's stage of graphic development and training has to be taken into consideration (Plokker, 1965).

Time, which is closely related to movement and space, is negated in the schizophrenic regression: time stands still or time also may be referred to as immemorial time or eternal time (Volmat, 1956).

Art Therapy with Chronic Schizophrenics

With the advent of psychotropic drugs and short hospitalizations, supportive therapy for schizophrenics takes place mainly in community day hospitalization centers. These changes, along with the availability of art and occupational therapists, have influenced the character of schizophrenics' visual expressions. The use of psychotropic drugs is assumed to be the main factor responsible for the presence of "empty" spaces in the work of chronic schizophrenics (Plokker, 1965). Their visual expressions lack the compressed and elaborate but obscure quality present in the early collections of schizophrenic work. The present work, however, still displays iterations and stereotypies expressive poverty and regressed forms.

In art therapy with schizophrenics the main emphasis is on structure, reality orientation, and socialization. Young (1975) compared the use of supportive and insight-oriented art therapy with chronic schizophrenics in a short-term psychiatric treatment center. The supportive therapy consisted of drawing self-images using instructions in art techniques and emphasis on the creative process. The insight-oriented psychotherapy program emphasized free visual expression and nonverbal communication of inner experiences. The supportive therapy produced increased evidence of self-esteem and realistic self-identity. The majority of the subjects were not able to relate to the insight-oriented therapy.

Reality orientation is enhanced through the sensory exploration and drawing of real objects or depictions of themes representing trips to the community. Socialization is increased through group work and murals

The stage of *development* determines whether the individual has the capacity to form symbolic images. A serious illness may precipitate a regressive trend which lowers the general level of intellectual and psychological functioning. The *ego strengths* and *coping* abilities present counteract this regressive trend. The intrapsychic and interpsychic *stresses* contribute to the acerbation of physical and psychological functioning.

The inquiry into the individual's *belief systems* may reveal the spiritual resources s/he can draw upon (Kuhn, 1988). Knowledge of the patient's beliefs about illness, life, and death helps the therapist to work more effectively within these beliefs, and also to deal with the misconceptions about the symptoms and disease (Achterberg & Lawlis, 1980).

Assessment of Alexithymic Characteristics

The practical approach of using imagery in healing with psychosomatic patients especially depends on their ability to be aware of and to be able to express their emotions, and the use a symbolic function in combining concrete images into metaphorical themes, i.e., the absence of alexithymic characteristics.

The presence of alexithymia can be evaluated by using the Shalling Sifneos Personality Scale (Apfel & Sifneos, 1979) of alexithymia. The Archetypal Test With 9 Elements (AT9) (Demers-Desrosiers, Cohen, Catchlove, & Ramsay, 1983) for alexithymia focuses on the ability to form symbolic structures combining drawing and verbalization. Because of their impoverished fantasy life and the inability to make a transition from the concrete references to symbolic images, alexithymics experience impairment in their ability to arrange symbolic images in an interrelated dynamic fashion. In visual representation the images remain concrete and separate from each other, and are portrayed in an isolated "comic strip" frame manner. The elements of the AT9 test operationalizes the symbolic inability present in alexithymia into expression through visual means. The individual is asked to integrate in a drawing nine items (fall, sword, refuge, devouring monster, something cyclical, a character, water, animal, and fire) to construct a myth. The nine items acquire a symbolic quality through their integration in a composite drawing representing a myth, which is then elaborated upon through a written explanation. The structuring of the nine elements and the force involved in this structure gives the visual representation a mythological infrastructure which helps to reduce an individual's anxiety. The alexithymic individual lacks the capacity to form such an infrastructure and the drawing reflects an organization without any projective elements. Alexithymics' references to the nine items represent concrete items which are often described in personal terms using the adjectives "my" and "mine," and the individual resorts to naming and numbering the items (Demers-Desrosiers, 1985, Demers-Desrosiers et al., 1983).

The core items for the AT9 test have been selected for their ability to elicit anxiety (fall, devouring monster), resolution of anxiety (sword, refuge, something cyclical), and a resolving agent (a character). Water, animal, and fire are considered accessories. According to Demers-Desrosiers, (1985), the anxiety can be resolved through different symbolic infrastructures. In the heroic infrastructure, the resolution focuses on the sword; in the mythical infrastructure, the focus is on the refuge, and in the synthetical, on the cyclical item.

The expressions of the alexithymic individuals are characterized either by representations with an infrastructure without a resolution of anxiety or by a lack of an infrastructure. When the infrastructure is present, individuals may express their anxiety by representing a flight, a destruction of the character, or a denial of an attack by the monster. A diminutive representation of the monster, for instance as a toy, or the monster being friendly may also represent a lack of resolution of anxiety (Demers-Desrosiers, 1982, 1985). The AT9 tests can differentiate between primary and secondary alexithymia, based on Freyberger's (1977) proposed division. Primary alexithymics are unable to create a mythological infrastructure, whereas the secondary alexithymics present an infrastructure, but fail to resolve the anxiety. Primary alexithymia represents an innate inability to use the symbolic function. Secondary alexithymia may be regression to an earlier mode of emotional functioning.

Demers-Desrosiers (1982) uses the graphic expression in the AT9 test as a preferred mode of expression of the symbolic imagery and its structuring into themes. The act of drawing may also enhance the dynamic/symbolic quality of integrating the images of the nine elements. A new symbol or a resolution of the conflict may emerge in the process of drawing before the individual is aware of it on a cognitive level.

Control of imagery can be tested with Gordon's (1949) test. Lack of control of imagery contributes to anxiety; thus it increases the stress experienced. The issue of control in general is especially important for cancer patients; being out of control is associated with poor prognosis (Achterberg & Lawlis, 1980). Internal locus of control as opposed to external locus of control (Rotter, 1967) is associated with better prognosis in psychosomatic illnesses.

Imagery-Based Assessment of Disease and Immune System

Diagnostic imagery is designed to obtain information about the disease, body defenses, and the way the individual perceives the effectiveness of the treatment. The disease and/or symptom may have an idiosyncratic meaning, which can be explored in the context of the client's belief systems. In the diagnostic approach the images are not interpreted and are not programmed (Achterberg & Lawlis, 1984).

Achterberg & Lawlis' (1984) imagery technique with cancer patients, IMAGE-CA, uses active imagination, drawing, and a structured interview to obtain information about the patient's experience of cancer. First, the patient is guided through relaxation exercises, and then s/he is instructed to imagine the cancer cells, and the medical treatment. The patient draws these images and then is asked to clarify the meanings of the drawn images in a structured verbal interview. The drawings and the interview are scored on the following dimensions along a 5-point scale: vividness, activity, and the strength of the cancer cells and the white blood cells; relative comparison of number and size of cancer cells to white blood cells; vividness and effectiveness of the medical treatment portrayed; concreteness vs. symbolism of the images; overall strength and emotional investment of imagery; estimated number of regular or daily imagery applications; clinician's estimate of the prognosis for disease.

The images that emerge can be either anatomically appropriate (if the patient is familiar with the medical concepts), or symbolic. For cancer patients, symbolic images have a better positive prognostic value than anatomically correct images. Similarly, a good outcome is related to cancer's being represented as weak animals or actual cells. Poor outcome is related to cancer cells drawn as immutable or ineradicable or represented symbolically as lumps of coal, ants, or submarines (Achterberg & Lawlis, 1984). The vividness, activity, and size of the imagery of the white blood cells are generally more predictive of the outcome of the disease than those of cancer cells. The white blood cells appear to represent symbolically the patient's belief in his/her ability to fight the disease. The estimated strength of the white blood cells is the most powerful predictor of a short-term disease state. Drawing images of white blood cells and cancer cells is used in monitoring the treatment progress. Imagery, along with sense of control, denial, and negative self-image, was found to be predictive of a positive or negative course of the therapy (Achterberg & Lawlis, 1984). Applied as an adjunct to the medical treatment, the different aspects of imagery are practiced daily. Achterberg and Lawlis (1980, 1984) use similar imagery approaches that involve the representations of the disease, immune system, and treatment in evaluation and adjunctive treatment of diabetes mellitus, low back pain, and rheumatoid arthritis.

The disease-specific inventory gives information to the therapist about the symptoms present and the patient's idiosyncratic way of experiencing and interpreting them. For the clients this inquiry into the symptoms is important as an acknowledgment of the experience. The therapist also needs to understand the basic principles of the disease and the role of medical treatment in order to help the clients with the imagery. As pointed out before, the imagery diagnosis and treatment is designed to supplement the regular medical treatment. The different images depicted during the assessment can be explored further in therapy.

PROGRESSIVE STEPS IN USING IMAGERY IN HEALING

Information and Instruction

The approach to the use of imagery in healing can be divided into several progressive steps, ranging from a cognitive information-sharing and instruction to supportive and psychodynamic in-depth oriented approach (Rhodes, Foard, & Dickstein, 1988).

In the *information*-sharing phase, the patient is provided with facts concerning the illness and the mechanisms involved. The patients also receive instructions for health-oriented behavior, including diet and exercise, information on patient's rights, peer counseling, support groups, and other related information. During this phase the patient's belief systems are further investigated and correct information is provided to substitute for any erroneous beliefs and misconceptions. Information is given to the patient concerning the role of stress and negative emotions in suppressing the immune system and the role of the positive emotions, laughter, and the natural opiates endorphin and enkephalin in stimulating the immune system. The information may be presented in the early part of each session for 10–15 minutes.

The *instructional* component exposes the patient to instructions in self-observation, relaxation techniques, deep breathing, sensory and emotional awareness, and imagery training. Assertiveness training and stress management techniques are part of the instructional component given to the patient.

Self-observational charts of tension-producing events during the day, with the patient's corresponding emotional, somatic, and cognitive responses, provide useful information on his/her reactions and problem-solving abilities. Self-observational charts of pain or symptom recurrence or flare-up also provide information about bodily reactions to different experiences. Daily practice of imagery and medication taken are some other variables that can be charted. Verbal or visual journals and dialogue with the images of the symptoms provide insight into one's physical and psychological functioning and the psychological meaning of the disease (Bresler & Trubo, 1979).

Relaxation is an important part of the use of imagery in healing. Stress and relaxation are incompatible with each other. Relaxation also becomes the basis for sensory awareness. The absence of the motor component facilitates the ability to concentrate on sensations present in different parts of the body. Jacobson's (1929) progressive relaxation consists of sequential contraction and relaxation of major muscle groups, with the subsequent awareness of the presence and release of tension. Schultz's (Luthe, 1969) autogenic training procedure emphasizes different parts of the body becoming warm and heavy. The images of warmth and heaviness enhance the relaxation. The images of a rag doll are useful in teaching relaxation to children. *Biofeedback* training is another approach to muscular tension reduction and vascular dilation. Relaxation deepens the levels of consciousness, and contributes to imagery formation (Achterberg & Lawlis, 1980).

Sensory awareness, in addition to relaxed self-observation, can be enhanced by external sensory exploration. A nature walk, with emphasis on the different sense perceptions, provides a rich source of sensory stimulation. Tactile exploration of different textures, including a walk in a park or in the country and touching plants and trees, emphasizes the sensory quality of external input. The visual and tactile aspects of such a walk can be reinforced by collecting different objects and constructing a collage afterwards, using these objects.

Internal sensory awareness can be enhanced through the imagery of "taking a trip through the body" which reveals the sensations present in different parts of the body, including tension and/or obstructions. Drawing the imagery experienced increases this awareness and also produces additional information about any tension or symptoms present. This approach presumes the ability to form images, and therefore may be initially too anxiety-provoking for alexithymic individuals. Similarly, the presence of blockages through tension and/or organic impairment may be too anxiety-provoking and require a gradual approach with supportive therapy. The emphasis on the sensory components of pain as represented in coloring areas within a body outline may be helpful in making a connection between physical distress and emotions (Fleming & Cox, 1989). The use of the same colors and lines without the body outline in a second drawing facilitates a transition to an image and feelings associated with it. This approach is particularly useful with alexithymics, since it starts with the representation of the physical experience of pain.

Movement therapy contributes to the awareness of body image and body sensations. Slow movement with attention to subtle changes in the body, as explored through Feldenkrais (1972) exercises, are especially helpful to increase awareness of body sensations.

Imagery training procedures were discussed previously in Chapter 2. The instruction in imagery formation can start on a perceptual level of the ETC (Kagin & Lusebrink, 1978) with an image of a simple object, such as an apple (Samuels & Samuels, 1975) or a flower (Leuner, 1984). Exploration of these objects through the sensory modality of touch enhances the ease of imagery formation. Drawing the objects reinforces the image through the concrete visual feedback, and also through the kinesthetic act of drawing itself. The rehearsal and reinforcement of these sensations helps to develop the sensory component of imagery. An extension of the image can be achieved by elaborating the object's environment. For example, a flower can be imagined to be in a garden or in a vase in a room. The exploration and description and/or depiction of the details in the environment elaborate on the imagery on perceptual and cognitive levels. The imagery based on elaborations of the environment often becomes the transition point between concrete imagery and fantasy or imagination imagery, some of which may have metaphorical or symbolic aspects. The mood of the pictures, especially the weather conditions and time of year, gives clues in regard to the affective component present. The therapist's reflection of the affect present in the patient's behavior and expression increases the patient's awareness of his/her emotions. Special associations and meaning related to the imagery add to its symbolic character.

Nature images, such as a peaceful scene in a meadow or by the ocean, are common and easily formed. Images of nature objects or scenes are associated with feelings of contentment and happiness (Lyman & Waters, 1989). The exploration of the perceptual details and kinesthetic/sensory images associated with the scenes enhances the imagery and increases its richness.

The informational and instructional components are basic steps in using imagery in healing. The extent of the instruction and information presented depends of the client's knowledge and skills in the different areas, and his/her resistance to imagery formation.

Supportive Therapy

In supportive therapy the therapist reinforces the patient's strengths, provides information, and facilitates support in the client's environment. As used with alexithymics, the interventions are anxiety-suppressive and reassuring (Sifneos, 1983). The patient's physical and psychological symptoms are accepted and the defenses are stabilized or converted into coping mechanisms.

Some of the information obtained from the patient during the instructional part is further elaborated in supportive therapy; for example, the charted objective self-observations or the KFD.

Exploration and improvement of self-image (Korn & Johnson, 1983), education about emotional process (Sifneos, 1983), and programmed imagery are some of the important aspects of supportive therapy using imagery with psychosomatic patients.

Self-image reflects the individual's concepts about him/herself as a person. An undifferentiated or poor self-image can contribute to increased experienced stress and ultimately to a disease. Developmentally, the body image precedes the self-image as a representaton of self. Body-image awareness can be increased through imagery and sensory-awareness training. Body-tracing is an effective way to increase the patient's awareness of his/her body and at the same time to deal with the anxieties of misperceptions associated with the body image. The concrete experience of body image becomes the basis for self-image and self-concept. Self-image evolves with increased self-awareness, differentiation of the social and work roles, and the different aspects of the self.

Drawing a whole person or the Draw-A-Person test reflects identification either with the self sex or the opposite sex, and thus indicates acceptance of or difficulties with one's gender (Ogdon, 1977). The size and placement on the page can reflect either low self-esteem, e.g., a small figure not centrally placed, or a grandiose self-concept, e.g., an oversized figure in relationship to the page. Collages about different aspects of self are helpful to explore and differentiate internalized and integrated self-images.

Ideal self, either in gender, social, or professional reference, also can be expressed and explored through collages of images obtained from magazines. Self-differentiation can be enhanced through lists of characteristics of the self, as compared to the characteristics of significant others. Abstract drawing of "how I see myself" and "how others see me" is useful in differentiating inner experience of self as compared to the feedback one perceives as given by others.

Improved self-image and assertiveness training contribute to the internalization of *locus of control*. As a result, individuals experience themselves as being in charge of their lives and circumstances surrounding them. The supportive aspect of therapy reinforces the *control of imagery*, whereby the patient is taught to deflect negative or anxiety-provoking images (Meichenbaum, 1977; Rossman, 1984).

The patient's education about *emotional processes* is approached from a cognitive level by listing words that describe emotions and then giving them form through images and colors expressed in art media. The different feelings and moods can be portrayed either abstractly or in reference to specific instances. The drawings of the images provide a visual feedback, which can be further elaborated with appropriate affective words by either the patient or the therapist. In general, images portrayed in art media provide some reflective and emotional distance. The reflective distance to the emotional images can be increased or decreased, depending on the media used, as was discussed in Chapter 2.

Painting with music integrates kinesthetic and affective expression with the visual aspects of a mood evoked by the music. The music provides rhythm and mood. The mood or affect experienced may be congruent with the music, or it may be opposed to it. An example of the latter case would be the individual who does not like slow rhythms and becomes upset while listening to such music. Music portraying different moods can be used to enhance the awareness and expression of emotions.

An emotional situation can be approached from the expressive viewpoint with emphasis on the affect and sensation associated with the situation. The same situation also can be approached from a cognitive viewpoint as a problem to be solved by exploring alternatives to the solution. For example, anger, either overt or repressed, is one of the characteristics associated with several psychosomatic illnesses (Friedman & Booth-Kewley, 1987). The direct expression of anger may be appropriate in some situations; but in an unchangeable situation, anger may be best dealt with either using imagery or cognitive problem solving. Free drawings and paintings help to express distress and also reflect the course of illness. Bach (1969) reports that severely ill children used black, red, and purple colors to depict their disease. Graves (1982) asked children with cancer to represent symbolically their experience of cancer and immune system in "battle" drawings. The power of the cancer images and those of the immune system was differentiated between high-risk and low-risk groups. In addition to their prognostic value, the battle drawings also were useful in coping with the disease.

Programmed imagery (Samuels & Samuels, 1975) is used in supportive therapy in the form of images specific to the mechanisms of the illness, such as the immune system interacting with the cancer cells, or warmth of hands increasing dilation of blood vessels. These images are not interpreted; only the qualities of the images are discussed in terms of what they mean for the patient's progress. Imagining desired outcomes may be more effective at times than programming the intermediate steps.

In supportive therapy images and their visual representations are used to focus on the somatic messages. The patient's illness and pain are given a concrete form through imagery and its representation in *art media*. A dialogue can be established with the concrete images in exploring the meaning of illness for the patient (Landgarten, 1981). Similarly, the images elaborate on the needs of the body.

Imagery helps the individual to train and trust his/her intuition. Similarly, an individual's spiritual strength can be explored and drawn upon through imagery. Both of these aspects are combined in the guided imagery of *inner guide* (Bresler & Trubo, 1979; Korn & Johnson, 1983; Lusebrink, 1988). The image of inner guide provides a voice for the innate, intuitive wisdom of the individual and his/her body which can be helpful in healing. The patient is encouraged to give a form to and establish a dialogue with this inner voice through the guided daydream.

The drawing of a *lifeline* depicting the highs and lows present at different ages can be used to illustrate the impact of stress and traumatic events. The comparison of this lifeline with one depicting the illnesses present at different ages often reveals striking correspondences. If appropriate, the references to traumatic events brought up through lifeline discussions can be further explored in insight-oriented therapy.

Supportive therapy is appropriate with alexithymic clients; it also serves well the severely physically impaired who lack the physical and emotional stamina to benefit from insight oriented therapy.

Insight-Oriented Psychotherapy in Healing

Insight *oriented or uncovering* therapy in healing is appropriate for patients with a healthy ego who possess the ability to symbolize, and who are also more aware of and able to express feelings than alexithymics. The emphasis in insight-oriented therapy is on the expression of feelings, especially reliving and expressing feelings associated with past conflicts and traumatic experiences. These feelings are brought to the level of consciousness, thus releasing the stress on the somatic level. Affect dissociated from memory images is reintegrated with the imagery. Patients with secondary alexithymic characteristics can eventually benefit from insight-oriented therapy. The insight-oriented approach focuses on working through conflicts and the associated affect and sensations. In insight-oriented therapy the therapist confronts the patient about present stresses and the secondary gains obtained from the illness behavior. Gestalt technique (Perls, 1969; Rhyne, 1973) can be used with imagery and art expressions.

The concrete visual expressions of the illness or pain can be explored for their messages and meaning. Through visual images one also can explore secondary gains from the illness or pain. Collage can be used effectively to illustrate the different aspects of these secondary gains (Landgarten, 1981). The in-depth exploration of the lifeline can be useful in insight-oriented therapy. The patient is asked to illustrate the different periods in his/her life with the corresponding images and then explore the feelings associated with these images.

Reentry into past memories can also be achieved through *guided imagery* that concentrates on images of looking over fences, exploring rooms, or other imagery with themes of going past the defenses. A deepened state of consciousness is beneficial for this type of introspective imagery. It can be achieved through counting to 10 while imagining going down an escalator (Rhodes, 1988).

The exploration of *dream images*, especially negative dream images and their substitution with positive images, is an important aspect of using imagery in healing. The inquiry about dream images is important in working with psychosomatic patients, such as asthmatic, arthritic, and hypertensive patients. In their repetitous dreams a character other than the dreamer is depicted as experiencing the affect, while the dreamer is actually expressing the affect through somatic manifestations, such as waking up from the dream crying (Levitan, 1980b). Sadness and terror are present repeatedly in the dreams of psychosomatic patients. Terror is predominant in dreams that culminate in migraine headaches (Levitan, 1984). Patients who have experienced significant loss project the affect onto another person who has experienced similar loss; in the absence of such a person the affect becomes deflected back onto the patient, contributing to the formation of a physical illness (Levitan, 1980b). Psychosomatic dreams present extreme cruelty and aggression against the dreamer, where the dreamer fails to protect the body from the aggression, as in being shot or stabbed (Levitan, 1980a). Levitan sees these dreams as indicating a lack of the normal defensive functions of the ego, which in dreams are manifested either as a call to action or by waking the dreamer. According to Levitan "psychological events including traumatic dreams can be as efficacious in producing stress disorders as events in real life" (1981, p. 6). The decreased awareness of negative affect allows the stress and trauma to progress too far and overstimulate the physiological system, thus precipitating and maintaining psychosomatic disorders (Levitan, 1978).

The lack of dream memories of psychosomatic, and especially alexithymic patients, creates difficulties in accessing the negative dream images. Imagery training as discussed above is an important part of the treatment because it increases the possibility of remembering dreams. The affect in dreams can be rediscovered by sequential dream-image drawings, followed by labeling the affect represented in each image (Lusebrink, 1987).

Expression of the affect and its reintegration with the images on a conscious level is one of the main goals in working with psychosomatic patients.

Summary

Images in a relaxed state provide a bridge between the body and mind. Thus, imagery becomes a healing agent that supplements conventional medical procedures. Imagery also is the intermediary between the physiological experience of emotion and its symbolic processing. Impairment in the ability to express emotions, or alexithymia, is characterized by an impairment in the symbolic function. Alexithymia contributes to the formation of psychosomatic illnesses in that the emotional stress is dealt with on a physiological instead of psychological level.

Emotions, like imagery, are conceptualized to consist of several subsystems: sensory-motor level, perceptive or schematic encoding level, and cognitive or conceptual level. The instruction in imagery training can start on a cognitive level, as can the differentiation of emotions. Imagery training can also start on a sensory, experiential, and reality-oriented level. The sensory cues are differentiated on the perceptual level into schemas that can be visually represented through form and color in images. This approach, with the help of cognitive feedback, helps to channel and differentiate the emotions. Ultimately, the images as symbols provide clues about the functioning of the body and its immune system. In turn, symbolic images can affect the physiological processes of the body.

The cognitive, supportive approach of using imagery in healing is more appropriate for alexithymics, whereas a symbolic and insight-oriented approach benefits clients who are aware of their symbolic processes. The goal for alexithymic clients is to be able to process emotions with the assistance of symbolic imagery and processes.

The visual expression of the images defines and reinforces the structure of the imagery themes, and elaborates the relationship between the symbolic images reflecting the bodily processes.

Overview
A Systems View of Imagery and Visual Expression

This book has covered different aspects of imagery and visual expression in therapy from various viewpoints.

Imagery is multileveled, as is visual expression. The order of these levels reflects the underlying hierarchical structures and developmental sequence. The Expressive Therapies Continuum (ETC) provides a model that accommodates the developmental sequence of imagery in a steplike manner, consisting of kinesthetic/sensory, perceptual/affective, cognitive/symbolic, and creative levels. Imagery in different modalities can be present on any of these levels. At the same time images at a given level can either have component parts on any of the other levels or evolve toward developmentally higher levels. For example, symbolic images have cognitive as well as perceptual/affective and kinesthetic/sensory components. A developmentally simpler level of information processing, such as kinesthetic/sensory, can evolve into more complex images, such as affective or perceptual schemata, or through further transformation, into symbolic images.

The levels of the ETC constitute a set of parts or subsystems of a system in that they interact in unique ways. The progressive emergence of a developmentally higher level leads to self-regulation through the interaction of the component parts. The opposite is true if the functioning on a level is disrupted, leading to deregulation of the system. For example, in alexithymia, the disrupted or ineffective functioning of the affective level influences the functioning on the symbolic level. Emergence is exemplified by the transformation of kinesthetic activity, which can be preempted by increasing the perceptual observations and descriptions (Leuner, 1984). Leuner's concept of synchronous transformation similarly points to the systemlike qualities of imagery. He reports that the changes of imagery on one level precipitate concurrent changes of imagery in other areas of functioning.

Impairment in affective functioning is a major disruption presented in therapy. The effects of strong emotions can be seen, for example, in visual expression on the perceptual level through distorted forms. The repression of affect is seen on the symbolic level as recurring fixed images. On the other hand, the self-regulatory aspects of affect are manifested in imagery through "mobile projection" (Leuner, 1978) or changes in the imagery. The same effect is observed in dreams (Klinger, 1981; Lusebrink, 1987) whereby the affect present in a dream segment influences the following segment. The disruption of affective expression in masked despression can be manifested on the kinesthetic level as acting out. Progression on the symbolic level through guided daydreams in depression, especially with adolescents, can be effective as an integrative strategy leading to self-regulation. The case vignette in Chapter 1 illustrates the expression of emotions through color and form and the emergence of symbolic images. Figure 1.1 is a spontaneous expression on the perceptual level of depression, or literally being "down." In elaborating on the barrier, the client turned the black horizontal line 90 degrees, so that it became the vertical line on the right hand side of Figure 1.2. The reference to the image changed from a barrier to "mother's breast," i.e., the image changed from a perceptual/affective image to a symbolic image.

As seen from the systems perspective on *art as therapy*, the visual expressions through art media lead to self-regulation. The visual expressions in art as therapy combine interaction on the different levels: The kinesthetic/sensory level is involved in the interaction with the media; the perceptual level provides the visual organization of stimuli into forms; the affect is amplified through the color and images used; the cognitive level of information processing deals with the organization of expression through sequencing of steps and problem solving; the symbolic level is manifested through the symbolic meaning of the images; and the final product of the expression attests to the presence of creative activity.

In *art psychotherapy* the emphasis may be on a particular level as a starting point for the exploration of the disruption of functioning. The intrinsic qualities of the media influence differentially the levels of information processing involved and the portrayal of the images on different levels of expression as discussed in chapters 5 and 6.

The multileveledness of imagery also can manifest itself through levels of depth of information processing, tapping the elemental and formal perceptual aspects, personal references, or archetypal roots of the psyche. The presence of archetypal images can be seen in acute psychosis and schizophrenia. The dynamic changes in these images during the course of recovery illustrate the innate self-regulatory tendencies of the human psyche. The connection to the biological roots of imagery is seen in the use of imagery in healing. The levels of the depth of the inner experiences and their manifestation through imagery are hierarchically ordered and can be considered as constituting a system. The visual representation of the images here again is recommended to organize the perceptual elements, to represent the manifest and latent meaning of personal references, or to depict the archetypal images, the description of which may defy words.

As with any theoretical model, further empirical evidence based on the use of a systems approach, as well as associated research, will attest to the validity or lack of validity of this model.

References

Achterberg, J. (1985). *Imagery in healing: Shamanism and modern medicine*. Boston: New Sciences Library.

Achterberg, J., & Lawlis, J. F. (1980). *Bridges of the bodymind: Behavioral approaches to health care*. Champaign, Ill: Institute for Personality and Ability Testing.

Achterberg, J., & Lawlis, G. F. (1984). *Imagery and disease*. Champaign, Ill: Institute for Personality and Ability Testing.

Ahsen, A. (1973). *Basic concepts in eidectic psychotherapy* (2nd ed.). New York: Brandon House.

Ahsen, A. (1982). Imagery in perceptual learning and clinical application. *Journal of Mental Imagery, 6*, 157–186.

Ahsen, A. (1984). ISM: The triple code model for imagery and psycho-physiology. *Journal of Mental Imagery, 8*(4), 15–42.

Albert-Puleo, N. (1980). Modern psychoanalytic art therapy and its application to drug abuse. *The Arts in Psychotherapy, 7*(1), 43–52.

American Psychiatric Association. (1987). *Diagnostic and statistical manual of mental disorders* (DSM III-R) (3rd ed.). Washington, DC: Author.

Anastasi, A., & Foley, J. P. (1940). A survey of the literature on the artistic behavior in the abnormal: III. Spontaneous productions. *Psychological Monographs, 52*(6), 1–71.

Anastasi, A., & Foley, J. P. (1941a). A survey of the literature on artistic behavior in the abnormal: I. Historical and theoretical background. *Journal of General Psychology, 25*, 111–142.

Anastasi, A., & Foley, J. P. (1941b). A survey of the literature on artistic behavior in the abnormal: II. Approaches and interrelationships. *Annals of the New York Academy of Sciences, 42*, 1–112.

Anastasi, A., & Foley, J. P. (1941c). A survey of the literature on artistic behavior in the abnormal. IV. Experimental investigations. *Journal of General Psychology, 25*, 187–237.

Anderson, J. R. (1978). Arguments concerning representations for mental imagery. *Psychological Review, 85*(4), 249–277.

Apfel, R. J., & Sifneos, P. E. (1979). Alexithymia: Concept and measurement. *Psychotherapy and Psychosomatics, 32*, 180–190.

Arena, G. J., Andrasik, F., & Blanchard, E. B. (1985). The role of personality in the etiology of chronic headache. *Headache, 25,* 296–301.

Arieti, S. (1967). *The intrapsychic self. Feeling, cognition and creativity in health and mental illness.* London: Basic Books.

Arieti, S. (1973). Schizophrenic art and its relationship to modern art. *Journal of American Academy of Psychoanalysis, 1*(4), 333–365.

Arieti, S. (1974). *Interpretation of schizophrenia* (2nd ed.). New York: Basic Books.

Arieti, S. (1976). *Creativity: The magic synthesis.* New York: Basic Books.

Arnheim, R. (1969). *Visual thinking.* Berkeley: University of California Press.

Arnheim, R. (1972). *Toward a psychology of art.* Berkeley: University of California Press.

Arnheim, R. (1974). *Art and visual perception* (rev. ed.). Berkeley: University of California Press.

Arnheim, R. (1977). The art of psychotics. *Art Psychotherapy, 4*(3/4), 113–120.

Arnold, O. H. (1953). Über schöpferische Leistungen im Beginn Schizophrener Psychosen. *Wiener Zeitschrift für Nervenheilkunde, 7,* 188–206.

Assagioli, R. (1965). *Psychosynthesis.* New York: The Viking Press.

Bach, S. (1969). *Spontaneous paintings of severely ill patients.* Basel, Switzerland: Geigy.

Bader, A. (1972). Zugang Zur Bildnerei der Schizophrenen vor und nach Prinzhorn. *Confinia Psychiatrica, 15,* 101–115.

Baker, L. L., & Jessup, B. A. (1980). The psychology of affective verbal and visual information processing in dysphoria. *Cognitive Therapy and Research, 4*(2), 135–148.

Barlow, G. C. (1983). Media potential: Its use and misuse in art therapy. In A. Di Maria, E. S. Kramer, & E. A. Roth (Eds.), *Art therapy: Still growing. Proceedings of the 13th Annual Art Therapy Conference* (p. 112).

Barlow, G. C., Shupe, L., & Niswander, V. (1977). Media therapy: Increased options within the creative process. In R. H. Shoemaker & S. E. Gonick-Barris (Eds.), *Creativity and the art therapist's identity. The Proceedings of the 7th Annual Art Therapy Association Conference* (pp. 111–112).

Barron, F. (1953). Complexity-simplicity as a personality dimension. *Journal of Abnormal and Social Psychology, 48,* 163–172.

Barten, S. S. (1980). How does the child know? Origins of the symbol in the theories of Piaget and Werner. *Journal of the American Academy of Psychoanalysis, 8*(1), 77–94.

Battle, J. (1980). Relationship between self-esteem and depression among high school students. *Perceptual and Motor Skills, 51*(1), 157–158.

Beck, A. T. (1967). *Depression: Clinical, experimental and theoretical aspects.* New York: Harper & Row.

Beck, A. T. (1970). Role of fantasies in psychotherapy and psychopathology. *Journal of Nervous and Mental Diseases, 150*(1), 3–17.

Beck, A. T. (1976). *Cognitive therapy and the emotional disorders.* New York: International Universities Press.

Beck, A. T., & Hurvich, M. S. (1959). Psychological correlates of depression: I. Frequency of "masochistic" dream content in a private practice sample. *Psychosomatic Medicine, 21,* 50–55.

Bell, S. M. (1970). The development of the concept of object as related to infant-mother attachment. *Child Development, 41,* 291–311.

Bertalanffy, L. von. (1968). *General systems theory.* New York: Braziller.

Betensky, M. (1973a). Patterns of visual expression in art psychotherapy. *Art Psychotherapy, 1*(2), 121–129.

Betensky, M. (1973b). *Self-discovery through self-expression.* Springfield, Ill: Charles C Thomas.

Betensky, M. (1977). The phenomenological approach to art expression and art psychotherapy. *Art Psychotherapy*, 4(3/4), 173–179.

Betensky, M. (1983). Media potential. Its use and misuse in therapy. In A. Di Maria, E. S. Kramer, & E. A. Roth (Eds.), *Art therapy: Still growing. Proceedings of the 13th Annual Conference of the American Art Therapy Association* (pp. 112–113).

Betensky, M. G. (1987). Phenomenology of therapeutic art expression and art therapy. In J. A. Rubin (Ed.), *Approaches to art therapy: Theory and technique* (pp. 149–166). New York: Brunner/Mazel.

Betensky, M., & Nucho, A. (1982). The phenomenological approach to art therapy. In L. Gantt & A. Evans (Eds.), *Focus on the future: The next ten years. Proceedings of the 10th Annual Conference of the American Art Therapy Association* (pp. 137–141).

Billig, O. (1966). Cross-cultural factors of schizophrenic art. *Excerpta Medica International, Congressional Series No. 150.*

Billig, O. (1968). Spatial structure in schizophrenic art. In I. Jakob (Ed.), *Psychiatry and art* (pp. 1–16). Basel: Karger.

Billig, O. (1970). Structures of schizophrenic forms of expression. *Psychiatric Quarterly, 44*, 187–222.

Billig, O. (1971). Is schizophrenic expression art? *Journal of Nervous and Mental Disease, 153*, 149–164.

Billig, O. (1973). The schizophrenic "artist's" expression of movement. *Confinia Psychiatrica, 16*, 1–27.

Billig, O., & Burton-Bradley, B. G. (1978). *The painted message.* New York: John Wiley & Sons.

Birren, F. (1961). *Color psychology and color therapy.* New York: Universal Books.

Blos, P. (1962). *On adolescence: A psychoanalytic interpretation.* New York: The Free Press.

Bogen, J. E., & Bogen, G. M. (1969). The other side of the brain III: The corpus callosum and creativity. *Bulletin of the Los Angeles Neurological Societies, 34*(4), 191–220.

Bolen, J. S. (1984). *Goddesses in everywoman: A new psychology of women.* San Francisco: Harper & Row.

Bolen, J. S. (1989). *Gods in everyman: A new psychology of men's lives and loves.* San Francisco: Harper & Row.

Bower, G. H. (1970). Analysis of a mnemonic device. *American Scientist, 58*(5), 496–510.

Brenner, C. (1955). *An elementary textbook of psychoanalysis.* New York: Doubleday.

Bresler, D. E., & Trubo, R. (1979). *Free yourself from pain.* New York: Simon and Schuster.

Bruner, J. S. (1964). The course of cognitive growth. *American Psychologist, 19*, 1–15.

Buchalter-Katz, S. (1989). "Barrier" drawings for depressed patients. In H. Wadeson, F. Durkin, & D. Perach (Eds.), *Advances in art therapy* (pp. 357–371). New York: Wiley.

Bugelski, B. R. (1983). Imagery and thought process. In A. A. Sheikh (Ed.), *Imagery: Current theory, research and application* (pp. 72–95). New York: Wiley.

Burns, R. C., & Kaufman, S. H. (1970). *Kinetic family drawings* (KFD). New York: Brunner/Mazel.

Burns, R. C., & Kaufman, S. H. (1972). *Action styles and symbols in kinetic family drawings* (KFD). New York: Brunner/Mazel.

Campos, J. J., & Barrett, K. C. (1984). Toward a new understanding of emotions and their development. In C. E. Izard, J. Kagan, & R. B. Zajonc (Eds.), *Emotions, cognition, and behavior* (pp. 229–263). Cambridge, England: Cambridge University Press.

Carlson, G. A., &, Garber, J. (1986). Developmental issues in the classification of depression in children. In M. Rutter, C. E. Izard, & P. B. Read (Eds.), *Depression in young people* (pp. 399–434). New York: Guilford Press.

Carnes, J. J. (1979a). Toward a cognitive approach to art therapy. In L. Gantt, G. Forrest, D.

Silverman, & R. J. H. Shoemaker (Eds.), *Art therapy: Expanding horizons. Proceedings of the 9th Annual Art Therapy Conference* (pp. 91–92).

Carnes, J. J. (1979b). Toward a cognitive theory of art therapy. *Art Psychotherapy, 6*(2), 69–76.

Cartwright, R. D., Lloyd, S., Knight, S., & Trenholme, I. (1984). Broken dreams: A study of the effects of divorce and depression on dream content. *Psychiatry, 47,* 251–259.

Cautela, J. R. (1979). Covert conditioning: Assumptions and procedures. In D. Upper & J. R. Cautela (Eds.), *Covert conditioning* (pp. 3–16). New York: Pergamon Press.

Cautela, J. R., & McCullough, L. (1978). Covert conditioning: a learning-theory perspective on imagination. In J. L. Singer & K. S. Pope (Eds.), *The power of human imagination* (pp. 227–254). New York: Plenum.

Celentano, F. (1977). Progression in paintings by schizophrenics. *American Journal of Art Therapy, 16*(2), 68–73.

Chartier, G. M., & Ranieri, D. J. (1984). Adolescent depression: Concepts, treatments, prevention. *Advances in Child Behavioral Analysis and Therapy, 3,* 153–193.

Chiles, J. A., Miller, M. L., & Cox, G. B. (1980). Depression in an adolescent delinquent population. *Archives of General Psychiatry, 37,* 1179–1184.

Cohen, D. B. (1977). Changes in REM dream content during the night: Implications for a hypothesis about changes in cerebral dominance across REM periods. *Perceptual and Motor Skills, 44,* 1267–1277.

Comfort, C. E. (1985). Published pictures as psychotherapeutic tools. *The Arts in Psychotherapy, 12*(4), 245–256.

Cytryn, L., & McKnew, D. H. (1972). Proposed classification of childhood depression. *American Journal of Psychiatry, 129*(2), 149–155.

Cytryn, L., & McKnew, D. H. (1974). Factors influencing the changing clinical expression of the depressive process in children. *American Journal of Psychiatry, 131*(8), 879–881.

Cytryn, L., & McKnew, D. H. (1979). Affective disorders. In J. D. Nospnitz (Ed.), *Basic handbook of child psychiatry* (Vol. II, pp. 321–340). New York: Basic Books.

Davidoff, J. (1976). Hemispheric sensitivity differences in the perception of colour. *Quarterly Journal of Experimental Psychology, 28,* 387–394.

Demers-Desrosiers, L. (1982). Influence of alexithymia on symbolic function. *Psychotherapy and Psychosomatics, 38,* 103–120.

Demers-Desrosiers, L. A. (1985). Empirical journey into the measurement of symbolic function in alexithymia. *Psychotherapy and Psychosomatics, 44,* 65–71.

Demers-Desrosiers, L. A., Cohen, K. R., Catchlove, R. F. H., & Ramsay, R. A. (1983). The measure of symbolic function as a dimension of alexithymic pain patients. *Psychotherapy and Psychosomatics, 39,* 65–76.

Denner, A. (1967). *L'Expression plastique: Pathologie et rééducation des schizophrenes.* Paris: Les Editions Sociales Francaises.

Dessoille, R. (1966). *The directed daydream.* New York: Psychosynthesis Research Foundation.

Dimond, S. J., & Beaumont, J. G. (1974). Experimental studies of hemisphere function in the human brain. In S. J. Dimond & J. G. Beaumont (Eds.), *Hemisphere function in the human brain* (pp. 48–88). New York: Halsted Press, Wiley.

Dumas, R., & Morgan, A. (1975). EEG asymmetry as a function of occupation, task, and task difficulty. *Neuropsychologica, 13,* 219–228.

Edinger, E. F. (1973). *Ego and archetype.* Baltimore: Penguin.

Edwards, B. (1979). *Drawing on the right side of the brain.* Los Angeles: J. P. Tarcher.

Ehrenzweig, A. (1971). *Hidden order of art.* Berkeley: University of California Press.

Ehrlichman, H., & Wiener, M. S. (1980). EEG asymmetry during covert mental activity. *Psychophysiology, 17*(3), 228–235.

Epstein, G. (1981). *Waking dream therapy: Dream process as imagination.* New York: Human Sciences Press.

Ey, H. (1973). *Traité des hallucinations* (Tome 1 et 2). Paris: Masson et Cie, Editeurs.

Faber, P. A., Saayman, G. S., & Papadopoulos, R. K. (1983). Induced waking fantasy. *Journal of Analytical Psychology, 28,* 141–164.

Feldenkrais, M. (1972). *Awareness through movement.* New York: Harper & Row.

Feldman, E. B. (1972). *Varieties of visual experience.* New York: Harry N. Abrams.

Fine, H. J., & Zimet, C. N. (1959). Process-reactive schizophrenia and genetic levels of perception. *Journal of Abnormal and Social Psychology, 59,* 83–86.

Fischer, K. W., & Pipp, S. L. (1984). Development of structures of unconscious thought. In K. S. Bowers & D. Meichenbaum (Eds.), *The unconscious reconsidered* (pp. 88–148). New York: Wiley.

Fleming, M. M. (1983). Early object loss and its relation to creativity as expressed through art therapy. In A. Di Maria, E. S. Kramer, & E. A. Roth (Eds.), *Art therapy: Still growing. Proceedings of the 13th Annual Conference of the American Art Therapy Association* (pp. 53–57).

Fleming, M. M., & Cox, C. T. (1989). Engaging the somatic patient in healing through art. In H. Wadeson, J. Durkin, & D. Petach (Eds.), *Advances in art therapy* (pp. 169–180). New York: Wiley.

Forisha, B. L. (1978). Mental imagery and creativity: Review and Speculations. *Journal of Mental Imagery, 2*(2), 209–238.

Fosshage, J. L. (1983). The psychological function of dreams: A revised psychoanalytic perspective. *Psychoanalysis and Contemporary Thought, 6*(4), 641–669.

Foulkes, D. (1977). Children's dreams: Age changes and sex differences. *Waking and Sleeping, 1,* 171–174.

Foulkes, D. (1978). *A grammar of dreams.* New York: Basic Books.

Foulkes, D. (1982). *Children's dreams: Longitudinal studies.* New York: Wiley.

Foulkes, D. (1985). *Dreaming: A cognitive psychological analysis.* Hillsdale, NJ: Lawrence Erlbaum.

Franz, von, M. L. (1968). The process of individuation. In C. G. Jung (Ed.), *Man and his symbols* (pp. 255–322). New York: Dell.

Frétigny, R., & Virel, A. (1968). *L'imagerie mentale.* Geneva: Mont Blank.

Freud, A. (1942). *The ego and the mechanisms of defense.* London: Hogarth Press.

Freud, A. (1965). *Normality and pathology in childhood: Assessments of development.* New York: International Universities Press.

Freud, S. (1967). *Interpretation of dreams.* New York: Avon-Discus Books.

Freyberger, H. (1977). Supportive psychotherapeutic techniques in primary and secondary alexithymia. *Psychotherapy and Psychosomatics, 28,* 337–342.

Friedman, B. J. (1974). The subjective experience of perceptual and cognitive disturbances in schizophrenia. *Archives of General Psychiatry, 30,* 333–340.

Friedman, H. S., & Booth-Kewley, S. (1987). The "disease prone personality." A meta-analytic view of the construct. *American Psychologist, 42*(6), 539–555.

Furth, H. G. (1981). *Piaget and knowledge* (2nd ed.). Chicago: The University of Chicago Press.

Gale, A., Morris, P. E., Lucas, B., & Richardson, A. (1972). Types of imagery and imagery types: An EEG study. *British Journal of Psychology, 63*(4), 523–531.

Galenson, E., Miller, R., & Roiphe, H. (1976). The choice of symbols. *Journal of the American Academy of Child Psychiatry, 15*(1), 83–96.

Gantt, L. (1979). The other side of art therapy. *American Journal of Art Therapy, 19*(1), 11–18.

Garai, J. E. (1976). New vistas in the exploration of inner and outer space through art therapy. *Art Psychotherapy, 3*(3/4), 157–167.

Garai, J. E. (1978). Birth, death, and rebirth in the struggle for creative expression. In B. K. Mandel, R. H. Shoemaker, & R. E. Hays (Eds.), *The dynamics of creativity. Proceedings of the 8th Annual Conference of the American Art Therapy Association* (pp. 8–13).

Garai, J. E. (1987). A humanistic approach to art therapy. In J. A. Rubin (Ed.), *Approaches to art therapy: Theory and technique* (pp. 188–207). New York: Brunner/Mazel.

Gates, C. (1978). *A manual for cancer.* Boston: American Cancer Society.

Gentry, W. D., Shows, W. D., & Thomas, M. (1974). Chronic low back pain: A psychological profile. *Psychosomatics, 15*, 174–177.

Gerard, R. (1964). *Psychosynthesis: A psychotherapy for the whole man.* New York: Psychosynthesis Research Foundation.

Getzels, J. W., & Csikszentmihalyi, M. (1975). From problem solving to problem finding. In I. A. Taylor & J. W. Getzels (Eds.), *Perspectives in creativity* (pp. 90–116). Chicago: Aldine.

Ghiselin, B. (Ed.). (1952). *The creative process.* New York: Mentor Books, New American Library.

Giambra, L. M., & Traynor, T. D. (1978). Depression and daydreaming: An analysis based on self-ratings. *Journal of Clinical Psychology, 34*, 14–25.

Gibson, G. (1966). *The senses considered as perceptual systems.* Boston: Houghton-Mifflin.

Gold, S. R., & Henderson, B. B. (1984). Adolescent daydreaming. In A. A. Sheikh (Ed.), *International review of mental imagery* (Vol. 1, pp. 139–157). New York: Human Sciences Press.

Gordon, R. (1949). An investigation into some factors that favor the formation of stereotyped images. *British Journal of Psychology, 39*, 156–167.

Gordon, R. (1950). An experiment correlating the nature of imagery with performance on a test of reversal of perspective. *British Journal of Psychology, 41*, 63–67.

Graves, S. L. (1982). *Children's drawings as predictors of prognosis in cancer.* Unpublished doctoral dissertation, University of Louisville, Louisville, Kentucky.

Graves (Kagin), S. L. (1983). Media potential: Its use and misuse in therapy. In A. Di Maria, E. S. Kramer, & E. A. Roth (Eds.), *Art therapy: Still growing. Proceedings of the 13th Annual Conference of the American Art Therapy Association* (p. 113).

Greenspan, S. I. (1979). Intelligence and adaptation. *Psychological Issues* (Vol. 12 [3/4, Whole Monographs 47/48]). New York: International Universities Press.

Griffis, S. L. (1978). *Bradley Y. Profile of an obsessive child.* Unpublished master's of art degree paper, University of Louisville, Louisville, KY.

Grof, S. (1976). *Realms of the human unconscious. Observations from LSD Research.* New York: E. P. Dutton.

Grossman, F. G. (1981). Creativity as a means of coping with anxiety. *The Arts in Psychotherapy, 8*(3/4), 185–192.

Halbreich, U., & Assael, M. (1979). Drawing of cephalopodes by schizophrenic patients, and their meaning. *Art Psychotherapy, 6*(1), 19–23.

Hall, D. C. (1974). Eye movements in scanning iconic imagery. *Journal of Experimental Psychology, 103*(5), 825–830.

Hammer, E. F. (1958). *The clinical applications of projective drawings.* Springfield, Ill: Charles C. Thomas.

Harrell, J. P. (1980). Psychological factors and hypertension: A status report. *Psychological Bulletin, 87*(3), 482–501.

Hauri, P. (1976). Dreams in patients remitted from reactive depression. *Journal of Abnormal Psychology, 85*(1), 1–10.

Hays, R. (1982). Dot to dot: Rationale for a "New Projective" for children under ten. In L. Gantt & A. Evans (Eds.), *Focus on the future: The next ten years. Proceedings of the 10th Annual Conference of the American Art Therapy Association* (pp. 116–121).

Henderson, J. L. (1973). The picture method in Jungian psychotherapy. *Art Psychotherapy, 1*(2), 135–140.

Henderson, B. B., Gold, S. R., & Clarke, K. (1984). Individual differences in IQ, daydreaming and moral reasoning in gifted and average adolescents. *International Journal of Behavioral Development, 7*(2), 215–230.

Herman, J. H. (1984). Experimental investigations of the psychophysiology of REM sleep including questions of lateralization. *Research Communications in Psychology, Psychiatry and Behavior, 9*(1), 53–75.

Hesse, P. P. (1981). Color, form, and silence: A formal analysis of drawings of a child who did not speak. *The Arts in Psychotherapy, 8*(3/4), 175–184.

Hillman, J. (1977). An inquiry into image. *Spring* (pp. 62–88). Zurich: Spring Publications.

Hillman, J. (1983). *Archetypal psychology*. Dallas, TX: Spring Publications.

Hoffman, A. L. (1974). Psychological factors associated with rheumatoid arthritis. *Nursing Research, 23*(3), 218–234.

Holmes, T. H., & Rahe, R. H. (1967). The social readjustment scale. *Journal of Psychosomatic Research, 11*, 213–218.

Holt, R. R. (1964). The return of the ostrasized. *American Psychologist, 12*, 254–264.

Holt, R. R. (1967). The development of the primary process: A structural view. *Psychological Issues* (Vol. 5, Monographs 18/19, pp. 345–383). New York: International Universities Press.

Honig, S. (1977). Art therapy in treatment of schizophrenia. *Art Psychotherapy, 4*(2), 99–104.

Honig, S., & Hanes, K. M. (1982). Structured art therapy with the chronic patient in long-term residential treatment. *The Arts in Psychotherapy, 9*(4), 269–289.

Hooke, J. F., Youell, K. J., & Etkin, M. W. (1975). Color preference and arousal. *Perceptual and Motor Skills, 40*, 710.

Horowitz, M. J. (1970). *Image formation and cognition*. New York: Appleton-Century-Crofts.

Horowitz, M. J. (1972). Image formation: Clinical observations and a cognitive model. In P. W. Sheehan (Ed.), *The function and nature of imagery* (pp. 282–309). New York: Academic Press.

Horowitz, M. J. (1978). Controls of visual imagery and therapist intervention. In J. L. Singer & K. S. Pope (Eds.), *The power of human imagination* (pp. 37–49). New York: Plenum.

Horowitz, M. J. (1983). *Image formation and psychotherapy* (rev. ed., *Image formation and cognition*). New York: Jason Aronson.

Howard, J. (1981). The expression and possible origins of depression in male adolescent delinquents. *Australian and New Zealand Journal of Psychiatry, 15*(4), 311–318.

Izard, C. E. (1972). *Patterns of emotions*. New York: Academic Press.

Izard, C. E. (1977). *Human emotions*. New York: Plenum.

Izard, C. E. (1984). Emotion-cognition relationships and human development. In C. E. Izard, J. Kagan, & R. B. Zajonc (Eds.), *Emotions, cognition and behavior* (pp. 17–37). Cambridge, England: Cambridge University Press.

Jacobi, J. (1959). *Complex/archetype/symbol in psychology of C. G. Jung*. Bollingen Series LVII. Princeton, NJ: Princeton University Press.

Jacobs, W., & Hustmyer, F. E., Jr. (1974). Effects of four psychological primary colors on GSR, heart rate and respiration rate. *Perceptual and Motor Skills, 38*, 763–766.

Jacobson, E. (1929). *Progressive relaxation*. Chicago, Ill: The University of Chicago Press.

Jacobson, E. (1930). Electrical measurements of neuromuscular states during mental activities: II. Imagination and recollection of various muscular acts. *American Journal of Physiology, 94*, 22–34.

Jones, D. L., & Rush, K. (1979). Treatment of psychotic patients with preoccupations of demon possession. *Art Psychotherapy, 6*(1), 1–9.

Jones, G. E., & Johnson, H. J. (1980). Heart rate and somatic concomitants of mental imagery. *Psychophysiology, 17*(4), 339–347.

Jung, C. G. (1956). *Two essays on analytical psychology.* New York: Meridian Books.

Jung, C. G. (1960). *The structure and dynamics of the psyche.* Bollingen Series XX (Vol. 8). New York: Pantheon.

Jung, C. G. (1968). *Man and his symbols.* New York: Dell.

Jung, C. G. (1969). *On the nature of psyche.* Princeton, NJ: Princeton University Press.

Jung, C. G. (1970). *Analytical psychology: Its theory and practice.* New York: Vintage Books, Random House.

Jung, C. G. (1972). *Mandala symbolism. Bollingen Series.* Princeton, NJ: Princeton University Press.

Kagin, S. (1969). *The effects of structure on the painting of retarded youth.* Unpublished master's thesis, University of Tulsa, Tulsa, Okla.

Kagin, S. L. (1978). Perception and the encephalopod: Human figure drawings by four year olds. *Art Psychotherapy, 5*(3), 143–147.

Kagin, S. L., & Lusebrink, V. B. (1978). The Expressive Therapies Continuum. *Art Psychotherapy, 5*(4), 171–179.

Kaufman, J. (1984). Mental imagery in problem solving. In A. A. Sheikh (Ed.), *International review of mental imagery* (Vol. 1, pp. 23–55). New York: Human Sciences Press.

Kazdin, A. E. (1978). Covert modeling: The therapeutic application of imagined rehearsal. In J. L. Singer & K. S. Pope (Eds.), *The power of human imagination* (pp. 255–278). New York: Plenum.

Kelly, G. A. (1955). *The psychology of personal constructs.* New York: Norton.

Kepecs, J. (1954). Observations on screens and barriers in the mind. *Psychoanalytic Quarterly, 23*, 62–77.

Kern, J. W. (1978). Countertransference and spontaneous screens: An analyst studies his own visual images. *Journal of American Psychoanalytic Association, 26*, 21–47.

Kieras, D. (1978). Beyond pictures and words: Alternative information processing models for imagery effects in verbal memory. *Psychological Bulletin, 85*(3), 532–554.

Klinger, E. (1971). *Structures and functions of fantasy.* New York: Wiley Interscience.

Klinger, E. (1978). Modes of normal conscious flow. In K. S. Pope & J. L. Singer (Eds.), *The stream of consciousness* (pp. 226–258). New York: Plenum.

Klinger, E. (1980). Therapy and the flow of thought. In J. E. Shorr, G. E. Sobel, P. Robin, & J. A. Connella (Eds.), *Imagery: Its many dimensions and applications* (pp. 1–20). New York: Plenum.

Klinger, E. (1987). The power of daydreams. *Psychology Today, 21*(10), 37–44.

Klüver, H. (1966). *Mescal and mechanisms of hallucinations.* Chicago: The University of Chicago Press.

Koestler, A. (1964). *The act of creation.* London: Hutchison.

Korn, E. R., & Johnson, K. (1983). *Visualization: The uses of imagery in health professions.* Homewood, Ill: Dow Jones-Irving.

Kosslyn, S. M. (1980). *Image and mind.* Cambridge, Mass: Harvard University Press

Kovacs, M., & Beck, A. T. (1979). Cognitive-affective processes in depression. In C. E. Izard (Ed.), *Emotions in personality and psychopathology* (pp. 417–442). New York: Plenum.

Kramer, E. (1958). *Art therapy in a children's community.* Springfield, Ill: Charles C Thomas.

Kramer, E. (1971). *Art as therapy with children*. New York: Schocken.

Kramer, E. (1979). *Childhood and art therapy*. New York: Schocken.

Kramer, M. (1982). The psychology of the dream: Art or science? *The Psychiatric Journal of the University of Ottawa*, 7(2), 87–91.

Kramer, M., Baldridge, B. J., Whitman, R. M., Ornstein, P. H., & Smith, P. C. (1969). An exploration of the manifest dream in schizophrenic and depressed patients. *Diseases of the Nervous System*, 30, 126–130.

Kramer, M., Whitman, R. M., Baldridge, B. J., & Lansky, L. (1966). Dreaming in the depressed. *Canadian Psychiatric Association Journal*, 11, 178–192.

Krantz, S. E., & Rude, S. (1984). Depressive attributions: Selections of different causes or assignment of dimensional meanings? *Journal of Personality and Social Psychology*, 47(1), 193–203.

Kreitler, H., & Kreitler, S. (1972). *Psychology of the arts*. Durham, NC: Duke University Press.

Kris, E. (1952). *Psychoanalytic explorations in art*. New York: International Universities Press.

Krystal, H. (1979). Alexithymia and psychotherapy. *American Journal of Psychotherapy*, 33(1), 17–31.

Kubie, L. S. (1961). *Neurotic distortion of the creative process*. New York: Noonday Press.

Kuhn, C. C. (1988). A spiritual inventory of the medically ill patient. *Psychiatric Medicine*, 6(2), 87–100

Kunkle-Miller, C., & Aach, S. (1983). Presymbolic levels of expression—their relation to the theory and practice of art therapy. In L. Gantt & S. Whitman (Eds.), *The fine art of therapy. Proceedings of the 11th Conference of the American Art Therapy Association* (pp. 55–57).

LaBerge, S. P. (1980). Lucid dreaming as a learnable skill. *Perceptual and Motor Skills*, 51(3, pt. 2), 1039–1042.

Landgarten, H. B. (1981) *Clinical art therapy*. New York: Brunner/Mazel.

Lang, P. J. (1979). Presidential address, 1978: A bio-informational theory of emotional imagery. *Psychophysiology*, 16(6), 495–512.

Lang, P. J. (1984). Cognition in emotion: Concept and action. In C. E. Izard, J. Kagan, & R. B. Zajonc (Eds.), *Emotions, cognition, and behavior* (pp. 192–226). Cambridge, England: Cambridge University Press.

Lang, P. J., Levin, D. N., Miller, G. A., & Kozak, M. J. (1983). Fear behavior, fear imagery and the psychophysiology of emotion: The problem of affective response integration. *Journal of Abnormal Psychology*, 92(3), 276–306.

Lanyon, R. I., & May, A. C. (1979). Relationship between spontaneous imagery distortions and schizophrenic psychopathology. *Journal of Mental Imagery*, 3, 43–52.

Lazarus, R. S. (1982). Thoughts on the relations between emotion and cognition. *American Psychologist*, 37(9), 1019–1024.

Lesse, S. (1974). Depression masked by acting-out behavior patterns. *American Journal of Psychotherapy*, 28, 352–361.

Lesse, S. (1981). Hypochondriacal and psychosomatic disorders masking depression in adolescents. *American Journal of Psychotherapy*, 35(3), 356–367.

Leuner, H. (1977). Guided Affective Imagery: An account of its development. *Journal of Mental Imagery*, 1, 73–92.

Leuner, H. (1978). Basic principles and therapeutic efficacy of Guided Affective Imagery (GAI). In J. L. Singer & K. S. Pope (Eds.), *The power of human imagination* (pp. 125–166). New York: Plenum.

Leuner, H. (1984). *Guided Affective Imagery*. New York: Thieme Stratton.

Leuner, H., Horn, G., & Klessmann, F. (1983). *Guided Affective Imagery with children and adolescents*. New York: Plenum.

Leventhal, H., & Mosbach, P. A. (1983). The perceptual-motor theory of emotion. In J. T. Cacioppo & R. E. Petty (Eds.), *Social psychophysiology* (pp. 353–388). New York: Guilford.

Leventhal, H., & Tomarken, A. J. (1986). Emotion: Today's problem. *Annual Reviews of Psychology, 37*, 565–610.

Levick, M. F. (1967). The goals of the art therapist as compared to those of the art teacher. *Journal of Albert Einstein Medical Center, 15*, 157–170.

Levick, M. F. (1980). Group dynamics of dependency and counterdependency manifested in drawings of graduate art, movement, and music therapy students. *The Arts in Psychotherapy, 7*(2), 87–96.

Levick, M. F. (1983). *They could not talk and so they drew: Children's styles of coping and thinking.* Springfield, Ill: Charles C Thomas.

Levick, M. F. (1984). Imagery as a style of thinking. *Art Therapy, 1*(3), 119–124.

Levitan, H. L. (1978). The significance of certain dreams reported by psychosomatic patients. *Psychotherapy and Psychosomatics, 30*, 137–149.

Levitan, H. L. (1980a). The dream in psychosomatic states. In J. M. Natterson (Ed.), *The dream in clinical practice* (pp. 225–236). New York: Jason Aronson.

Levitan, H. L. (1980b). Traumatic events in dreams of psychosomatic patients. *Psychotherapy and Psychosomatics, 33*, 226–232.

Levitan, H. L. (1981). Failure of the defensive functions of the ego in dreams of psychosomatic patients. *Psychotherapy and Psychosomatics, 36*, 1–7.

Levitan, H. L. (1984). Dreams which culminate in migraine headaches. *Psychotherapy and Psychosomatics, 41*, 161–166.

Levy, B. I. (1980). Research into the psychological meaning of color. *American Journal of Art Therapy, 19*(4), 87–91.

Levy, J., Treverthen, C., & Sperry, R. W. (1972). Perception of bilateral chimeric figures following hemispheric disconnexion. *Bruin, 95*, 61–78.

Lewis, M., & Michalson, L. (1983). *Children's emotions and moods: Developmental theory and measurement.* New York: Plenum.

Ley, R. G. (1983). Cerebral laterality and imagery. In A. A. Sheikh (Ed.), *Imagery: Current theory, research and application* (pp. 252–287). New York: Wiley.

Ley, R. G., & Freeman, R. J. (1984). Imagery, cerebral laterality, and the healing process. In A. A. Sheikh (Ed.), *Imagination and healing: Imagery and human development series* (pp. 51–68). Farmingdale, NY: Baywood Publishing.

Lowenfeld, V., & Brittain, W. L. (1970). *Creative and mental growth* (5th ed.). New York: Macmillan.

Lusebrink, V. B. (1974). *Visual expression, creativity and reconstitution in psychosis.* Presentation at the 5th Annual Conference of the American Art Therapy Association, New York.

Lusebrink, V. B. (1975). *A study of the formal elements of the abstract pictorial expression of self: Preliminary research report.* Paper presented at the 6th Annual Conference of the American Art Therapy Association, Louisville, Ky.

Lusebrink, V. B. (1977). *Psychotic art.* Presentation, Grand Rounds, University of California Medical School, Sacramento, Calif.

Lusebrink, V. B. (1980). *Visual expression in chronic and acute psychosis.* Unpublished manuscript.

Lusebrink, V. B. (1982). Transformations and gates through art media. In A. E. Di Maria, E. S. Kramer, & I. Rosner, (Eds.), *Art therapy: A bridge between worlds. Proceedings of the 12th Annual Conference of the American Art Therapy Association* (pp. 63–67).

Lusebrink, V. B. (1983). Expressive styles in art and art therapy. In L. Gantt & S. Whitman (Eds.), *The fine art of therapy. Proceedings of the 11th Annual Conference of the American Art Therapy Association* (pp. 57–60).

Lusebrink, V. B. (1986–1987). Visual imagery: Its psycho-physiological components and levels of information processing. *Imagination, Cognition, and Personality, 6*(3), 205–218.

Lusebrink, V. B. (1987). *Cognitive integration of dream sequences and affect.* Paper presented at the 18th Annual Conference of the American Art Therapy Association, Miami Beach, Fla.

Lusebrink, V. B. (1988). Inner guide. *Art Therapy, 5*(3), 99–105.

Lusebrink, V. B., Agell, G. L., Barlow, G. C., Betensky, M., Graves, S., Rosenberg H., & Rubin, J. A. (1983). Media potential: Its use and misuse in art therapy. In A. Di Maria, E. S. Kramer, & E. A. Ross (Eds.), *Art therapy: Still growing. Proceedings of the 13th Annual Conference of the American Art Therapy Association* (pp. 111–115).

Luthe, W. (1969). *Autogenic therapy,* (Vol. 1). New York: Grune & Stratton.

Luthe, W. (1976). *Creativity mobilization technique.* New York: Grune & Stratton.

Lyddiatt, E. M. (1971). *Spontaneous painting and modeling.* London: Constable.

Lyman, B., & Waters, C. E. (1989). Patterns of imagery in various emotions. *Journal of Mental Imagery, 13*(1), 63–74.

MacKinnon, D. W. (1975). IPAR's contribution to the conceptualization and study of creativity. In I. A. Taylor & J. W. Getzels (Eds.), *Perspectives in creativity* (pp. 60–89). Chicago: Aldine.

Maddi, S. R. (1975). The strenuousness of the creative life. In I. A. Taylor & J. W. Getzels (Eds.), *Perspectives in creativity* (pp. 173–190). Chicago: Aldine.

Mahler, M. S. (1963). Thoughts about development and individuation. *The Psychoanalytic Study of the Child, 18,* 307–324.

Mahler, M. S. (1965). On the significance of the normal separation-individuation phase: With reference to research in symbiotic child psychosis. In M. Schur (Ed.), *Drives, affects, behavior* (Vol. 2, pp. 161–169). New York: International Universities Press.

Marks, D. F. (1973a). Visual imagery differences and eye movements in the recall of pictures. *Perception and Psychophysics, 14*(3), 407–412.

Marks, D. F. (1973b). Visual imagery differences in the recall of pictures. *British Journal of Psychology, 64*(1), 17–24.

Marks, D. F. (1983). Mental imagery and consciousness: A theoretical review. In A. Sheikh (Ed.), *Imagery: Current theory research and application* (pp. 96–130). New York: Wiley.

Martin, J. B., & Pihl, R. O. (1985). The stress-alexithymia hypothesis: Theoretical and empirical considerations. *Psychotherapy and Psychosomatics, 43,* 169–176.

Maslow, A. H. (1971). *The farther reaches of human nature.* New York: Viking.

Masters, R. E. L., & Houston, J. (1968). *Psychedelic art.* New York: Blanche House.

McConeghey, H. (1980). *The body of the image.* Unpublished manuscript.

McGuigan, F. J. (1978a). *Cognitive psychophysiology: Principles of covert behavior.* Englewood Cliffs, NJ: Prentice-Hall.

McGuigan, F. J. (1978b). Imagery and thinking: Covert functioning in the motor system. In G. E. Schwartz & D. Shapiro (Eds.), *Consciousness and self regulation: Advances in research and theory* (Vol. 2, pp. 37–100). New York: Plenum.

McNiff, S. A. (1977). Motivation in art. *Art Psychotherapy, 4*(3/4), 125–136.

McNiff, S. A. (1981). *The arts and psychotherapy.* Springfield, Ill: Charles C Thomas.

Meichenbaum, D. (1977). *Cognitive-behavior modification: An integrative approach.* New York: Plenum.

Meichenbaum, D. (1978). Why does using imagery in psychotherapy lead to change? In J.

L. Singer & K. S. Pope (Eds.), *The power of human imagination* (pp. 381–394). New York: Plenum.

Meichenbaum, D., & Gilmore, J. B. (1984). The nature of unconscious processes: A cognitive-behavioral perspective. In K. S. Bowers & D. Meichenbaum (Eds.), *The unconscious reconsidered* (pp. 273–298). New York: Wiley.

Miljkovitch, M., & Irwine, G. M. (1982). Comparison of drawing performances of schizophrenics, other psychiatric patients and normal schoolchildren on a Draw-a-Village task. *The Arts in Psychotherapy, 9*(3), 203–216.

Miller, L. (1988). The emotional brain. *Psychology Today*, Feb., 35–42.

Molinari, S., & Foulkes, D. (1969). Tonic and phasic events during sleep: Psychological correlates and implications. *Perceptual and Motor Skills*, Monograph Supplement, I-V29, 334–368.

Morgan, A. H., McDonald, H., & Hilgard, E. R. (1974). EEG alpha: Lateral asymmetry related to task and hypnotizability. *Physiopsychology, 11*(3), 275–282.

Morgan, A. H., McDonald, P. J., & McDonald, H. (1971). Differences in bilateral alpha activity as a function of experimental task, with a note on lateral eye movement and hypnotizability. *Neuropsychologia, 9*, 459–469.

Motokawa, K. (1970). *Physiology of color and pattern vision.* Berlin–New York: Springer Verlag.

Muuss, R. E. (1980). Peter Blos' modern psychoanalytical interpretation of adolescence. *Journal of Adolescence, 3*, 229–252.

M'Uzan, de M. (1974). Psychodynamic mechanisms in psychosomatic symptom formation. *Psychotherapy and Psychosomatics, 23*, 103–110.

Naumburg, M. (1950). *Schizophrenic art: Its meaning in art therapy.* New York: Grune & Stratton.

Naumburg, M. (1953). *Psychoneurotic art: Its function in psychotherapy.* New York: Grune & Stratton.

Naumburg, M. (1966). *Dynamically oriented art therapy: Its principles and practice.* New York: Grune & Stratton.

Naumburg, M. (1973). *An introduction to art therapy* (rev. ed.). New York: Teachers College Press.

Navratil, L. (1969). Psychose und Kreativität. *Hippokrates, 40*, 597–602.

Navratil, L. (1976). Die schizophrenen Gestaltungstendenzen. Im A. Bader und L. Navratil, *Zwischen Wahn und Wirklichkeit: Kunst, Psychose, Kreativität.* Luzern: Verlag C. J. Bucher.

Neisser, U. (1967). *Cognitive psychology.* New York: Appleton-Century-Crofts.

Neisser, U. (1978). Anticipations, images and introspection. *Cognition, 6*, 169–174.

Noy, P. (1979). The psychoanalytic theory of cognitive development. *Psychoanalytic Study of the Child, 31*, 169–216.

Nucho, A. O. (1982). Client resistance to art therapy: Where does it come from and what can be done about it? In A. E. Di Maria, E. Kramer, & I. Rosner (Eds.), *Art therapy: A bridge between worlds. Proceedings of the 12th Annual Conference of the American Art Therapy Association* (pp. 27–30).

Nucho, A. O. (1983). Art therapy with depressed adults. In A. Di Maria (Ed.), *Proceedings of the 13th Annual Conference of the American Art Therapy Association* (pp. 25–29).

Nucho, A. O. (1987). *The psychocybernatic model of art therapy.* Springfield, Ill: Charles C Thomas.

O'Connor, K. (1986). The interaction of hostile and depressive behaviors: A case study of a depressed boy. *Journal Child and Adolescent Psychotherapy, 3*(2), 105–108.

Ogdon, D. P. (1977). *Psychodiagnostics and personality assessment: A handbook* (2nd ed.). Los Angeles, CA: Western Psychological Services.

Ogilvie, R. D., Hunt, H. T., Tyson, P. D., Lucescu, M. L., & Jeakins, D. B. (1982). Lucid dreaming and alpha activity: A preliminary report. *Perceptual and Motor Skills, 55*, 795–808.

Ornstein, R. (1972). *The psychology of consciousness.* San Francisco: W. H. Freeman.

Paivio, A. (1971). *Imagery and verbal processes.* New York: Holt, Rinehart & Winston.

Peek, L., & Sawyer, F. P. (1988). Utilization of family drawing depression scale with pain patients. *The Arts in Psychotherapy, 15*(3), 207–210.

Pennal, B. E. (1977). Human cerebral asymmetry in color discrimination. *Neuropsychologia, 15*, 563–568.

Perls, F. S. (1969). *Gestalt therapy verbatim.* Moab, Utah: Real People Press.

Perry, J. W. (1953). *The self in psychotic process.* Berkeley: University of California Press.

Perry, J. W. (1962). Reconstitutive process in the psychopathology of the self. *Annals of the New York Academy of Sciences, 96*(3), 853–876.

Perry, J. W. (1973). The creative element in madness *Art Psychotherapy, 1*(1), 61–65.

Petti, T. A. (1981). Depression in children: A significant disorder. *Psychosomatics, 22*(5), 444–447.

Piaget, J. (1962). *Play, dreams, and imitation in childhood.* New York: Norton.

Piaget, J., & Inhelder, B. (1971). *Mental imagery in the child.* New York: Basic Books.

Pickford, R. W. (1971). "Stilwandel" (or radical change of style) in a normal artist. *Japanese Bulletin of Art Therapy, 3*, 113–129.

Plokker, J. H. (1965). *Art from the mentally disturbed.* Boston: Little, Brown.

Popkin, L. (1980). *Communication and growth through art: A case study.* Unpublished master's of art degree paper, University of Louisville, Louisville, Ky.

Portner, E. S. (1982). Depressive themes in children's fantasies. *Journal of Children in Contemporary Society, 15*(2), 29–39.

Prinzhorn, H. (1972). *Artistry of the mentally ill.* New York: Springer-Verlag. (Original English translation published 1922.)

Progoff, I. (1963). *The symbolic and the real.* New York: Julian Press.

Rad, von, M., Lalucat, L., & Lolas, F. (1977). Differences of verbal behaviour in psychosomatic and psychoneurotic patients. *Psychotherapy and Psychosomatics, 28*, 83–97.

Ray, W. J., Morell, M., Frediana, A. W., & Tucker, D. (1976). Sex differences and lateral specialization of hemispheric functioning. *Neuropsychologia, 14*, 391–394.

Reardon, J. P., & Tosi, D. J. (1977). The effects of rational stage directed imagery on self-concept and reduction of psychological stress in adolescent delinquent females. *Journal of Child Psychology, 33*(4), 1084–1092.

Redden, C. (1979). *Rita: A case study. Individual art psychotherapy with a 15 year old girl.* Unpublished master's of art degree paper, University of Louisville, Louisville, Ky.

Rennert, H., & Mode, H. (1969). Mischwesen und Monstern in der Vorstellung und Ausdruckswelt der archaischen und psychotischen Menschen. *Der Nervenarzt, 40*(1), 8–17.

Reyher, J. (1977). Spontaneous visual imagery: Implications for psychoanalysis, psychopathology, and psychotherapy. *Journal of Mental Imagery, 1*(2), 253–274.

Reyher, J. (1978). Emergent uncovering psychotherapy: The use of imagoic and linguistic vehicles in objectifying psychodynamic process. In J. L. Singer & K. S. Pope (Eds.), *The power of human imagination* (pp. 51–93). New York: Plenum.

Reyher, J., & Smeltzer, W. (1968). Uncovering properties of visual imagery and verbal association: A comparative study. *Journal of Abnormal Psychology, 73*, 218–222.

Rhinehart, L., & Engelhorn, P. (1982). Pre-image considerations as a therapeutic process. *The Arts in Psychotherapy, 9*(1), 55–64.

Rhinehart, L., & Engelhorn, P. (1984). The full rainbow—Symbol of individuation. *The Arts in Psychotherapy, 11*(1), 37–44.

Rhinehart, L., & Englehorn, P. (1987). The Sun Wheel: Bridge to the unconscious. *Art Therapy, 4*(3), 105–111.

Rhodes, J. T. (1988). Rheumatoid arthritis—a dialogue with pain: From subjective experience to objective observation. In P. I. Ahmed (Ed.), *Coping with arthritis* (pp. 107–125). Springfield, Ill: Charles C Thomas.

Rhodes, J. T., Foard, T., & Dickstein, L. (1988). Professional peer group counseling in the management of rheumatoid arthritis: A clinical trial. In P. I. Ahmed (Ed.), *Coping with arthritis* (pp. 73–106). Springfield, Ill: Charles C Thomas.

Rhyne, J. (1970). Gestalt art experience. In J. Fagan & I. L. Shepherd (Eds.), *Gestalt therapy now* (pp. 274–284). Palo Alto, Calif.: Science and Behavior Books.

Rhyne, J. (1973). *The gestalt art experience.* Monterey, Calif.: Brooks/Cole.

Rhyne, J. (1979a). Drawings as personal constructs: A study in visual dynamics. *Dissertation Abstracts International, 40*(5), 2411B. (University Microfilms International No. Tx 375–487).

Rhyne, J. (1979b). *Gestalt art experience.* In L. Gantt, G. Forrest, D. Silverman, R. J. H. Shoemaker (Eds.), *Art therapy: Expanding horizons. Proceedings of the 9th Annual Conference of the American Art Therapy Association* (pp. 125–126).

Rhyne, J. (1983). Personal dramas of transition. In L. Gantt & S. Whitman (Eds.), *The fine art of therapy. The Proceedings of the 11th Annual Conference of the American Art Therapy Association* (pp. 31–38).

Rhyne, J. (1987). Gestalt art therapy. In J. A. Rubin (Ed.), *Approaches to art therapy: Theory and technique* (pp. 167–187). New York: Brunner/Mazel.

Richardson, A. (1969). *Mental imagery.* London: Routledge & Kegan Paul.

Richardson, A. (1983). Imagery: Definitions and types. In A. A. Sheikh (Ed.), *Imagery: Current theory, research and application* (pp. 3–42). New York: Wiley.

Riley, S. (1979). Techniques of adolescent art therapy. In L. Gantt, G. Forrest, D. Silverman, & R. Shoemaker (Eds.), *Art therapy: Expanding horizons. Proceedings of the 9th Annual Conference of the American Art Therapy Association* (pp. 60–61).

Robbins, A. (1983). Expressive therapy: A creative arts approach to depth oriented treatment. In L. Gantt & S. Whitman (Eds.), *The fine art of therapy. Proceedings of the 11th Conference of the American Art Therapy Association.*

Robbins, A. (1987). An object relations approach to art therapy. In J. A. Rubin (Ed.), *Approaches to art therapy: Theory and technique.* (pp. 63–74). New York: Brunner/Mazel.

Robbins, A., & Sibley, L. B. (1976). *Creative art therapy.* New York: Brunner/Mazel.

Robbins, D., Lusebrink, V. B., & Rhyne, J. (1979). A study of color associated with stages of life. In L. Gantt et al. (Eds.), *Art therapy: Expanding horizons. Proceedings of the 9th Annual Conference of the American Art Therapy Association* (pp. 98–100).

Robbins, K. I., & McAdam, D. W. (1974). Interhemispheric alpha symmetry and imagery mode. *Brain and Language, 1,* 189–193.

Rogers, C. (1971). Toward a theory of creativity. In C. Jordan, L. Levenson, & R. Holsinger (Eds.), *The creative encounter.* Glenview, Ill: Scott, Foresman and Co.

Rosal, M. L. (1985). *The use of art therapy to modify the locus of control and adaptive behavior of behavior disordered students.* Unpublished doctoral dissertation, University of Queensland, Australia.

Rosal, M. L., & Lehder, D. M. (1983). The effects of tempo upon form and reflective distance. In A. Di Maria, E. S. Kramer, & E. A. Roth (Eds.), *Art therapy: Still growing. Proceedings of the 13th Annual Conference of the American Art Therapy Association.*

Rosenberg, H. (1982). Modular drawing: A clinical technique which explores the drawings within drawing. In L. Gantt & A. Evans (Eds.), *Focus on the future: The next ten years. Proceedings of the 10th Annual Conference of the American Art Therapy Association.*

Rossman, M. L. (1984). Imagine health! Imagery in medical self-care. In A. A. Sheikh (Ed.), *Imagination and healing.* Farmingdale, NY: Baywood Publishing.

Roth, E. A. (1978). Art therapy with emotionally disturbed—mentally retarded children: A technique of reality sharing. In B. K. Mandel, R. H. Shoemaker, & R. E. Hays (Eds.), *The dynamics of creativity. Proceedings of the 8th Annual Art Therapy Association Conference.*

Roth, E. A. (1987). A behavioral approach to art therapy. In J. A. Rubin (Ed.), *Approaches to art therapy: Theory and technique* (pp. 213–232). New York: Brunner/Mazel.

Rotter, J. B. (1967). Generalized expectancies for internal versus external control of reinforcements. *Psychological Monographs; General and Applied. 80,* (1, whole no. 609).

Rubin, J. A. (1978). *Child art therapy: Understanding and helping children grow through art* New York: Van Nostrand Reinhold.

Rubin, J. A. (1980). *Imagery and psychoanalysis: Reflections and visions.* Submitted in partial fulfillment of the requirements for graduation, Pittsburgh Psychoanalytic Institute.

Rubin, J. A. (1983). Media potential. Its use and misuse in therapy. In A. Di Maria, E. S. Kramer, & E. A. Roth (Eds.), *Art therapy: Still growing. Proceedings of the 13th Annual Conference of the American Art Therapy Association* (pp. 114–115).

Rubin, J. A. (1984). *The art of art therapy.* New York: Brunner/Mazel.

Rubin, J. A. (1987). Freudian psychoanalytic theory: Emphasis on uncovering and insight. In J. A. Rubin (Ed.), *Approaches to art therapy: Theory and technique* (pp. 7–25). New York: Brunner/Mazel.

Rusch, C. W. (1970). On understanding awareness. *Journal of Aesthetic Education, 4*(4), 57–59.

Samuels, M., & Samuels, N. (1975). *Seeing with the mind's eye: The history, techniques, and uses of visualization.* New York: Random House.

Schnake, A. M. (1980). *Case study: Johnny.* Unpublished master's of arts degree paper, University of Louisville, Louisville, Ky.

Schultz, D. (1978). Imagery and the control of depression. In J. L. Singer & K. S. Pope (Eds.), *The power of human imagination* (281–307). New York: Plenum.

Schwartz, G. E. (1984). Psychophysiology of imagery and healing: A systems perspective. In A. A. Sheikh (Ed.), *Imagination and healing: Imagery and human development series* (pp. 35–50). Farmingdale, NY: Baywood Publishing.

Schwartz, G. E., Weinberger, D. A., & Singer, J. A. (1981). Cardiovascular differentiation of happiness, sadness, anger and fear following imagery and exercise. *Psychosomatic Medicine, 43*(4), 343–364.

Schwartz, D., Weinstein, L., & Arkin, A. M. (1978). Qualitative aspects of sleep mentation: Psychophysiological parallelism. In A. M. Arkin, J. S. Antrobus, & S. J. Ellman (Eds.), *The mind in sleep* (pp. 143–241). New York: Wiley.

Seamon, J. G., & Gazzaniga, M. F. (1973). Coding strategies and cerebral laterality effects. *Cognitive Psychology, 5,* 249–256.

Segal, J. S. (1972). Assimilation of a stimulus in the construction of an image: The Perky effect revisited. In P. W. Sheehan (Ed.), *The function and nature of imagery* (pp. 203–230). New York: Academic Press.

Shaw, B. A. (1978). Obsessional defenses and reading disabilities in adolescence as seen through art therapy. *Art Psychotherapy, 5*(2), 61–69.

Sheehan, P. W. (1967). Visual imagery and the organizational properties of perceived stimuli. *British Journal of Pyschology, 58*(3/4), 247–252.

Sheehan, P. W. (Ed.). (1972). *The function and nature of imagery.* New York: Academic Press.

Sheikh, A. A. (1978). Eidectic psychotherapy. In J. L. Singer and K. S. Pope (Eds.), *The power of human imagination* (pp. 197–224). New York: Plenum.

Sheikh, A. A. (Ed.). (1986). *Anthology of imagery techniques.* Milwaukee, Wis.: American Imagery Institute.

Sheikh, A. A., & Jordan, C. H. (1983). Clinical uses of mental imagery. In A. A. Sheikh (Ed.), *Imagery: Current theory, research, and application* (pp. 391–435). New York: Wiley.

Sheikh, A. A. & Kunzendorf, R. G. (1984). Imagery, physiology, and psychosomatic illness. In A. A. Sheikh (Ed.), *International review of mental imagery* (Vol. 1, pp. 95–138). New York: Human Sciences Press.

Shepard, R. N., & Cooper, L. A. (1982). *Mental images and their transformations.* Cambridge, Mass.: The MIT Press.

Shoemaker, R. H. (1978). The significance of the first picture in art therapy. In B. K. Mandel, R. H. Shoemaker, & R. E. Hays (Eds.), *The dynamics of creativity. Proceedings of the 8th Annual Art Therapy Association Conference* (pp. 156–162).

Shorr, J. E. (1978). Clinical use of categories of therapeutic imagery. In J. L. Singer & K. S. Pope (Eds.), *The power of human imagination* (pp. 95–121). New York: Plenum.

Siegel, L. J., & Griffin, N. J. (1984). Correlates of depressive symptoms in adolescents. *Journal of Youth and Adolescence, 13*(6), 475–487.

Siegel, R. K., & Jarvik, M. E. (1975). Drug induced hallucinations in animals and man. In R. K. Siegel & L. J. West (Eds.), *Hallucinations: Behavior, experience and theory* (pp. 81–161). New York: Wiley.

Sifneos, P. F. (1973). The prevalence of "alexithymic" characteristics in psychosomatic patients. *Psychotherapy and Psychosomatics, 22,* 255–262.

Sifneos, P. E. (1983). Psychotherapies for psychomatic and alexithymic patients. *Psychotherapy and Psychosomatics, 40,* 66–73.

Sifneos, P. E., Apfel-Savitz, R., & Frankel, F. H. (1977). The phenomenon of "alexithymia." *Psychotherapy and Psychosomatics, 28,* 47–57.

Silberman, E. K., & Weingarten, H. (1986). Hemispheric lateralization of functions related to emotion. *Brain and Cognition, 5,* 322–353.

Silver, R. (1978). *Developing cognitive and creative skills through art.* Baltimore, Md.: University Park Press.

Silver, R. (1988). Screening children and adolescents for depression through draw-a-story. *American Journal of Art Therapy, 26,* 119–124.

Simon, R. M. (1970). The significance of pictorial styles in art therapy. *American Journal of Art Therapy, 9*(4), 159–175.

Simon, R. M. (1974). Pictorial style as a means of communication. *American Journal of Art Therapy, 13*(4), 275–292.

Simonton, O. C., Simonton, S., & Creighton, J. (1978). *Getting well again.* Los Angeles, Calif.: P. Tarcher.

Sinclair, H. (1970). The transition from sensory-motor behavior to symbolic Activity. *Interchange, I,* 119–126.

Singer, J. L. (1966). *Daydreaming.* New York: Random House.

Singer, J. L. (1973). *The child's world of make-believe.* New York: Academic Press.

Singer, J. L. (1974). *Imagery and daydream methods in psychotherapy and behavior modification.* New York: Academic Press.

Singer, J. L. (1975a). *The inner world of daydreaming.* New York: Harper & Row.

Singer, J. L. (1975b). Navigating the stream of consciousness: Research in daydreaming and related inner experience. *American Psychologist, 30,* 727–738.

Singer, J. L. (1976). *Daydreaming and fantasy.* London: George Allen & Unwin Ltd.

Singer, J. L. (1978). Experimental study of daydreaming and the stream of thought. In K. S. Pope & J. L. Singer (Eds.), *The stream of consciousness* (pp. 187–223). New York: Plenum.

Singer, J. L. (1979). Affect and imagination in play and fantasy. In C. E. Izard (Ed.)., *Emotions in personality and psychopathology,* (pp. 13–34). New York: Plenum.

Singer, J. L. (1988). The conscious and unconscious stream of thought. In D. Pines, (Ed.), *Emerging syntheses in science* (pp. 142–180). New York: Wiley.

Singer, J. S., Greenberg, S., & Antrobus, J. S. (1971). Looking with the mind's eye: Experimental studies of ocular motility during daydreaming and mental arithmetic. *Transactions of the New York Academy of Science, 33,* 694–709.

Singer, J. L. & Pope, K. S. (1978). The use of imagery and fantasy techniques in psychotherapy. In J. L. Singer & K. S. Pope (Eds.), *The power of human imagination* (pp. 3–34). New York: Plenum.

Singer, J. L., & Kolligian, J., Jr. (1987). Personality developments in the study of private experience. *Annual Review of Psychology, 38,* 553–574.

Spergel, P., Ehrlich, G. E., & Glass, D. (1978). The rheumatoid arthritic personality: A psychodiagnostic myth. *Psychosomatics, 19*(2), 79–86.

Starker, S. (1974). Daydreaming styles and nocturnal dreaming. *Journal of Abnormal Psychology, 83,* 52–55.

Starker, S. (1977). Daydreaming styles and nocturnal dreaming. Further observations. *Perceptual and Motor Skills, 45* 411–418.

Starker, S. (1978). Dreams and waking fantasy. K. S. Pope & J. L. Singer (Eds.), *The stream of consciousness* (pp. 301–317). New York: Plenum.

Starker, S. (1982). *Fantastic thoughts: All about dreams, daydreams, hallucinations and hypnosis.* Englewood Cliffs, N.J.: Prentice-Hall.

Starker, S. (1984–1985). Daydreams, nightmares, and insomnia: The relation of waking fantasy to sleep disturbances. *Imagination, Cognition and Personality, 4*(3), 237–248.

Starker, S., & Hasenfeld, R. (1976). Daydream styles and sleep disturbance. *Journal of Nervous and Mental Disease, 163*(6), 391–400.

Starker, S., & Singer, J. L. (1975). Daydreaming and symptom patterns of psychiatric patients: A factor-analytic study. *Journal of Abnormal Psychology, 84*(5), 567–570.

Stember, C. J. (1977). Printmaking with abused children: A first step in art therapy. *American Journal of Art Therapy, 16*(3), 104–109.

Stember, C. J. (1978). Use of art therapy in child abuse/neglect: Are there graphic clues? In B. K. Mandel, R. H. Shoemaker, & R. E. Hayes (Eds.), *The dynamics of creativity. Proceedings of the 8th Annual Art Therapy Association Conference* (pp. 73–78).

Sternbach, R. (1978). Psychological dimensions and perceptual analysis. In M. Friedman & E. Cartevette (Eds.), *Handbook of perception 6B.* New York: Academic Press.

Storr, A. (1972). *The dynamics of creation.* New York: Atheneum.

Strosahl, K. D., & Ascough, J. C. (1981). Clinical uses of mental imagery: Experimental foundations, theoretical misconceptions, and research issues. *Psychological Bulletin, 89*(3), 422–438.

Summerville, P. (1983, October) *Three-dimensional dream house.* Paper presented at the 14th Annual American Art Therapy Conference, Chicago, Ill.

Taylor, I. A. (1975). An emerging view of creative actions. In I. A. Taylor & J. W. Getzels (Eds.), *Perspectives in creativity* (pp. 297–325). Chicago: Aldine.

Taylor, P. L., & Fulcomer, M. (1979). Adolescent daydreaming. The I.Q. effect. *Journal of Mental Imagery, 3*(1,2), 107–122.

Taylor, P. L., Fulcomer, M., & Taylor, F. Z. (1978). Daydreaming in the adolescent years: Instrument development factor analysis and sex differences. *Adolescent, 13*(52), 735–750.

Tokuda, Y. (1973). Image and art therapy. *Art Psychotherapy, 1*(3/4), 169–176.

Tokuda, Y. (1980). Theory and practices of image art psychotherapy. *Confinia Psychiatrica, 23*, 193–208. Basel: S. Karger, AG.

Tomkins, S. (1962). *Affect, imagery, consciousness* (Vol. I). New York: Springer.

Tower, R. B. (1983). Imagery: Its role in development. In A. A. Sheikh (Ed.), *Imagery: Current theory, research, and application* (pp. 222–251). New York: Wiley.

Trenholme, I., Cartwright, R. D., & Greenberg, G. (1984). Dream dimension differences during a life change. *Psychiatry Research, 12*, 35–45.

Tucker, D. M. (1976). Sex differences in hemisphere specialization for synthetic visio-spatial functions. *Neuropsychologia, 14*, 447–454.

Tucker, D. M. (1981). Lateral brain function, emotion and conceptionalization. *Psychological Bulletin, 89*(1), 19–46.

Tucker, D. M., Stenslie, C. E., Roth, R. S., & Shearer, S. L. (1981). Right frontal lobe activation and right hemisphere performance decrement during depressed mood. *Archives of General Psychiatry, 38*, 169–174.

Uhlin, D. M., & De Chiara, E. (1984). *Art for exceptional children* (3rd ed.). Dubuque, IA: Wm. C. Brown.

Ulman, E. (1961). Art therapy: Problems of definition. *Bulletin of Art Therapy, 1*(2), 10–20.

Ulman, E. (1965). A new use of art in psychiatric diagnosis. *Bulletin of Art Therapy, 4*(3), 91–116.

Ulman, E. (1975a). Art therapy: Problems of definition. In E. Ulman & P. Dachinger (Eds.), *Art therapy in theory and practice* (pp. 3–13). New York: Schocken Books.

Ulman, E. (1975b). Therapy is not enough: The contribution of art to general hospital psychiatry. In E. Ulman & P. Dachinger (Eds.), *Art therapy in theory and practice* (pp. 14–32). New York: Schocken Books.

Uttal, W. R. (1973). *The psychology of sensory coding.* New York: Harper & Row.

Vaillant, G. E. (1976). V. Natural history of male psychological health. *Archives of General Psychiatry, 33*, 535–545.

Volmat, R. (1956). *L'Art psychopathologique.* Paris: Presses Universitaires de France.

Volmat, R. (1967). Methodes de la Psychopathologie de l'expression. *Schweizer Archiv für Neurologie, 99*(1), 118–133.

Wachter, H. M., & Pudel, V. (1980). Kontrollierte Untersuchung einer extremen Kurzpsychotherapie (15 stunden) mit dem katathymen Bilderleben. *Psychotherapie und Medicinishe Psychologie, 30*, 193–205.

Wadeson, H. (1980). *Art psychotherapy.* New York: Wiley.

Wadeson, H. (1987). An eclectic approach to art therapy. In J. A. Rubin (Ed.), *Approaches to art therapy: Theory and technique* (pp. 299–313).

Wallas, G. (1926). *The art of thought.* New York: Harcourt & Brace.

Watkins, M. (1984). *Waking dreams* (3rd ed.). Dallas, TX: Spring Publications.

Webb, W. B., & Cartwright, R. D. (1978). Sleep and dreams. *Annual Reviews of Psychology, 29*, 223–252.

Webster's new collegiate dictionary. (1976). Springfield, Mass: G. B. C. Merriam Co.

Weiss, E. (1981). *The case of Larry.* Unpublished master's of art degree paper, University of Louisville, Louisville, Ky.

Werner, H., & Kaplan, B. (1963). *Symbol formation.* New York: Wiley.

Whitmont, E. C. (1973). *The symbolic quest.* New York: Harper Colophon Books.

Wilson, L. (1977). Art therapy with the mentally retarded. *American Journal of Art Therapy*, *16*(3), 87–97.

Wilson, L. (1985a). Symbolism and art therapy: I. Symbolism's role in the development of ego functions. *American Journal of Art Therapy*, *23*(3), 79–88.

Wilson, L. (1985b). Symbolism and art therapy: I. Symbolism's relationship to the basic psychic functioning. *American Journal of Art Therapy*, *23*(4), 129–133.

Wolff, P., & Levin, J. R. (1972). The role of overt activity in children's imagery production. *Child Development*, *43*(2), 537–547.

Wolpe, J. (1958). *Psychotherapy by reciprocal inhibition*. Stanford, Calif.: Stanford University Press.

Wolpe, J. (1973). *The practice of behavior therapy* (2nd ed.). New York: Pergamon.

Wright, J. H., & McIntyre, M. P. (1982). The family drawing depression scale. *Journal of Clinical Psychology*, *38*(4), 853–861.

Yanish, D. L., & Battle, G. (1985). Relationship between self-esteem, depression and alcohol consumption among adolescents. *Psychological Reports*, *57*(1), 331–334.

Yarbus, A. L. (1967). *Eye movements and vision*. New York: Plenum.

Young, N. A. (1975). Art therapy with chronic schizophrenic patients of a low socioeconomic class in short-term treatment facility. *Art Psychotherapy*, *2*(1), 101–117.

Zajonc, R. B., & Markus, H. (1984). Affect and cognition: The hard interface. In C. E. Izard, J. Kagan, & R. B. Zajonc (Eds.), *Emotions, cognition, and behavior* (pp. 73–102). Cambridge, England: Cambridge University Press.

Author Index

Subject Index